IRE
AN
MIDD

IRELAND
AND THE
MIDDLE EAST

Trade, Society and Peace

Editor
RORY MILLER
King's College, London

Foreword by
FRED HALLIDAY

IRISH ACADEMIC PRESS
DUBLIN • PORTLAND, OR

First published in 2007 by
IRISH ACADEMIC PRESS
44, Northumberland Road, Dublin 4, Ireland

and in the United States of America by
IRISH ACADEMIC PRESS
c/o ISBS, Suite 300, 920 NE 58th Avenue
Portland, Oregon 97213-3786

www.iap.ie

British Library Cataloguing in Publication Data
An entry can be found on request

ISBN 978 0 7165 2867 8 (cloth)
ISBN 978 0 7165 2868 5 (paper)

Library of Congress Cataloging-in-Publication Data
An entry can be found on request

Typeset in 10/12pt Caslon 540 by FiSH Books, Enfield, Middx.
Printed by Biddles Ltd., King's Lynn, Norfolk

Contents

Acknowledgements

I would like to thank Lisa Hyde, my editor at Irish Academic Press, for the enthusiasm with which she greeted the idea of this book of essays on Ireland and the Middle East and then for her commitment to the project once it got underway. I would also like to thank Professor Fred Halliday for writing the Foreword and Róisín Heneghan of Heneghan Peng architects for allowing the use of the firm's design for Egypt's new Grand Museum in Cairo on the cover of this book. Finally, I would like to thank all those who took the time, and made the effort, to provide chapters for this book. All have added to our understanding of Ireland's role in, and contribution to, the Middle East region.

Rory Miller, London, January 2007

List of Abbreviations

ALN	Armée de Libération Nationale
AML	Amis du Manifeste et de la Liberté
ANC	African National Congress
BAM	Border Assistance Mission
BIRD	Binational Industrial Research and Development
CCCA	Churchill College Cambridge Archives
CFSP	Common Foreign and Security Policy
CG&CS	Government Code and Cipher School
CID	Criminal Investigations Department
CSP	Country Strategy Programme
DBA	Direct Budgetary Assistance
DEA	Department of External Affairs
DFA	Department of Foreign Affairs
DIFP	*Documents on Irish Foreign Policy*
DOI	Digital Opportunity Index
DUP	Democratic Unionist Party
ENA	Étoile Nord-Africaine
ETA	Euskai ta Askatasuna (Basque Homeland and Freedom)
EU BAM	EU Border Maintenance Mission
FDI	Foreign Direct Investment
FLN	Front de Libération Nationale
FO	Foreign Office
GC&CS	Government Code & Cipher School
GCI	Global Competitiveness Index
GDP	Gross Domestic Product
GNI	Gross National Income
HMSO	Her Majesty's Stationery Office
IB	Intelligence Bureau
ICT	Information and Computer Technology
IDA	Industrial Development Agency
IDF	Israeli Defence Force
IFSC	International Financial Services Centre
IMC	Independent Monitoring Commission
IMF	International Monetary Fund
INLA	Irish National Liberation Army
IOR	India Office Records and Library
IPI	Indian political Intelligence

IPLO	Irish People's Liberation Organisation
IRA	Irish Republican Army
IRB	Irish Republican Brotherhood
IT	Information Technology
IZL	Irgun Tsvai Leumi
MEDA	Mediterranean Development Assistance
MERIP	Middle East Research and Information Project
MK	Member of the Knesset
MRF	Mobile Reconnaissance Force
NAI	National Archives, Ireland
NBER	National Bureau of Economic Research
NGO	Non-Governmental Organisation
NLI	National Library, Ireland
NZO	New Zionist Organisation
OCHA	Office for the Co-ordination of Humanitarian Affairs
OECD	Organisation for Economic Co-operation and Development
PA	Palestinian Authority
PAA	Palestinian Administered Areas
PFLP	Popular Front for the Liberation of Palestine
PIF	Palestinian Investment Fund
PLO	Palestine Liberation Organisation
PP	Partido Popular
PPA	Parti du Peuple Algérien
PPP	Purchasing Power Parity
PRO	Public Records Office
R&D	Research and Development
RIRA	Real Irish Republican Army
RTI	Research, Technology and Innovation
RUC	Royal Ulster Constabulary
SAS	Special Air Service
SCF	Special Cash Facility
SDLP	Social Democratic and Labour Party
SIS	Secret Intelligence Service
SOE	Special Operations Executive
TNA	The National Archives
UCDA	University College Dublin Archives
UDA	Ulster Defence Association
UFF	Ulster Freedom Fighters
UNDP	United Nations Development Programme
UNOGIL	United Nations Observer Group in Lebanon
UNRWA	United Nations Relief and Works Agency
UNSC	United Nations Security Council
UUP	Ulster Unionist Party
UVF	Ulster Volunteer Force
WBG	World Bank Group

Notes on Contributors

Steven David is Professor of Political Science, Director of the International Studies Programme and Vice Dean for Programmes and Centres at the Zanvyl Krieger School of Arts and Sciences, Johns Hopkins University, Baltimore, Maryland. He is the author of *Choosing Sides: Alignment and Realignment in the Third World* (1991) and *Third World Coups d'Etat and International Security* (1987).

John Doyle is co-Director of the Centre for International Studies in the School of Law and Government, Dublin City University. He is Director of the School's MA programmes in International Relations, Globalisation and International Security and editor of the Royal Irish Academy journal *Irish Studies in International Affairs*. Recent publications include 'Irish Diplomacy on the UN Security Council 2001–2' in *Irish Studies in International Affairs* (2004) and 'The aftermath of 11 Sept – increasing international insecurity', in *Development Review* (2002) (co-authored with Eileen Connolly).

Jonathan Githens-Mazer is a lecturer in Politics at the University of Exeter, Cornwall Campus. His research interests include theories of ethnicity and nationalism and the role of national identity in constituting a basis for radical and/or violent political mobilisation. This includes the examination of how myths, memories and symbols of nations form popular bases of radical nationalism. He is the author of *Myths and Memories of the Easter Rising: Cultural and Political Nationalism in Ireland* (2006).

Constantin Gurdgiev is editor of *Business & Finance Magazine*. He is also Director of the Open Republic Institute, a Research Fellow at Trinity College, Dublin, a Fellow at the International Pharmaceutical Economics and Policy Council and an Honorary Research Fellow at the Copenhagen Institute. He is the editor of 'Historic, Theoretical and Institutional Perspectives of the Debt Problem' (2007) and author of 'Trade in Services' (2007).

Michael Kennedy is Executive Editor of the Royal Irish Academy's *Documents on Irish Foreign Policy* series, the fifth volume of which was published in 2006. He is a Research Associate of the Centre for Contemporary Irish History at Trinity College, Dublin, an Adjunct Associate Professor of History at University College, Dublin, and is currently secretary of the Royal Irish Academy's Committee for International Affairs. He has published widely on Irish diplomatic history, including *Division and Consensus: The Politics of Cross Border Relations in Ireland* (2000) and *Obligations and Responsibilities: Ireland and the United Nations 1955–2005* (2005), a book of essays marking fifty years of Irish membership of the United Nations co-edited with Dr Deirdre McMahon.

Gary Kent has worked in the House of Commons since 1987, since which time he has been heavily involved in the British-Irish peace movement. Currently he is Director of Labour Friends of Iraq in the UK and Westminster correspondent for New American Liberalism – the US equivalent of the Euston Manifesto group. He also works for the integrated education movement in Northern Ireland and is an adviser to the Northern Ireland Committee of the Irish Congress of Trade Unions. He writes in a personal capacity.

Michael Kerr is a Leverhulme Research Fellow in the International History Department of the London School of Economics. He is author of *Imposing Power-Sharing: Conflict and Coexistence in Northern Ireland and Lebanon* (2005) and *Transforming Unionism: David Trimble and the 2005 General Election* (2005).

Simon Kingston is an Executive Director in the London office of Russell Reynolds Associates. A former Irish Government Senior Scholar at Oxford University, his doctoral studies dealt with Ulster and western Scotland in the late mediaeval and early modern periods. He is the author of *Ulster and the Isles in the Fifteenth Century: The Lordship of the Clan Domhnaill in Antrim* (Dublin, 2004) and writes occasionally in the media about contemporary Irish politics. He sits on the executive committee of the British Irish Association.

John Maher is a prize-winning author and doctoral candidate at the School of Oriental and African Studies (SOAS), at the University of London, where he is working on his thesis 'Slouching Towards Jerusalem: The Representation of Political Violence in the Irish, Israeli and Palestinian Novel, 1990–2005.' His novel, *The Luck Penny*, was published by Brandon Books in March 2007. It is based on the life of the Irish Assyriologist Dr Edward Hincks.

Rory Miller is a senior lecturer in Mediterranean Studies, King's College, University of London, where he teaches courses on the EU and US involvement in the Middle East. He is author of *Divided Against Zion: Anti-Zionist Opposition to a Jewish State in Palestine, 1945–48* (2000) and *Ireland and the Palestine Question, 1945–1948* (2005). He is also associate editor of the academic journal *Israel Affairs*.

Jonathan Moore is principal lecturer in Irish Studies at London Metropolitan University. He has written widely on the conflict in Northern

Ireland and is a frequent contributor to British, Irish, American and Canadian television and radio programmes. He is currently writing a history of the Northern Irish electorate.

Eunan O'Halpin is Bank of Ireland Professor of Contemporary Irish History at Trinity College, Dublin, where he is also Director of the Centre for Contemporary Irish History. His recent publications include the edited volume *MI5 and Ireland, 1939–1945: The Official History* (2003) and *Defending Ireland: The Irish State and its Enemies Since 1999* (2002). He is also co-editor, with Robert Armstrong and Jane Ohlmeyer, of *Intelligence, Statecraft and International Power* (2006).

Jonathan Spyer is a Research Fellow at the Global Research in International Affairs Centre in Herzliya, Israel. The Centre is the international affairs think-tank of the Inter-Disciplinary Centre, Herzliya. He has a PhD. in International Relations from the London School of Economics. His articles and analysis of political processes in Israel and the modern Middle East are published widely and he is a regular contributor to *The Guardian* and *Ha'aretz*.

Foreword

No-one with the slightest knowledge of both can fail to notice the many points of intersection, of influence, symbolism, policy, comparison, and, not least, tragedy, between the modern history of Ireland and that of the two dozen or so countries of the Middle East. Whether it be in formulation of nationalist and protest ideologies that draw on international sources while packaging themselves as authentic and indigenous, in the rhetoric and supposed heroism of armed struggles, in the role of the clergy in politics, in the generation of a literature that embodies nationalist values and themes, in the mutual delegitimation of competing peoples, in the rise of 'revisionist' or 'new' and later 'anti-revisionist' historians, not to mention in a love of horses, good company, vibrant music and the odd engaging scoundrel, the two regions seem in many ways to mirror and rival each other.

Ireland and the Middle East have had, for many decades past, a range of interactions, ones that are discussed, with much wonderful scholarship and interlacing, in this book. How far, beyond the interchange of mythologies, from James Connolly to Bobby Sands, they have actually influenced each other is harder to say, but there are some concrete and in their own way important instances of this. The story of the Irish Army in Lebanon is an important part of the history of peace-keeping in general and had its impact in the Republic; the malign charity of Colonel Qaddafi, enraged by British support for the US air raids on Tripoli of April 1986, in the form of, it is believed, hundreds of tons of weapons, took its toll in suffering and increased intransigence in the North, in the years that followed. That the Colonel, in a policy of ecumenical irresponsibility, sent arms to both Catholic and Protestant paramilitaries, on the grounds that they were all 'strugglers', *munadhilin*, only compounded the problem.

As someone born and brought up in the Republic, and who has spent these four and more decades past studying and visiting the Middle East, I have my own special feelings and some analytic insights on the matter of the Irish-Middle Eastern interconnection. There are also anecdotes and incidents that stick particularly in my mind. First in line must be the story retailed by Dr Conor Cruise O'Brien, the first Irish diplomat to take his seat in the UN General Assembly when Ireland was finally admitted in 1955, a story he tells in his classic book on the Congo crisis, *To Katanga and Back*. As he sat in the allotted place, this determined by alphabetical order, the man on his left took him warmly by the hand, and expressed the undying affection and respect of his nation for the people of Ireland. Then the man on his right did the same thing. It turned out that these were, respectively, the representatives of Iraq and of Israel: hitherto they had been condemned to sit next to each other, now, thanks to the imaginative intervention of Ireland in what must count as one of the finest examples of conflict resolution, this was no longer necessary.

A second incident is one retailed to me by an old and wise friend, Colonel Ned Doyle of the Irish army, veteran of peace-keeping missions in the Congo, Sinai and Lebanon. The Irish involvement in Lebanon deserves wide study for the impact it had on Ireland's perception of the Middle East, particularly in alienating public opinion from Israel because of the responsibility of its client, the South Lebanese Army, in Irish casualties, and for the exemplary way in which, despite casualties, Irish public opinion continued to support the country's commitment to the UN. Among his many other postings, Colonel Doyle was appointed commander of the joint Soviet-American peace-keeping force in Sinai after the 1973 war, the first officer of any country ever to serve in such a role. By all accounts, he kept the two reasonably in order, although he was once heard to remark on the differential drinking cultures of the two groups under his command. In keeping with a practice first introduced in the Congo, when the Belgians and Katangans listened in on Irish military radio traffic conducted in English, the Irish army radio operators assigned to work with Colonel Doyle conducted their business in Gaelic. One day, he noticed a strange, and unexpected, pre-emptive movement by Israeli troops and, after some reflection, concluded that it could only be explained by their having been listening to the conversations of the Irish radio operators. Next time he met his IDF opposite number he queried him on this, and got a confirmatory reply: the Israeli army had indeed been recruiting former pupils of Stratford College, the Jewish school in Dublin, to serve for exactly this purpose, in their military intelligence corps. The problem was, as Colonel Doyle's IDF counterpart freely admitted, that the boys from Dublin had been taught the literary Irish of the official school curriculum, somewhat removed from the colloquial of the Irish army signals operators from Galway and Kerry.

One of my stranger experiences in this domain involved the political programme of the left-wing opposition group in North Yemen during the 1980s, the National Democratic Front. In keeping with the custom of those times, the NDF, which was an offshoot of the Marxist regime in South Yemen but well implanted in the central part of the North, issued a programme with the ritual passage denouncing the various enemies of the Yemeni people. The usual suspects were indeed there: imperialism, Zionism, Saudi reaction, Iranian expansionism and so on, but I was rather surprised to find a further denunciation, this time of what were termed *al-andhuma al-jasusia al-irlandia*, to wit 'Irish espionage organisations'. Some questioning at a Trocaire conference in Dublin in 1987 where the guest of honour was Archbishop Casey of Galway, a dedicated and much maligned man, and a mild altercation with Jairullah Omar, the leader of the NDF, in Sanaa in 1994, later assassinated by an Islamist gunman, brought me to the conclusion that this was a reference to some entirely innocuous little Irish aid NGO, which had been trying to bring water and some education to a mountainous part of Yemen. Such aid had, however, challenged the power of some tribal leader, and the sheikh had as a result spread rumours throughout Yemen about the perfidious activities of this hitherto unknown imperialist power.

This claim had, moreover, a curious sequel. Years later, in a lecture in 1994 in St Stephen's Green to a meeting of the International Committee of the Royal Irish Academy, on the subject of 'Irish Questions in International Perspective', I got to tell this story to a Dublin audience for the first time. They were perhaps most taken with my quote from *Irisches Tagebuch*, the travel book on Ireland in the 1950s by Heinrich Boll, where he arrives off the Dun Laoghaire boat to find the whole of Dublin closed. Shocked by an encounter with the van of the Swastika Laundry, which in grand and politically most incorrect style still bore its red and white emblem through the streets of the capital, he observed that Ireland was *ein Land wo man das Fruhaufstehen hasst*, 'a country where people hate to get up early'. But the Yemeni incident did not go unnoticed, and at the end a man of unspecific but clearly Middle Eastern opinion came up to me and, smiling, said to me in Arabic that he had really liked the Yemeni story. I could not quite place him, but my instinct said he was from Iraq. 'Are you from the land of the two rivers?' I asked, using the conventional term for Iraq. Indeed he was. At that point I began to wonder what an obviously well appointed Iraqi agent was doing in Ireland: we had not nuclear weapons for Saddam to buy and it seemed an odd deployment. Such people were usually based in Knightsbridge, Geneva or Cannes. 'Who are you?' I gingerly asked, to which he replied, with a laugh: *ana al-safir al-israeli*, 'I am the Israeli ambassador'. Such, it would seem, is the cunning of history.

Finally, I would recall a chance encounter, at a seminar on Cyprus at the Turkish Embassy in London, with a cheerful Unionist MP. He seemed unusually at home and at ease in this setting and it transpired, in the course of our conversation, that he had 'a wee house' in Northern Cyprus, a villa that he visited at least half a dozen times a year. Picking up on the drift of my questions, he opined, with much gusto, that the best friends of the Ulster people were no longer the Israelis, but indeed the Turks of Northern Cyprus. Indeed, it turned out that no less than six other Unionist politicians had such houses in the north of the island. As for the Greek Cypriots, they were an utterly untrustworthy bunch, priest-ridden and violent. In words with an uncanny relevance to another divided island he told me: 'I would never go down to the south, they could cut your throat if you did' He was, in his way, an honest and decent fellow, and I was later to share a platform with him at a meeting in Dundalk, where he talked a lot of sense, but I forbore to ask on what commercial terms the 'wee house' was acquired and maintained, and strongly suspected that whenever, on any of his half dozen or more long weekend trips to the island, he opened the kitchen door, there would be a good pile of fresh olives, vegetables and, no doubt, wine provided by unnamed local friends on the table. The house may well once have belonged to Greeks, but this would probably not have bothered him: they had, as it were, gone back to where they came from.

No study can do justice to the full richness and diversity of Ireland's relationship to the Middle East and to the conjoining of reality and myth that surround this question. The place to start is, of course, with the origins of Christianity in Ireland when the influences of Eastern Christianity, driven westwards by the Muslim advance of the seventh century, were felt in the island: what in Ireland is considered to be an authentic national symbol, the Celtic cross, is, in fact, a variant of the design earlier used by Copts, and, to this day, by Ethiopians and Armenians, as a symbol of their religion and identity. No account of the ideological dimension of Cromwell's bloody campaigns in Leinster in the 1640s would be complete without mention of the way the Biblical term 'Amalekite' was used to justify the slaughter of the Irish, as it was later to be used on the West Bank by some right-wing Israelis to preclude the rights of Palestinians.

The history of Ireland in modern centuries bears many points of comparison with that of the Middle East, from the imposition of colonial rule on hitherto separated tribes and regions (it was, after all, Henry VIII who first united Ireland), the installation for a mixture of strategic, political and religious reasons of settler populations, the destruction of indigenous economic, social and linguistic institutions, and the rise, in rejection of this domination, of nationalist and protest movements that took their very vocabulary and goals from the available international, metropolitan, lexicon of politics, but turned them to nationalist use. Whether in the programme and vocabulary of national-ism, in the aspiration to purify and revive language, in the design of flags, in the very tactics used to advance, or oppose, the nationalist cause, there is much which Ireland shares with the Middle East. Ultimately the comparisons and intersections rest on one overarching consideration, the fact that modern Ireland, like all the countries of the modern Middle East, was shaped by its simultaneous incorporation into, and rejection of, the imperial and hegemonic systems of the last two centuries, and the impact of great power conflict, be this in the French Revolution, World War I, or, in the 1960s, Vatican II and the US Civil Rights Movement, on the Irish political system.

In any social science perspective, at least three issues bear comparison and further study. One is that of state and society formation, of the way in which British rule shaped the growth of the administration, of the institutions in society, of education and public attitudes and, in so doing, left a legacy that long outlived the period of direct colonial rule. That part of this legacy involving poisoned relations between either pre-existing communities, or between older and more recently established communities, as in Ulster and Palestine, is part, but only part, of the whole story.

The second is the issue of inter-ethnic conflict, and the degree to which meaningful comparisons, as well as lines of influence, can be established between the Irish and, most evidently, the Arab-Israeli case. Chapters in this book look in detail at the uses and abuses of the 'Irish struggle' by forces in the Middle East, as Ireland also served to inspire rebels in India, Cyprus and Kenya. There are, for sure, important differences between Ireland and Palestine, but the core issue, of mutual recognition and compromise, is evident in both. Here, a decade on from the Oslo Accords and the first IRA ceasefire, the Irish process seems to have advanced much further than that in Israel and Palestine. The Irish process now appears to be nearer that of South Africa, which has endured, and less like that of Israel-Palestine, which has not. Hence the wisdom of the remark made by Israeli Prime Minister Rabin when he met John Major on a visit to London, and which an Israeli diplomat present at the occasion retailed to me: 'You have a ceasefire without a peace agreement. I have a peace agreement without a ceasefire. I know which one I would prefer'. No one claimed the Oslo Accords were perfect, but the analogy with the Anglo-Irish Treaty of 1922 is evident: one of the reasons why I, for my part, was 'pro-Treaty' over Oslo was precisely because of that analogy.

Thirdly there is the issue of rights, and of the status of parties in ethnic conflicts, where each, while proclaiming to the skies its own rights as a nation, denies recognition of the rights of the other, indeed that the other is a national group at all. Anyone familiar with the argument that the Protestants, or the Catholics, in the North of Ireland, or the Jews or the Palestinians are not a national group will know the points of overlap: *we are an ancient people, with title to this land, they are colons, fascists, immigrants, agents of imperialism and should go back to where they came from.* The linkage between Ireland and the Palestine question is of special relevance to the evolution of attitudes towards both conflicts on the left in Britain. In both cases, while the majority of international and particularly left-wing sentiment sided unequivocally with one side or the other (the nationalist 'struggle' in the North, Israel up to 1967, the Palestinians thereafter), a minority sought to develop and maintain a position that recognised the rights, and follies, of both communities and sought to establish some bi-national solution, what in the debates on the British and Irish left after 1968 came to be known as 'the two nations theory'.

That the Palestine question became an object of active debate and concern on the international left after the Arab-Israeli war of 1967, and the Irish conflict erupted a year later, with the Burntollet March of 1968, generated a discussion, and set of comparisons, that served greatly to clarify the issues involved. Of course, the majority of the left regarded any recognition of the Protestants as a legitimate national grouping as collusion with imperialism. I well recall an argument with a Marxist supporter of the Provisional IRA in a pub in West Belfast in 1969. Surely, I argued, in good and in this case quite appropriate Leninist fashion, the Protestants, bigoted as they were, had 'a right to self-determination'. The reply was devastating: 'The Protestants can have their fuckin right to self-determination', and she paused, '*provided* they go and do it somewhere else'. This reply is one that could be immediately translated into

Arabic, Hebrew, Serbo-Croat, Greek, Turkish, Sinhalese, Amharic, Hindi, Chinese and all the languages that have served in recent times to make claim to national rights on one side and deny them to the ethnic opponent.

Here, as with so much nationalism, was expressed in a specific national and nationalist form a sentiment that has, with terrible costs, been universally expressed in the modern world. The process of inter-ethnic delegitimation is, like nationalism, itself modular, adopting a specific garb in each case, but with an underlying, and necessarily common, structure. Sometimes this goes even to detail: the Irish nationalist derogation of Protestants as 'soupers', people who converted from Catholicism during the famine because the English offered them soup, is matched in the Serbian denunciation of Bosnian Muslims as just Serbs who were bribed with food and land by the Ottomans. The Bosnian-Serb conflict struck many observers as having Irish parallels, hence the remark of one senior UN official from Belfast, Cedric Thornberry, about this conflict: 'It is just like Northern Ireland, each side is worse than the other'.

Here too, and as a negative example, may be one of the more pertinent, and long-term, lessons of Ireland for the Middle East, as well as for former Yugoslavia, Sri Lanka, Kashmir and elsewhere. And it may point to the most important underlying contribution that Ireland, in good times and bad, has contributed, and can contribute, to understanding and resolving the conflicts of the modern world. Ireland has produced its armed strugglers, fanatical clergy and nationalist demagogues, but it has also, out of the experience of its history, produced others, diplomats, conciliators, sceptics, universalists, not least in the writers, such as Swift and Burke, later Joyce and O'Casey, more recently Conor Cruise O'Brien, Roddy Doyle, Mary Robinson, Tom Paulin and many others, who have questioned the nationalist narrative and its myths and advocated a more universal approach. At times, as in the case of Conor Dr Cruise O'Brien and his views on the North of Ireland and on Palestine, there may be an element of overshoot, but this is hardly surprising in such a polarised context, and the basic instinct, to critique the myths of one's own tribe, is an eminently healthy one, all the more needed in an age where 'community', 'identity', 'roots', 'authenticity' and 'tradition' have acquired new, and pernicious, legitimation.

This philosophy, tough-minded, principled and engaged, may, more than leprechauns or armed struggle, and indeed more than U2, Guinness or the Cliffs of Moher, be Ireland's greatest contribution to the world at large. In its very particularity, and in the debates and divisions its history has produced, Ireland has generated controversies and ideas that are of universal relevance. It is as a unique, most informative and long overdue contribution to the discussion and understanding of this question that the following volume is so particularly to be welcomed.

Fred Halliday
London School of Economics and Institut Barcelona d'Estudis
Internacionals
30 March 2007

Introduction:
Ireland and the Middle East:
Trade, Society and Peace

The thirteen chapters making up this volume offer the most comprehensive and wide-ranging work yet published on Ireland's involvement
in, and relationship with, the Middle East region over a period of almost 100
years. Specifically, the historians, commentators and foreign policy experts
who have contributed to this work examine Ireland's varied relationship with
eight Middle Eastern states – Afghanistan, Algeria, Egypt, Israel, Iraq,
Lebanon, the Palestinian Authority and Sudan.

It is true that Ireland's earliest official involvement in Middle East
diplomacy began with the eloquent and important contribution by Minister
for External Affairs Liam Cosgrave, and the Irish delegation headed by
Freddy Boland, at the United Nations General Assembly during the Suez
crisis of late 1956. However, as Michael Kennedy shows in a fascinating and
entertaining first chapter, for one Irish diplomat at least, Middle East diplomacy began twenty years earlier. Joseph Walshe, secretary of the Department
of External Affairs during the inter-war period, visited Egypt, Palestine and
the Sudan in the summers of 1937 and 1938. Walshe, a remarkable figure,
even by the standards of an Irish foreign service, which in its early decades
prided itself on the eccentrics, polymaths and strong-willed individuals who
made up its numbers, was intrigued by what he encountered on his sojourns
in the region and his reports back to Dublin throw much light on Irish
attitudes to the geopolitical issues preoccupying the Middle East at the time
– from the nascent Arab nationalist movement in Egypt to the debate over
the partition of Palestine.

The following chapter by Eunan O'Halpin explores the experience
between 1939 and 1945 of Ireland and Afghanistan. Two neutral states, both
of whom managed to stay out of Britain's war despite sharing land borders with
her or her possessions, and despite considerable diplomatic and economic
pressure from more than one of the major belligerents – in Ireland's case
Britain and the United States, in Afghanistan's Britain and (after June 1941)
the Soviet Union.

The chapter not only compares and contrasts British and German relations
with Ireland and Afghanistan both on the eve of, and during, the war, but

O'Halpin also draws on his scholarly research to bring to light what he calls the 'personal links' and 'bureaucratic coincidences' which reflect the intersecting nature of Ireland's role within the British Empire. For example, the British minister in Kabul from 1941 to 1943 was Sir Francis Wylie, an Irishman and a graduate of Trinity College, Dublin. Another Trinity graduate, the gifted linguist Philip Vickery, was the head of Indian Political Intelligence (IPI), a small London-based organisation which acted as a clearing house for all intelligence pertaining to India and to Indians. When he originally accepted the IPI post in 1926 Vickery's acceptance was sent from 'Carraig na Mara, Killiney'. He was succeeded in his post by yet another Trinity man, the Calcutta police officer Sir Charles Tegart.

The next two chapters by Jonathan Spyer and Jonathan Githens-Mazer both compare aspects of the Irish struggle for independence from the British with similar anti-colonial struggles by the Jewish Revisionist–Zionist Irgun group in British Palestine in the 1930s and 1940s and Algerian nationalists in their struggle against the French during the 1940s and 1950s. Both shed much new light on the issues addressed. Spyer's chapter is one of the first scholarly attempts to examine the influence of the Irish nationalist struggle on the ideology and policies of the Irgun. In doing so he draws on Hebrew documents never previously translated into English to explain just how these young Jewish radicals, who began to formulate the idea of revolt against British rule in the 1930s, looked to the Irish model, which at the time represented the only example of successful insurrection against the British Empire in the twentieth century, and the twentieth century's first example of a successful national liberation struggle.

In his chapter Githens-Mazer shows how the Irish Easter Rising of 1916 and the 1955 Philippeville Massacre in Algeria are illuminating examples of specific events in history which subsequently triggered the radicalisation of previously moderate nationalist movements. In particular, he shows how these 'tipping points' were popularly understood to correspond to the repression of the Irish and Algerian nations and nationalisms in history. As such, both events were significant and potent because they were closely, and popularly, associated with Irish and Algerian national myths, memories and symbols of disasters, defeats and massacres. Finally, Githens-Mazer makes a strong argument that both the Easter Rising and Philippeville Massacre are significant, not solely because the British and French authorities, and Unionist and *Colons* communities, pursued policies detrimental to the indigenous populations, but because these actions were understood by Irish and Algerian members of the nation through the prism of the preceding colonial/inter-nation relationship.

Northern Ireland, like most conflict-zones, has long drawn comparisons with other high-profile global conflicts. The seven chapters that follow Spyer and Githens-Mazer deal with issues relating to the 'The Troubles' in Northern Ireland by examining the conflict in the North with various past, and ongoing, conflicts in the Middle East region.

John Maher's examination of how the issue of 'territoriality' is dealt with in the novels of some of the leading Irish, Israeli and Palestinian writers – including Israeli author A.B. Yehoshua; Irish writers Pat McCabe and Glen Patterson and Palestinian writers Yahyia Yakhlif and Said Kashua – is not only highly original but shows how conflict and related issues such as territory have deeply influenced not only the politics, but the culture and literature of crisis zones.

John Doyle addresses a more conventional aspect of conflict in Ireland and Israel/Palestine by examining the manner in which Irish nationalists have attempted to link their struggle with the Israel–Palestinian conflict. It analyses two separate components of Irish nationalism. The foreign policy of the Republic of Ireland is analysed not only as the official expression of moderate Irish nationalism but also because it sets a broader ideological context within which even more radical voices are situated. Second, it examines how Sinn Féin, as the largest expression of radical Irish nationalism, and the majority party among the nationalist community in Northern Ireland, has sought to utilise comparisons with the Palestinian cause in its political discourse over the period of the recent conflict and peace process.

The chapters by Simon Kingston and Steven David take a look, respectively, at British counter-insurgency tactics in Northern Ireland and those of Israel in the Occupied Territories. As David notes, since the outbreak of the second intifada in September 2000, the Israeli authorities have identified, located and then killed alleged Palestinian terrorists with fighter aircraft, helicopter gun-ships, tanks, car bombs, booby traps and bullets. Over 200 Palestinian militants (and more than 100 innocent bystanders) have been killed prompting international condemnation, domestic soul-searching and bloody retaliation. As such, David asks whether the policy has been effective in reducing Palestinian attacks on Israeli civilians and whether the Israeli national interest has been served by this policy. Moreover, he examines whether a counter-insurgency approach that adopts a strategy of targeted killings is acceptable in moral terms or under international law.

Kingston asks similar questions in regard to the British counter-insurgency effort in Northern Ireland. As he notes, from the mid-1970s onwards, a number of covert groups were created by the RUC, the British army and various intelligence organisations to 'take the fight to the terrorists'. They did not always co-operate effectively and some were short-lived, but the evidence suggests that in the end they made a considerable difference. Intelligence-gathering and the running of informers ('touts' in Northern Irish slang) was a major focus of activities. By the mid-1980s, this intelligence was capable of being used to apprehend or engage IRA active service units in the preparation and prosecution of their operations. Most frequently, this direct engagement fell to the Special Air Service (SAS) to carry out. As in the Israeli case, Kingston shows that careful intelligence-led targeting of terrorist suspects, though slow to develop, did ultimately contribute positively to creating the environment that made a peace process possible.

This culminated with the Good Friday Agreement of 1998 and the next three chapters by Jonathan Moore, Michael Kerr and Gary Kent focus primarily on the lessons of the peace-making experience in Northern Ireland for various conflicts in the Middle East region from Palestine, to Lebanon to Iraq.

Moore asks whether the success of the Irish republican movement in moving from armed conflict to strictly peaceful means provides any lesson for the Islamist group Hamas, winner of the Palestinian parliamentary elections in January 2006. While he acknowledges that there are dangers in applying the Irish template to other groups involved in armed struggle across the globe, he sees one overwhelming lesson of the IRA's experience over the last two decades that Hamas would do well to learn: Militarism can produce a response but it is very rarely enough to force a powerful state to surrender. As such, if a group is to make political progress, it needs a sophisticated political strategy and must seriously analyse those with whom it is in conflict.

In 2006, Northern Ireland and Lebanon reached critical junctures in their approaches to power-sharing. Thus, Michael Kerr provides an extremely timely examination of the similarities and differences between the approaches to power-sharing in Northern Ireland and Lebanon since the 1970s. Both territories clearly share a history of power-sharing, brought about by internationally sponsored constitutional agreements between rival ethno-national or religious communities. As Kerr shows, consociational arrangements have repeatedly been used to regulate ethnic conflict in these divided societies by intervening powers. Many lessons can be learned from the varied approaches intervening states have taken towards implementing power-sharing in these two cases. For internationally brokered consociational agreements to stabilise, long-term support is essential. If external powers are to negotiate and implement power-sharing accords, they must act as stanchions between the rival communities in order to create and maintain a political environment where inter-communal antagonisms may be regulated through political co-operation.

Gary Kent's essay is no less topical, dealing as it does with conflict resolution and civil society in Northern Ireland and Iraq. The author is both a senior figure in the Labour Friends of Iraq in the United Kingdom and a long-time member of the British-Irish peace movement, and his attempt to draw on his experience in both conflict-zones is both fascinating and disturbing. As he notes in both Northern Ireland and Iraq there were, and are, people of all religions and forces in civil society who can do much to stabilise society, assist government, and eradicate and reverse extremism.

However, much of the Irish and British Left, who should be natural allies for those Iraqis risking their lives to prevent Iraq falling apart and descending into civil war, has embraced the 'anti-imperialist' terror in Iraq as they did previously in Northern Ireland. In the latter this meant accepting that the primary cause of terror was partition and in the case of Iraq it means accepting that the primary cause of violence is the 'occupation' and the presence of foreign troops. In both cases, a vociferous minority wanted the immediate withdrawal of troops and tended to franchise its thinking to extremist forces, rather than the majority in the two polities who wanted the troops withdrawn or scaled down but only when it was safe to do so. As Kent passionately argues, victory for the Sunni and Shia extremists and al-Qaeda would help condemn Iraq, and the wider Middle East, to languish in its own oil wealth without having to nurture a civil society or create the jobs for a restless youth who may then become more susceptible to the millenarian claims of Islamic totalitarianism.

The final two chapters in the volume by Constantin Gurdgiev and myself deal with recent Irish economic involvement in the Middle East. In his chapter Gurdgiev examines the impact (both positive and negative) of Irish aid to the Palestinian Authority since the beginning of the Oslo peace process in 1993. By the mid-1990s, at the height of the Oslo era, Ireland had significantly increased its bilateral financial aid to the Palestinian Authority (PA). The majority of Irish aid to the PA since that time falls into three categories – direct bilateral aid; NGO administered aid; and aid flows through EU programmes. But as Gurdgiev, an economist by training, clearly shows, it is not a lack of aid, but a lack of proper governance and reforms, that is the primary cause of the miserable economic situation faced by the Palestinian population. In contrast with the rest of the region, in PA-administered territories even the first trench of reforms, primarily comprising of regulatory reforms which are easy to adopt, such as streamlining court and collections procedures; taxation rates and collection; exchange rate and central banking regulations; and zoning and development regulations are all lagging behind regional norms. Similarly, even the first round of trade tariffs and barriers reforms were not implemented in the PA-administered areas.

Ireland's economic commitment to the Middle East over the last decade and a half can be seen not only in growing aid contributions to the Palestinian people, but also in the growing involvement of Irish firms from numerous economic sectors in the Middle Eastern economy. For example, the Irish capacity to compete in the region in the area of cultural and creative industries was highlighted by the success of the Irish architectural firm Heneghan Peng, in beating off 1557 competitors from eighty-three different countries in 2003 to win the contract to design Egypt's new Grand Museum in Giza. The subsequent design for this flagship building adorns the cover of this book. Since the success of Heneghan Peng in 2003, Irish companies in the region have gone from strength to strength – as evidenced by the largest ever trade delegation to the region, led by Taoiseach Bertie Ahern, in January 2007. As such, my own concluding chapter examines this newest aspect of Ireland's Middle Eastern involvement by focusing on the extent to which three of the region's nations – Egypt, Lebanon and Israel – have come to perceive the 'Celtic Tiger', the Irish economic 'miracle', as an important model for their own economic development. It also assesses whether the Irish achievement in harnessing an educated, English-speaking workforce to a number of progressive economic policies – most notably low tax rates, flexible business practices and a strategic goal of promoting a competitive enterprise environment – is relevant to the development of these three nations.

Recent research into Irish foreign policy, in particular studies examining Ireland's role at the United Nations and as a member of the European Union, have underlined the fact that despite its small size and location on the margins of the European continent, its policy of military neutrality, and its complex and often contradictory relationship with the United Kingdom, Ireland has contributed much to international affairs since its establishment as a Republic in the late 1940s. We hope that this varied and wide-ranging book of essays on Ireland's involvement in, and ties with, the Middle East will show that the same is true for our involvement in this most fascinating and volatile of regions even prior to this date. But more than this, we also hope that it will whet the appetite for further research on this still underexplored area of Irish foreign policy.

Rory Miller, London, January 2007

'A voyage of exploration':[1] Irish diplomatic perspectives on Egypt, Sudan and Palestine in the inter-war years

Michael Kennedy

During the inter-war period between 1919 and 1939 Irish diplomats rarely ventured beyond the borders of Europe. With the exception of the United States, contact with the wider world was minimal.[2] The inter-war Irish Free State diplomatic service showed little of the enthusiasm of its Dáil Éireann predecessor to post envoys to the four corners of the globe. Strapped for cash and focused on British–Irish relations, it set its sights closer to home. Ireland's membership of the League of Nations enabled contact with the fifty or so members of that body, most of them states in which Ireland did not have a diplomatic mission. Even then, vital missions such as the Office of the Permanent Delegate to the League of Nations at Geneva were targeted for cutbacks by the Department of Finance.[3]

In this period Ireland maintained its formal contact with the Middle East through the office of the Irish Permanent Delegate at Geneva. As there were no Irish diplomatic missions in the Middle East until the mid-1970s, External Affairs relied on information from third parties, mostly League of Nations and Foreign Office sources, to get an understanding of the region's affairs. Two trips by Joseph Walshe, the Secretary of the Department of External Affairs, to the Middle East provided a personal informal dimension to the formal contacts developed at Geneva and also gave an Irish perspective to the affairs of the region.

In the summers of 1937 and 1938 Walshe visited Palestine, a British Mandate; Egypt, a former protectorate now a nominally independent state under strong British influence; and the Sudan, an Anglo-Egyptian condominium, where, after 1924, the Egyptian influence was vigorously snuffed out. He used his contacts in the Foreign Office to meet senior British officials in the three countries.

A former Jesuit seminarian who found his vocation in diplomacy, the 'eternal city' of Rome and the Holy Land were the two centres of his world. For Walshe, in Rome and 'in the Africa of Augustine, was where his world lay; where his world had its beginning and where it would, he hoped, have its end'.[4] He had a profound interest in the Holy Places in Jerusalem and was strongly Christian. Writing to Eamon de Valera from Khartoum in 1938 he reminded the Taoiseach that 'this whole area was Christian long before St. Patrick came to Ireland'.[5]

A keen observer of British involvement in Palestine, Egypt and Sudan, his annual vacations in 1937 and 1938 became fact-finding missions 'encouraged' by de Valera.[6] Walshe kept de Valera 'informed of conditions' wherever he went. When he met the British Ambassador in Cairo, Sir Miles Lampson, in 1938, Lampson 'assumed during his whole talk with me that I had been sent – this year and last – by the Government on a voyage of exploration'.[7] These visits, ostensibly private holidays, in fact augmented contacts via the League of Nations and were the first sustained contact, albeit unofficial and only over two years, between Irish diplomats and their counterparts in the Middle East since low-intensity contacts between Irish and Egyptian nationalists at the Paris Peace Conference after the First World War.

IRELAND AND EGYPT, 1919–36

Egyptians and Irish enthusiastically welcomed US President Woodrow Wilson's innovative Fourteen Point programme which he introduced during the First World War. By the end of that conflict Britain had conceded that self-government would be granted to Ireland, but not Egypt. Representing strong nationalist movements, Irish and Egyptian delegations made their cases for independence to the victorious powers at Paris. De Valera instructed the Irish to 'get into the closest possible contact' with the 'oppressed nations' including Egypt seeking independence from Britain.[8]

The task of the Egyptian delegation to Paris, the Wafd, led by Said Zaghlul, was similar to the Irish delegation as it was 'empowered by the nation and expressing its will about a matter which it has assigned to us... complete independence'.[9] Yet there were few beneficial contacts between the Irish and the Egyptians in Paris. Arab nationalism was a potent force in Egypt, but when the head of the Irish delegation in Paris, Seán T. O'Ceallaigh, made contact with the Wafd, he found that the Irish had to act 'in an advisory capacity' to the Egyptians who looked to the Irish 'for aid and assistance in drawing up their documents and presenting their claims'.[10]

Nevertheless, the Irish planned 'joint action' in conjunction with the Egyptians and 'some other of the smaller oppressed nations' against Britain.[11] However, it was feared that contact with the Egyptians might damage the Irish case at Paris by diluting it and the general view was that it was averse from identifying Ireland's case with that of the other victims of the Empire ... of course they have our full sympathy and any mutual assistance that can be rendered without definitely aligning our position with theirs is very desirable.[12]

O'Ceallaigh replied that 'whatever action we took in regard to the working arrangement with the Egyptians and South Africans was taken with full knowledge of the relative strength of our case'. He tellingly added

I do not expect much to come from our consultations with either of these people. We can be of much more service to them than they can be to us. We were glad to be able to offer them helpful advice and suggestions and to assure them ... our cordial support and sympathy in their fight.[13]

Within the ranks of the 'oppressed nations' there were, it seemed, hierarchies of the oppressed, and for Irish nationalists the Egyptian case for independence ranked below the Irish. A common bond never formed between the Irish and the Egyptians at Paris. This is surprising when compared to the considerable contacts between Irish and Indian nationalists in the same period. It may have been that Irish and Indian forms of nationalism were more developed than their Egyptian counterpart and bonds were easier to forge, and perhaps future research will explore this matter further. It must have dawned on O'Ceallaigh that the Irish and Egyptian delegations to Paris did have one important area of common ground: both were unsuccessful in winning the support of the victorious powers in their struggle for independence from Britain.

GEOPOLITICAL COMPARISONS BETWEEN IRELAND AND EGYPT

Britain unilaterally declared Egyptian independence in 1922, though 'it failed to satisfy Egyptian national aspirations'.[14] Thereafter, an 'uneasy and ultimately unworkable balance of forces' between the monarchy, parliament and the British, governed Egypt through an 'unstable façade of parliamentary democracy'.[15] In Ireland, those who rejected the 1921 Anglo-Irish Treaty argued that the Irish Free State had little independence from Britain due to the Oath of Allegiance to the Crown, but compared to Egypt, the Irish Free State had a distinct international identity and was a stable democracy. Its dominion status notwithstanding, the Irish Free State was admitted to the League of Nations in September 1923 as a fully independent state, but as will be seen below, Egyptian membership of the League was more problematic.

Lacking representation in Cairo, the best channel of information on Egypt for Dublin was through John Dulanty, Ireland's High Commissioner in London. When Dulanty spoke with British Foreign Secretary Anthony Eden in January 1936, Eden 'doubted whether anybody outside the inner political circles in Egypt could have much idea of the amount of intrigue existing there'.[16] Egypt was a continual 'political maelstrom', with 'British soldiers there in reserve if trouble should arise'; a synopsis which absolved Britain from all blame for fomenting intrigue. When Dulanty inquired about British plans for Egypt, Eden told him that Britain 'would seek to get a Treaty in which the British position, particularly concerning military occupation and defence was recognised and regularised'. It would be 'an extremely difficult Treaty to negotiate', but the British High Commissioner in Cairo, Sir Miles Lampson 'seemed reasonably hopeful'. Dulanty had no instructions from Dublin on Egypt, but he 'thought they would be interested' and sought further information from Eden.

Lampson settled the question which had 'defied all previous attempts' in the Anglo-Egyptian Treaty of 1936.[17] Under its terms the British occupation of Egypt formally ended. Britain would withdraw all troops except those protecting the Suez Canal zone. There were solid geopolitical reasons for Egypt accepting the treaty. Dependent on Britain for its defence, Egypt was worried by Italian imperial ambitions in Africa. Italy had recently conquered Ethiopia to the southeast and was in control of Libya to the west. The British garrison would strengthen Egypt against Italian ambitions. In the short term the treaty secured Egypt's defence and the 'presence of British armed forces in Egypt was...as essential to Egypt as to Great Britain'.[18] Ultimately, the 1936 Treaty became a liability for Egypt during the Second World War. Egypt's fate showed why de Valera had acted wisely in ensuring the complete evacuation of British military forces from Ireland through the return of the Treaty ports to Ireland under the 1938 Anglo-Irish agreements. A Department of External Affairs memorandum prepared for de Valera on British relations with Egypt and Iraq explained that:

> In the event of war or an imminent menace of war or apprehended emergency Iraq and Egypt will furnish to Britain all facilities and assistance in their power, including the use of ports, aerodromes, railways and other means of communication.[19]

It was not unlike Article 7 of the 1921 Anglo-Irish Treaty under which similar facilities were available for Britain in time of war. Britain assumed that its use of military facilities in Egypt 'would not be impaired by a hostile or even unenthusiastic Egyptian government'.[20] But when ostensibly neutral Egypt made contact with the Axis in 1942 as Rommel advanced across North Africa, Lampson sent troops to the Abdin Palace in Cairo and forced a change of government in favour of the Allies. While British forces remained in Egypt Cairo had no real power to follow an independent foreign policy. As External Affairs noted, Egypt along with Iraq were merely satellite states of Great Britain. They are permanently occupied by considerable bodies of British forces, and they are obliged to take part in some manner in all British wars, no matter how small the extent to which their own interests are involved. Their position is worse than ours even now.

This was written in November 1937, a little under a year before the return of the Treaty ports to Irish control. A comparison between British action in Egypt in 1942 and Britain's inability to force Ireland to grant Britain access to Irish ports in 1939–40, except by invasion of Ireland, which London rejected for fear of the reaction in the United States and the Dominions, shows how Ireland ensured its neutrality and the freedom to follow its own foreign policy during the Second World War. It also shows the failure of Egypt to act in a similar manner. Egypt finally declared war on Germany in February 1945. Ireland remained neutral, though with a distinctly pro-Allied disposition. The ultimate proof of international sovereignty is an independent foreign policy. By removing British forces in 1938, Ireland could prove her independence, Michael Yapp concludes that seventeen years later it was similar for Egypt: 'by 1955 British troops had also gone from Egypt and the country was at last truly independent'.[21]

EGYPT JOINS THE LEAGUE OF NATIONS

In an attempt to prove her international sovereignty, Egypt sought membership of the League of Nations in 1937. For Egypt, as well as for Iran and Turkey, 'to be in the League enhanced their security, not simply by bringing them under the now uncertain protection of the Covenant, but by making it easy for them to insist in exercising the same rights as those of other members'.[22] Much the same argument could be applied to Ireland when she joined the League in 1923. Before formally applying to the League, Egypt asked to be invited to join by existing members. Britain backed Egypt and informed Ireland that they would 'much appreciate it' if any Dominion governments 'were able to extend to [the] Egyptian Government an invitation to apply for election as a member of the League and would notify the Secretary-General of the League simultaneously of the action' they were taking.[23] On showing the telegram to Walshe, his officials noted: 'Seen by Secretary. No action by S.[aorstát] E.[ireann].'[24]

Dublin was not going to get involved in this British-sponsored process. In a time of British–Irish antagonism, Ireland was loath to support Britain over Egypt as Egypt would be little more than another vote for British policies at Geneva. Support for Egypt would be an unnecessary show of support for Britain and would cast doubt on Ireland's independence, the achievement of which had been the key theme of Irish foreign policy from 1919. When the Egyptian minister for foreign affairs highlighted 'the Egyptian people's

attachment to the high ideals of justice, concord and fraternity between all
nations' and submitted Egypt's League application, Ireland, though
expressing similar sentiments at the core of her foreign policy, was unmoved
and did not send a despatch to invite Egypt into the League.[25] Walshe
explained that there did

> not seem to be any particular point why we in this country should send an
> invitation to Egypt. She was bound to receive invitations from the States
> Members of the Commonwealth such as India, Australia, New Zealand
> and South Africa, for reasons which are evident, from the Mohammedan
> States and from certain European States which have close trade or other
> relations with Egypt.[26]

For Ireland, 'an invitation from us would have been a departure from our
conservative policy of not interfering with things that do not really concern
us'.[27]

Ireland agreed to an Extraordinary Assembly meeting to admit Egypt.
The Irish Permanent Delegate to the League, Frank Cremins attended as
the sole Irish delegate.[28] He 'of course' voted in favour of Egypt's admission.[29]
Cremins later informed Dublin that 'there was of course no opposition, and
Egypt was unanimously elected'.[30] The Egyptian delegation 'immediately
entered the Assembly and took their places, and all the delegations
proceeded, in speeches, long or short, to voice their welcome'. Cremins 'said
a few words... joining the name of Ireland to the welcome that was being
extended'. He added that 'the speeches were almost interminable'. The
social side was similar as 'many delegations vied with each other' in
honouring the Egyptians. Ireland was not one of them.

PARTITION AND PALESTINE

The unanimous admission of Egypt to the League contrasted with 'the tragic
conflict of wills in Palestine' between Jews and Arabs.[31] The Palestine
Mandate came into existence in 1923; mandates 'were not colonies, but
rather a form of trust in which the mandatory power administered the
territory under the supervision of the League of Nations'.[32] Ireland had no
mandates and took little interest in the mandates system until events in
Palestine worsened. The Arab rebellion of 1936, provoked by fears that
Jewish immigration would lead to Zionist dominance in Palestine, caused
conditions in Palestine 'to arouse anxiety throughout the world'.[33]

The Peel Commission investigated reasons behind the uprising,
concluding 'that Britain's obligations to the Arabs and the Jews were
irreconcilable and the mandate unworkable'.[34] The July 1937 report of the
Commission proposed the partition of Palestine into independent Jewish and

Arab states, with the Holy Places and Jerusalem remaining under British control. The Arab governments and the Arabs of Palestine rejected the proposal, while the Twentieth Zionist Congress rejected the proposed boundaries but reluctantly agreed in principle to partition.

In Ireland the Commission's report 'met with an overwhelmingly negative response...both because it was viewed as another case of British colonial malfeasance...and because Ireland's own experience had left her population with grave doubts that partition was a viable solution to territorial conflict'.[35] Ireland had been partitioned under the Government of Ireland Act of 1920 and the result had few supporters in the Irish Free State. Palestine's post-1918 history was 'a tragedy of errors beginning with a colossal blunder'; the *Irish Times* called the proposed partition 'a desperate remedy...the last desperate expedient'.[36] In Geneva, Cremins was unimpressed by the 'gratuitously insulting references to Ireland' in the Commission's report.[37] Page 135 explained that

> Acts of 'terrorism' in various parts of the country have long been only too familiar reading in the newspapers. As in Ireland in the worst days after the War or in Bengal, intimidation at the point of a revolver has become a not infrequent feature of Arab politics. Attacks by Arabs on Jews, unhappily, are no new thing.[38]

As 'any protest would give much greater prominence to the objectionable references than they otherwise would receive', Dublin let the matter sit.[39] The *Irish Independent* nonetheless remarked that 'the sundering of Ireland is far from being on all fours with Palestine and it has none of the justification which is claimed for the policy of dealing with the Jews and the Arabs'.[40]

As the Peel Commission reported, Walshe left Dublin for the Middle East. He passed through Cairo on 22 July, calling in on Lampson. 'Just a courtesy call' the ambassador noted in his diary.[41] The two men spoke for about an hour, Walshe commenting that he 'had been struck by the friendly feeling obviously existing towards [Britain] now in Egypt' since the 1936 Treaty. The British diplomat thought Walshe was 'a pleasant well spoken individual...I rather liked the fellow'.

In Walshe's absence, External Affairs commenced preparations for the 1937 League Assembly. Pessimistic about the value of the League after its failure to counter the Italian invasion of Abyssinia, Head of the League Section, Michael Rynne, concluded that 'difficult questions, such as...Palestine are essentially matters that the Great Powers prefer to settle out of the Assembly, which since 1935, is tending to become more and more formal and ineffective'.[42i]

Rynne wrote to Cremins that 'the Secretary is still away on leave, and I have no reason (and probably no right!) to anticipate his mind on the matter of the Delegation'.[43] But if de Valera chose to attend the Assembly and 'if

Palestine was to loom large on the Agenda, there's no knowing but the Secretary might also attend'. Rynne jocularly continued that if Walshe chose to travel to Geneva he would be well prepared, being 'just back from the scene of action and should be fully equipped with the "low-down" on the whole Jew–Arab situation'.

Walshe returned to Dublin in early September, passing through London on 7 September. The research for this chapter has not discovered any report of his trip in the Department of External Affairs archives in Dublin or the Foreign Office records at the British National Archives, Kew, while a search of Eamon de Valera's papers likewise revealed nothing. Walshe did not join the delegation to Geneva, though de Valera was the Primary Delegate. Cremins knew that it was unlikely that 'the Palestine question would come in concrete form before the Assembly... apart from discussions in the Sixth Committee', and from another source that 'the British would not be at all anxious that the matter should come before the Assembly – quite the contrary'.[44]

When the Iraqi Minister hoped that the Irish would 'support the Arab point of view', at the Assembly Cremins replied that he was 'at present collecting all the information [he] could get in order to put it before [his] Minister'.[45] The Irish Minister to the Vatican was to ascertain in light of the Peel Commission report, 'any views of the Holy See in the proposals therein contained relative to the future of the Holy Places'.[46] Minister William Macaulay replied that 'the Holy See attitude was 'unfavourable' as the partition of Palestine was not believed to be the only solution and the abandonment of some of the Holy Places, common as they are to all Christians, is considered at the Vatican as most deplorable'.[47] In a strongly worded section, Macaulay continued:

> The Holy See has little sympathy with Jewish claims to a National Home in Palestine... once the Jews are in control of the territory allocated to them the Holy Places therein will not be respected and difficulties created for pilgrims and those Christians living there.

The report immediately went to the Irish delegation in Geneva and the sentiments incorporated into its thinking.

On 23 September, without briefing the British or any other delegation of his intentions, de Valera attacked the Peel Commission's report at the Sixth Committee. He prefaced his remarks by attacking the committee for 'prejudicing' a solution in Palestine by adopting a position whereby it appeared that 'the Committee had given its approval in advance to a partition scheme'.[48] He called for a solution in Palestine with 'open terms of reference', and

> did not want the search to begin with an agreement that the solution was to be sought along the lines of partition. He did not believe it could be found along such lines. Partition was no solution.

Neither Jews nor Arabs, nor, with reference to the Holy See, 'the Christian world interested in the Holy Places'[49] wanted partition, 'it was not going to bring peace but rather would result in future problems even more complex than those being dealt with at that moment.'[1] De Valera also highlighted 'the consequences of partition' for Iraq after Britain carved the Emirate of Kuwait out of the British mandate for Mesopotamia and he reiterated that these consequences 'had been very clearly indicated in the speech by the representative of Iraq. Partition of their territory was the cruellest wrong that could be done to any people'.[50] Referring to British policy in Palestine, de Valera

> did not, of course, believe that there could be any really satisfactory solution of the problem which had been created. If promises were given, which by their nature could not be kept, at least no cynical attempt should be made now to pretend to reconcile the irreconcilable on the basis of these promises. That would satisfy nobody.

The comments could just as equally apply to the remit of the Irish Boundary Commission, which under the Anglo-Irish Treaty attempted to 'reconcile the irreconcilable' by determining 'in accordance with the wishes of the inhabitants, so far as may be compatible with economic and geographic conditions, the boundaries between Northern Ireland and the rest of Ireland.' Later Britain learned that if de Valera had 'known that the question of the partition of Palestine was to come up at the meeting in the form in which it did he would certainly before the meeting have told Mr. Eden and Mr. MacDonald what his views were'.[52] Yet there was praise for de Valera not only from the Arab world, but also from the pro-Arab Foreign Office in London who, though angry that de Valera had 'intervened'[53] in the discussion at the Sixth Committee, noted that there was 'unfortunately a great deal of truth in what Mr de Valera said'.[54] A subsequent minute agreed that de Valera's speech had 'a great deal of sense in it – but one would hardly expect it to be very constructive'.[55]

While the Foreign Office assumed that de Valera had been referring to the partition of Ireland rather than the partition of Iraq, de Valera in fact made no reference to Ireland. The speech was nothing like the hawkish speeches de Valera made on partition in Ireland. References to Iraq and Palestine meant more on the international stage than references to Northern Ireland. In concluding at Geneva, de Valera reiterated his main point on partition and Palestine; he wished to protest 'against any proposal for a solution by partition'.

De Valera certainly got through to his audience, supportive telegrams came from bodies such as an Arabian convention in Detroit representing half a million Americans of Arab descent who passed a vote in thanks:

> Ireland has tasted this bitter cup before we did and cannot be deceived by the machinations and the confidence game being played ... we thank God for Ireland and the little nations.[56]

Judah Magnes, the President of the Hebrew University of Jerusalem and a leading Jewish opponent of partition, wrote of his 'greatest interest' in de Valera's speech.[57] De Valera replied that he did not 'know the Palestine problem' as Magnes knew it, yet he knew 'from a knowledge of what partition means in Ireland now, and what I am convinced it will mean in the future', that partition was 'the worst of the many solutions' for Palestine and 'only by negotiation and free agreement between Jew and Arab, and having due regard to the interests of Christians ... can there be a satisfactory solution'.[58] This was 'not prompted by any feeling of hostility towards the great Jewish people'. Former Chief Rabbi of the Irish Free State, Dr Isaac Herzog, now Chief Rabbi of Palestine, wrote to de Valera, appealing to de Valera's 'natural, inborn sympathy for an unfortunate, homeless, historic race' and to de Valera's 'historic sense, to your lofty idealism, to you as the great regenerator of the Irish race, whose history, as you once remarked to me, offers so many parallels with the history of Israel' to support the case of 'the most unfortunate of races, of that homeless race, a wanderer for nearly two thousand years'.[59] Herzog was a close friend of de Valera's, but despite his views, when the letters of support for de Valera stopped arriving, Irish policy on Palestine reverted to a watching brief; the 1937 speech became a once off. De Valera remained opposed to partition, but took little further interest in Palestine; he had far more important matters relating to British–Irish relations to deal with in 1938.

Passing through Cairo in June 1938 Walshe again met Lampson. They discussed the future of Palestine over 'a very long chat'. Lampson told Walshe that

a proposal for a ten-year truce is in the air. The Arabs and Jews will thus have time to come to some understanding. No doubt G.B. will consolidate her position in the meantime with both sides. The policy of divide and conquer is to be abandoned being over worked and too crude to achieve any lasting results.[60]

De Valera agreed, telling the Dáil that 'no solution involving the partition of that country should be sanctioned in any way by the League of Nations'.[61] The Arab rebellion died down in 1939. Under the subsequent British White Paper on Palestine partition was replaced by proposals for an independent Palestine with Arabs in the majority. The Mandates Commission, unimpressed, implied that partition would be the wisest solution. Its views were merely advisory opinions for the council. Before the Council could meet, war broke out in Europe.

WALSHE'S 1938 TRAVELS IN EGYPT AND SUDAN

Walshe visited Egypt and Sudan in the summer of 1938, a colleague writing candidly that the trip 'certainly surprised me. [Walshe] is apparently in the mind of going Arab'.[62] He arrived in Egypt in early May, made courtesy calls in Cairo, including on Lampson, and then left for Alexandria 'for a few days'.[63] Returning to Cairo Walshe took a flying boat to Khartoum to explore east-central Sudan. After a week he had 'done quite a lot of exploring in spite of a shade temperature of 105 degrees during the day and 95 degrees at night'. Omdurman, to the north of Khartoum, Walshe found 'very interesting', meeting 'some old warriors' who had fought the British in 1898. It was peaceful, 'the Festival of the Birthday of the Prophet is on at the moment and although there are tens of thousands of Arabs in the two adjoining cities of Khartoum and Omdurman there isn't a trace of disorder'.

In a sharp comment on the nature of British rule in Sudan Walshe explained that the 'Sons of the Mahdi and of the Khalif who succeeded him are local potentates...no doubt enjoying fat salaries from the British'. He speculated that they were 'close friends of the Governor General', Sir Stewart Symes who came to Sudan in 1934 'at a critical period in its evolution' as the government 'was conscientiously endeavouring to train the country for eventual independence'.

Walshe travelled southeast from Khartoum to Al-Aswat 'in an old Ford car ...following a desert track along the line of the Blue Nile' to Barakat, 'the centre and the administrative headquarters of the great cotton growing area'. He was keen to see how British rule was administered and Symes obliged him, providing 'every facility to see and understand'. The desire to explore further was now overwhelming, and 'were it not for the intense heat' his party 'should have given in to [the] temptation to continue for another two hundred miles to the Abyssinian border'. Walshe was moving into terra incognita and told de Valera how 'the people, who get blacker and blacker as you go further south are invariably very courteous and you are not in the least disturbed at not meeting any white people'.

Returning to Khartoum, Walshe met with Symes and 'the principal Government officials'. Walshe found Symes to be 'a very decent fellow' and 'a close friend' of Paschal Robinson, the Papal Nuncio in Dublin. Showing a strong interest in Symes' policies, Walshe cast Symes as an 'idealist' with 'very long experience in the Near East Africa' which had not made him 'the narrow minded imperialist one expects to find in a post such as this'.

In contrast to the last decades of British rule in Ireland, Symes could 'go where he likes here with a few unarmed policemen'. The nature of British rule in Sudan appealed to Walshe, he told de Valera that 'the British could stay here for centuries if they had always men of Symes' type to do the Governing for them'. In an apparently genuine aside to de Valera, though one which goes against all the norms of Irish foreign policy, Walshe suggested to the Taoiseach that he 'give a little thought to the question of a colony when you have leisure. It would be a splendid training ground for our people, and colonial budgets can be made to balance without subsidies from the home Government.' The two sentences stand out sharply in the history of Irish foreign policy as probably the only time any Irish diplomat seriously suggested that Ireland should develop an empire.

While Symes' obituary described him as having 'a friendly surface manner' and as being 'an excellent host', he 'was not an easy man to get to know'.[64] A sympathy for Italy, a pro-Catholic outlook, particularly towards the work of Italian Catholic missionaries in southern Sudan and connections with Italian nobility by marriage all made Symes an appealing figure for Walshe, the Italophile. There is no indication in Walshe's correspondence that he understood that Symes was strengthening traditional local patterns of authority in north Sudan to further reduce the Egyptian influence on the pro-Egyptian Sudanese middle classes. In 1938 Symes had concluded his 'initial period of very direct and patriarchal administration' and was now favouring native administration 'in principle and in its proper place as local government'.[65] Walshe saw this process positively and in contrast to British 'Anglicisation' and the decline of the Irish language in Ireland in the second half of the nineteenth century:

> he and his successors will be advisers to the Sheiks. He is making no effort to anglicise the people. English is not taught in the schools though no doubt it will be when a Sunday school system has been established. He makes all the officials learn and speak Arabic and the local dialects.[66]

Neither did Walshe make any reference to the policy of running Sudan as two separate colonies, the three provinces of 'Southern Sudan' being a 'Closed District', or to the development of native governing bodies merely to lighten the load on the British and diminish the pro-Egyptian influence in the north. Walshe seemed to be coming speedily to the simplistic conclusion that British policy in Sudan was the enlightened opposite to 'Killing Home Rule by Kindness' as tried by Britain in late nineteenth-century Ireland.

Despite his favourable view of Symes, Walshe did not see a long-term future for British rule in Egypt and Sudan, speculating that with the Arab populations

> coming under the growing power especially cultural of Arabia which is only just across the Red Sea and is their Religious homeland ... whether any white nation can hold out in these regions for more than another fifty years.[67]

The cultural and political force of Arabia would snuff out British rule and influence. Walshe's friend Michael MacWhite, a former French foreign legionnaire who had fought in Mesopotamia and was now Ireland's Minister in Rome, was also conscious of the growing power of Arabia, writing to Walshe:

the seriousness of the Egyptian situation... and of the situation on the other side of the Red Sea... Ibn Saud, the powerful ruler of the Arab tribes... has gradually veered against the British because of the possibility of conquering Irak and its large oil fields with Italian support.[68]

MacWhite also linked the problems in Palestine with Arab nationalism as 'the strife in Palestine has roused Moslem feeling to a state of exaltation unprecedented in our time'.[69]

A RETURN TO IRISH–EGYPTIAN RELATIONS

On 14 May Walshe returned to Cairo, meeting Lampson and other officials. Lampson 'emphasized how enormously important it was for any country interested in world peace to keep in touch with this region of the world'. Walshe replied that de Valera 'realized, in particular, the importance of Egypt as one of the chief sensitive areas in the world' and was 'fully conscious' of the 'problems involved in the renaissance of the Jewish and Arab peoples'.[70] Lampson spoke 'very highly' of de Valera's 'work at Geneva' and Walshe 'got confirmation' of this 'from officials and others'. He met 'a great many people with Irish blood among the officials – who all expressed unfeigned delight at the Anglo-Irish rapprochement... naturally they are very proud of the results achieved by you in the Agreement with the British'.

Finding Lampson 'communicative' and with the external association of Ireland with the Commonwealth in mind, Walshe 'mentioned the possibility of Egypt coming into a group more broadly based than the present Commonwealth group'. To Walshe's 'surprise', Lampson replied that 'he had given the subject a good deal of thought'. He told Walshe that he found the Foreign Office 'impervious to new ideas' and 'agreed instantly that no red tape or precedent should be allowed to make serious difficulties about the adhesion of separate monarchies or republics to a new Commonwealth'. It was a novel idea that would see fruition with India in the 1940s.

Walshe also met Sharara Pasha, head of the Egyptian Department of Foreign Affairs, whom he found 'very friendly'. Other 'higher civil servants' he viewed less positively as they had 'interests in commercial concerns... to the detriment of the general welfare of the State'. He told de Valera that they 'are all with a few splendid exceptions very much on the make and their work for the State is neither zealous nor efficient'. Zealous, efficient officials working selflessly for the greater good of the state was Walshe's image of the ideal civil servant, an image he tried to cultivate in External Affairs. As for the Egyptians, 'this appalling defect leaves them completely at the mercy of foreign or private interests and nothing but an extremely strong national movement will afford a remedy.' He continued that

Egypt has unfortunately one great weakness...she has no really patriotic
leaders and the Service as well as the Cabinet is venal to the last degree.
This is recognised by all good Egyptians and they look forward to the time
when they will have a Leader who will be simpleminded and ruthless with
corruption.

The implied, but unstated, compliment to de Valera was clear.

Walshe and Sharara Pasha discussed the establishment of diplomatic
relations between their countries. Sharara Pasha was 'strongly convinced, as I
am, that, in the course of the next few years, there ought to be an exchange of
legations between the two countries'. The need for diplomatic relations was
due to the 'certain similarity of relationship vis-à-vis Great Britain' and the
'instinctive sympathy for Ireland and Irishmen' in Egypt. An embassy would
also gain the support of the small Irish ex-patriot community in Egypt, headed
by the brothers Arthur and Gerald Delaney, both of whom were known to de
Valera. There was also the need to provide support for the 'many Irish citizens
[who] go on pilgrimage to the Holy Land' and 'almost invariably pass through
Egypt' and the 'tourists who pass the winter season in Egypt'.[71]

Together these were not the most substantial reasons, but there were few
other ties between Ireland and Egypt necessitating the establishment of
bilateral relations. Walshe returned to the establishment of bilateral relations
with Egypt when he returned to Dublin. In a draft letter to Sharara Pasha,
unsent, but written in the context of hoping to interest the Egyptian army in
purchasing horses from Ireland, Walshe wrote that 'pending the establishment
of diplomatic relations between us I hope that it will be possible in due course
to begin doing something to make Egypt better known in Ireland'.[72] The
Egyptians had taken on board recent events in Ireland and 'the hundreds of
papers in Egypt in various languages' gave the appointment of Douglas Hyde
as President of Ireland 'great publicity'. Walshe found the 'interest displayed in
Ireland by everybody one meets here' a 'constant cause of surprise'.

The development of some rather surprising wider ties with Egypt was
suggested. A 'brother of the Minister for the Interior' hoped that Ireland could
provide 200 officers to train the Egyptian army. Walshe found 'all concerned'
in favour of 'concluding a treaty of friendship with us' and 'with the other
countries associated in varying degrees with the Commonwealth'. But there
was a harder edge to this woolly concept as the Egyptians understood

the advantage of linking up with the individual associated States rather
than with G.B. alone. Egypt could form the first unit of the new group
which would change the Commonwealth's character and give us an
opportunity of sliding quietly out of the King's orbit.

Bilateral relations with Egypt would bring Dublin into the 'will and confidence
of the Egyptian Government' and Walshe told de Valera he would not be
'surprised if our influence with them became greater than that of the British

Embassy. If that position were realized…our prestige and influence here would react favourably on our more immediate position vis-à-vis the British at home.' Both Egypt and Ireland were playing each other off for their own ends.

Before leaving Egypt Walshe explored 'the southern Sinai area with my friend', possibly Gerald Delaney, driving 'through desert tracts and river beds to the Holy Mountain some three hundred miles from here'.[73] The route through the mountains of Sinai was 'a fitting setting for the greatest drama of our race', and Walshe was 'more impressed on the mountain of the Ten Commandments than in Palestine.' He and his companion 'stayed two nights in the Greek Monastery at the foot of the mountain and discussed age-old problems including the procession of the Holy Ghost (on which they were not very enlightening)'. While to Walshe the monks seemed 'to live outside time', in a surreal sentence Walshe added that they were not so removed 'as not to know about our new constitution, and the appointment of Dr. Hyde as President.'

Leaving Egypt by flying boat Walshe arrived in England on 6 June, passing through London where he intended to 'to remain over Tuesday in order to pay a few visits of courtesy to officials who kindly secured me facilities in the Near East'.[74] He returned to Dublin 8 June, glad that the Dáil had passed the 1938 Anglo-Irish Agreement and thrilled that the country was heading into a general election in which he hoped de Valera would gain an overall majority.

CONCLUSIONS

The story has a curious postscript. When Walshe retired as Ambassador to the Vatican in 1954 he planned to live in Rome. To improve his health he temporarily moved to Kalk Bay, Cape Province, South Africa. While returning to Rome in early 1956, he was taken ill and died in Cairo on 6 February 1956. He was buried in a simple grave in the city's Commonwealth War Graves Cemetery. Walshe had expressed the wish that he was to be buried wherever he died. He had expected this would be Rome. In a strange twist of fate the land he had explored almost twenty years before became his final resting place.

But Walshe's trips aside, for the Department of External Affairs the Middle East between the wars hardly featured on their diplomatic radar. Palestine was a specific case, where interest was fuelled by the resonance of the Irish troubles as partition and events in the Holy Land touched a raw nerve for de Valera and the Irish people, or at least those interested in international relations. There was never enough in common between Ireland and Egypt for the two countries to forge bonds between 1919 and 1939. The Irish–Egyptian relations paradigm is perhaps an example of what might have been or what could have been had Ireland had a better resourced diplomatic service between the wars.

There are hints, but not more than that, of how the Commonwealth would eventually develop post-1948 in Walshe's conversations with Lampson and Sharara Pasha. The reality was that the two states had little in common at this stage in their development beyond a shared history of an unwanted relationship with Britain forced upon them through British geopolitical desires. Irish-Egyptian bilateral relations would not be established until the 1970s.

As for Sudan, Walshe's apprenticeship in colonial administration and the source of his pipedream colony, it was perhaps evidence of a personal kind of Walshe's mercurial nature, caught up in the spirit of the moment he relished the desire to run a small portion of the globe as an Irish colony. Walshe's Sudanese adventure combined with the inability to develop relations with Egypt due to the lack of real common interests and the view of Palestine as a projection of the partition of Ireland shows that Ireland had yet to develop a real understanding of the wider Middle Eastern region. The norms of Irish foreign policy did not apply there and the combined rhetoric of Irish and Arab nationalism could not create common bonds.

NOTES

1 Walshe to de Valera, 2 June 1938, P150/2183, University College Dublin Archives Department (hereafter, UCDA).
2 For further details on this see Michael Kennedy and Joseph Skelly (eds), *Irish Foreign Policy 1919–1969*, Dublin, 2000.
3 For an account of Ireland's membership of the League of Nations see Michael Kennedy, *Ireland and the League of Nations 1919–1946*, Dublin, 1996.
4 Mary C. Bromage, 'Roman Love Story', *Michigan Quarterly Review* (Winter, 1963), pp. 18–21, p. 18.
5 Walshe to de Valera, 13 May 1938, UCDA, P150/2183.
6 Ibid., Walshe to de Valera, 2 June 1938.
7 Ibid.
8 Ronan Fanning, Michael Kennedy, Dermot Keogh and Eunan O'Halpin (eds), *Documents on Irish Foreign Policy* (hereafter, *DIFP*) I (1919–1922), No. 11, O'Ceallaigh to Dublin, p. 14 and p. 19.
9 M.E. Yapp, *The Near East Since the First World War*, Harlow, 1991, quoting Albert Hourani, *Arabic Thought in the Liberal Age, 1798–1939*, Oxford, 1962, p. 221.
10 *DIFP I*, No. 11, O'Ceallaigh to Dublin, p. 14.
11 Ibid., p. 19.
12 Ibid., No. 17, O'Hegarty to O'Ceallaigh, p. 35.
13 Ibid., No. 15, O'Ceallaigh to Dublin, p. 31.
14 Lampson to Eden, 28 July 1937, [T]he [N]ational [A]rchives FO 371/20919.
15 Peter Mansfield, *A History of the Middle East*, London, 1992, pp. 179–80.
16 *DIFP* IV (1932–1936), No. 313, Dulanty to Walshe, 17 January 1936, pp. 406–7.
17 *The Times*, 19 September 1964.
18 Lampson to Eden, 28 July 1937, PRO/FO 371/20919.
19 See 'The relations between Great Britain and (a) Iraq (b) Egypt, in particular relations to matters of defence', 23 November 1937, National Archives Ireland, Department of Foreign Affairs (hereafter, NAI DFA) miscellaneous files of memoranda by senior officials.
20 Yapp, *Near East*, p. 60.
21 Ibid., p. 68.
22 F.P. Walters, *A History of the League of Nations*, London, 1952, p. 739.
23 See Circular Telegram, 16 February 1937, NAI DFA 126/22.
24 Ibid., marginal note by Murphy.

25 Ibid., 'Communication from the Egyptian Government', 8 March 1937.
26 Ibid., Walshe to Dulanty, 13 March 1937.
27 Ibid.
28 Rynne (for Walshe) to Cremins, 16 March 1937, NAI DFA 126/35.
29 Ibid., memorandum, (undated), 're Special Assembly'.
30 Ibid., Cremins to Walshe (Confidential), 28 May 1937.
31 Walters, *League*, p. 745.
32 Mansfield, *History*, p. 196.
33 Walters, *League*, p. 746.
34 Mansfield, *History*, p. 206.
35 Rory Miller, *Ireland and the Palestine Question 1948-2004*, Dublin, 2005, p. 7.
36 *Irish Times*, 6 July 1937.
37 Cremins to Walshe, 12 July 1937, NAI DFA 227/13.
38 *Palestine Royal Commission. Summary of Report (With Extracts)* (Colonial No. 135), London, 1937, p. 10, reprinting p. 135 of report.
39 Cremins to Walshe, 12 July 1937, NAI DFA 227/13.
40 *Irish Independent*, 9 July 1937.
41 M.E. Yapp (ed.), *Politics and Diplomacy in Egypt. The Diaries of Sir Miles Lampson 1935–1937*, Oxford, 1997, p. 878.
42 Memorandum on the 18th session of the League Assembly, 16 August 1937, NAI DFA, 126/37.
43 Ibid., Rynne to Cremins (Confidential), 19 August 1937.
44 Cremins to Walshe, 31 August 1937, NAI DFA 227/13.
45 Ibid.
46 Ibid., Hearne (for Walshe) to Macaulay, 2 September 1937.
47 Ibid., Macaulay to Walshe, 6 September 1937.
48 Ibid., Eighteenth Ordinary Session of the Assembly. Sixth Committee. Provisional Minutes. Sixth Meeting, 23 September 1937, p. 17.
49 Ibid.
50 Miller, *Palestine*, pp. 7–8.
51 Eighteenth Ordinary Session of the Assembly. Sixth Committee. Provisional Minutes. Sixth Meeting, 23 September 1937, p. 17, NAI DFA 227/13.
52 Confidential Report, Dulanty to Walshe, 16 December 1937, NAI DFA 2006/39.
53 Elliot to Eden, 2 October 1937, PRO/ FO 371/20816.
54 PRO/ FO 371/20814, minute 1 October 1937
55 Ibid., minute, 2 October 1937.
56 Telegram from Fawwaz and Berry to de Valera, 28 September 1939, NAI DFA 227/13.
57 Ibid., Magnes to de Valera, 25 September 1937.
58 Ibid., de Valera to Magnes, 30 September 1937.
59 Herzog to de Valera, 20 October 1937, ibid.
60 Walshe to de Valera, 2 June 1938, UCDA, P150/2183.
61 *Dáil Eireann Debates*, Vol. 72, No. 718, 13 July 1938.
62 Macaulay to Murphy, 31 May 1938, NAI DFA Joseph Walshe–Miscellaneous Semi-Official Correspondence-1938.
63 Walshe to de Valera, 13 May 1938, UCDA P150/2183. All unattributed quotes in this and the following paragraphs are from this source.
64 *The Times*, 7 December 1962.
65 Ibid.
66 Walshe to de Valera, 2 June 1938, UCDA, P150/2183.
67 Ibid., Walshe to de Valera, 13 May 1938.
68 *DIFP* IV, No. 310, MacWhite to Walshe, p. 401.
69 MacWhite to Walshe, 9 September 1938, UCDA, P194/536.
70 Walshe to de Valera, 2 June 1938, UCDA, P150/2183. All subsequent unattributed quotes from this source.
71 Gallagher to Walshe, 5 July 1938, NAI DFA 117/54.
72 Unsent draft letter by Walshe, undated, but 1938, NAI DFA 132/229.
73 Abu Zenima.
74 Walshe to de Valera 2 June 1938, UCDA, P150/2183.

Britain's neutral neighbours: Ireland and Afghanistan compared, 1939–45

EUNAN O'HALPIN

This chapter explores the experience between 1939 and 1945 of two neutral states which on the face of it had in common only one notable achievement: the fact that they each managed to stay out of Britain's war despite sharing land borders with her or her possessions, and despite considerable diplomatic and economic pressure from more than one of the major belligerents – in Ireland's case Britain and the United States, in Afghanistan's Britain and (after June 1941) the Soviet Union.

In recent years the experience of European neutrals has received some comparative attention, in particular through the collection of essays edited by Neville Wylie, *European Neutrals and Non-belligerents in the Second World War*, and through Christian Leitz's study of relations between European neutrals and belligerents (a book which does not discuss Ireland at all). Such comparative work has complemented national studies of neutral states, such as William Carlgren on Sweden, Robert Fisk on Ireland, and Neville Wylie on Switzerland.[1] There is an obvious geopolitical logic to studying European neutrals as a comparative group, even though the different states faced very different challenges and had very varied experiences depending on location, history, ideology and opportunity. But why pair Ireland and Afghanistan, and then for good measure bring both Persia and Iraq into the discussion?

The first reason is the straightforward one that contiguity and patterns of migration greatly influenced the two relatively newly recognised states in their relations with their powerful neighbours. Each had highly permeable land borders, Afghanistan with British India, Ireland with the United Kingdom. Afghanistan's frontier with British India was a theoretical legal construct, largely ignored by the people whose customary territories, ways of life and kith and kin spanned the Durand line effectively imposed by the British in 1893.[2] Ireland's border with Northern Ireland was equally porous. In addition, since independence, Ireland and the United Kingdom had shared a common travel area, and Ireland was an important manpower reservoir both for British industry and for the British armed services. Many people and groups in both Ireland and Afghanistan regarded their legal borders as unilateral British impositions which cut them off from territory and people who rightfully belonged with them. Irish nationalists regarded the six counties of Northern Ireland as a lost province which should some day be recovered, while the Durand line divided historic tribal areas and peoples, and ensured that Afghanistan was entirely landlocked whereas Afghans aspired to control Baluchistan, and so secure access to the Arabian sea.

A second reason which justifies a comparative approach is a political one: independent Ireland and Afghanistan had respectively asserted their independence from British control or successfully maintained it through the use of force. Here there is also a coincidence of dates, as 1919 was both the first year of the Irish War of Independence, and the year of the third Afghan war (which ended with a ceasefire followed by an agreement signed at Rawalpindi which acknowledged Afghan independence beyond the Khyber Pass). Britain finally, and fully, recognized Afghanistan as an independent state in November 1921, just a month before the Anglo-Irish treaty granted Irish independence.

A third reason is that during the war, in respect both of Afghanistan and of Ireland, Germany let it be understood that the certain reward for helping to defeat Britain would be the achievement of historic territorial ambitions (just as, in 1917, it had attempted to lure Mexico into the war with the promise of the restoration to it of lands lost to the United States in the nineteenth century).[3]

A fourth reason for looking at the wartime experiences of the two neutral states is that they each had to deal with what appeared to be a real threat of invasion from one or more of the belligerents in the early years of the war. Both Ireland and Afghanistan had to balance their determination to maintain diplomatic relations with the Axis powers, in their eyes a badge of sovereignty, with the necessity of preventing their territories being used to mount espionage, sabotage and subversive operations respectively against the United Kingdom and British India. Both states found that their most constant difficulties in remaining neutral and maintaining their sovereignty came from Britain.

In the case of Afghanistan these pressures were added to after 22 June 1941 by the Soviet Union, which was anxious about the security threat to its southern border posed by émigré groups in Afghanistan, and which rightly feared that the Axis legations in Kabul were up to no good; in the case of Ireland, after Pearl Harbor the United States played a somewhat similar role, adopting a pose of outright hostility to Irish neutrality and to the presence of

Axis missions in Dublin which was somewhat at odds with the more nuanced approach developed in London where, for a variety of reasons, officials argued the need to persuade the Irish rather than to confront them. So carefully calibrated did British policy towards Ireland become, particularly in the crucial area of the security of war information, that the British security service (MI5) concluded that on balance Irish neutrality probably served Allied interests better than participation on Britain's side in the war would have done.[4]

A final reason for studying the two countries in parallel are the somewhat unlikely personal links which emerge. The appointments of the German ministers Hempel and Pilger, who were to serve in Dublin and Kabul respectively throughout the Second World War, were announced on the same day in Berlin in 1937: the British ambassador reported that Pilger

> does not give the impression of any particular ability and he has a somewhat scrubby and unprepossessing appearance, but he has always shown himself friendly to this Embassy in the transaction of the tiresome business which falls to the lot of a Near Eastern expert. Despite the promotion involved he views his translation to Kabul without enthusiasm.[5]

Pilger's gloomy response to his elevation was well judged. Hempel was to sit out the war in Ireland unharmed, and at its end to be treated with great consideration by the Irish, despite British and American pressure for him and his staff to be quickly handed over to Allied custody. In the same year, the British decided not to oppose Soviet demands that Pilger and his staff be handed over to them for interrogation in Russia. When the Afghan government politely enquired in the spring of 1946 if Pilger had reached Germany, the Foreign Office thought it wisest 'not to provoke' the Russians, who had already refused to answer similar queries from both Britain and the United States.[6] Thanks to American and French pressure, the Soviets eventually allowed Pilger and his party back to Germany. Pilger probably joined his family in Switzerland, as their Berlin home had been destroyed by allied bombing.[7]

We may note other bureaucratic coincidences which reflect the intersecting nature of Irish engagement with the British Empire. The British minister in Kabul from 1941 to 1943 was Sir Francis Wylie, an Irishman and a graduate of Trinity College, Dublin. Like Hempel in the German legation in Dublin, Wylie was very concerned lest any clandestine activities run from the British legation in Kabul might compromise him in the eyes of the Afghan government. He consequently obstructed intelligence gathering by legation staff. This was somewhat to the irritation of Philip Vickery, the head of Indian Political Intelligence (IPI), a small London based organisation which acted as a clearing house for all intelligence pertaining to India and to Indians. When he originally accepted the IPI post in 1926 Vickery's acceptance was sent from 'Carraig na Mara, Killiney'. A gifted linguist and Trinity graduate, he succeeded yet another Trinity man, the Calcutta police officer Sir Charles Tegart. Finally, we may note that one of the two Delhi Intelligence Bureau (IB) officers who ran the crucial double agent Silver, the link between the Indian nationalist underground and the German legation in Kabul, was William Magan from Meath, while Sir John Maffey, British Representative in Dublin from 1939, was also an expert on Afghanistan.[8]

The discussion which follows is based mainly on British and Indian government records, including those of the Government Code & Cipher School (GC&CS), the India Office, Indian Political Intelligence (IPI), the security service MI5, and the Special Operations Executive (SOE), together with the diaries of Leo Amery, Secretary of State for India from 1940 to 1945.

Long before the Soviet Union was established, Britain had regarded Afghanistan as a necessary buffer between its Indian possessions and Russia. Whatever the reality and extent of Tsarist designs in the late nineteenth and early twentieth centuries, mutual Anglo-Russian suspicion and jealousy about Afghanistan was enduring (although the two powers did co-operate in the region during the First World War, jointly occupying parts of neighbouring Persia, and Russia would have had a strong post-war claim to have its interests there properly recognised, had the 1917 revolution not taken it out of its alliance with France and Britain). During the First World War, Germany had sent a military mission to Kabul. It was the first diplomatic contact between the two states. The German aim was to lure the Afghans into a pact to expel the British from India.

The Niedermayer mission stayed in Kabul for seven months in 1915–16, leaving in May 1916 when it became clear that while apparently well-disposed towards Germany and hostile and resentful towards the British in India, the Afghans would not commit themselves (it appears their main aim was to use the threat posed by the German mission to force Britain to recognise Afghan independence). One of the key figures in the mission, Otto Werner von Hentig, a specialist in Islamic questions, was to feature once more in the Second World War (early in 1941 SOE was repeatedly told to kill him and his assistants in Syria and the Lebanon, shortly before he was nominated to replace Pilger in Kabul, an appointment which the Afghans refused to accept at British insistence (the 'high authorities were most disappointed' about his failure to kill him, but he survived the war, publishing his memoirs and visiting Afghanistan as a guest of the king in 1970).[9]

The parallel with Ireland is not exact – Afghanistan was already effectively an independent state, although not formally recognised as such by Britain – but the German design derived from broadly the same principle as did their encouragement and support for the Irish rebellion of 1916, i.e. that any trouble that could be caused away from the main fronts distracted British attentions and sucked away military resources. In the Irish case the results were spectacular, particularly in political terms, although Germany seemed barely to notice this; in the case of Afghanistan, while the Niedermayer mission did not succeed in its primary aim, it ensured that Britain had to keep much stronger forces to guard India's Northwest frontier than she would otherwise have done.[10]

Both Ireland and Afghanistan experienced an influx of German professionals in the inter-war years, such as medical specialists, engineers, teachers, accountants and others with technical qualifications. In neither case should this be seen as evidence of a conscious strategy of penetration for political purposes; rather, it reflected two main factors: a conscious desire in each state to reduce dependence on Britain for necessary technical expertise, and for the Germans a hope that new markets could be developed. Germany put rather more effort into its attempts to use expertise to build up economic and commercial links with Afghanistan than with Ireland, for reasons not of geopolitics but of location and potential: Afghanistan was but the remotest of a group of Middle Eastern countries including Turkey, Persia and Iraq where Germany sought to revive pre-war economic links and to develop new ones. Diplomatic relations were established in 1922, and in 1923 a German minister was accredited to Kabul.

The governments of Weimar Germany were at pains not to antagonize the British, repeatedly emphasising that their interest was solely in developing trade and economic links in the Middle East generally and intended no threat to British interests.[11] Britain remained somewhat hostile towards such penetration and nervous about German influence generally. This was illustrated in 1924 when Wilhelm Wassmuss, the former German consular official who had earned a reputation as a Middle Eastern irregular fighter during the war second only to T.E. Lawrence, sought British approval for his return to Bushire in Persia to recover his possessions. The India Office was acutely alarmed at the prospect, and even the German minister in Tehran 'foresaw no good, and possible trouble for himself', despite Wassmuss' assurances to the British minister in Tehran: 'neither by acts nor by words I shall give utterance to anything unfriendly... the unfortunate war between England and Germany during which I have only done my duty towards my country is a thing of the past'.[12] Britain was also concerned generally that the Soviet–German rapprochement of the mid-1920s might have implications for her colonial interests in the Middle East.

Anglo-Afghan relations improved during the 1930s, as Kabul grew more confident that Britain would not seek to interfere in Afghanistan's affairs. Kabul sought to maintain passable relations with the two great, and menacing, powers on her northern and southern frontiers, while at the same time developing as many links as possible with other states which might act as a counter-balance. Afghanistan joined the League of Nations at the same time as the Soviet Union in 1934, and appointed a minister in Rome. This led to some Italian involvement, including the provision of aircraft and trainers for the Afghan air force (which, confusingly, by 1939 also had British trainers and some aircraft).[13] Once Hitler came to power, the nature of the German engagement with Afghanistan inevitably changed. The 'resurgence of Germany... with its imposing industrial potential and its strident militarism, was a particularly attractive factor' for the Afghans, particularly as Hitler was perceived to be well disposed towards Muslim interests and identity.[14] As in Ireland, the German colony was put under a form of political control. Lufthansa established a regular Kabul–Berlin route in 1937, although this was suspended when war broke out, and the Organisation Todt oversaw major roads and public works programmes.[15]

However, Britain was more concerned at the apparent growth of Soviet influence, and the possibility of a Soviet attack on India through Afghanistan.[16] Afghanistan, itself concerned that the Soviets might attack, sought a British guarantee of its territorial integrity in 1938, but that was not forthcoming. With the outbreak of war, the British general staff speculated that Hitler might encourage the Soviet Union to strike for India. This idea had in fact gained currency in Berlin, where the military pondered a 'joint Nazi–Soviet strategy against the British Empire in the Middle East and Asia', using the ex-King Amanullah, a modernizer in exile in Europe since his ouster in 1929 by more conservative elements, as a figurehead leader in Afghanistan.[17]

Compared to these complexities, Ireland seemed in very secure circumstances on the eve of war. Britain and France stood between it and the only conceivable military threat, and the likelihood of being drawn into a general European war had greatly decreased in April 1938 when Britain relinquished its defence rights under the Anglo-Irish treaty of 1921 as part of a general settlement of economic, financial and political issues. The US minister in Dublin remarked that this 'was an outstanding outstanding triumph and marks de Valera as the greatest Irish leader', while de Valera was at pains to thank US President Roosevelt for sending a message 'at a critical moment in... the negotiations'.[18] The grievance of partition aside, Ireland's geostrategic position must have appeared enviable to other neutrals intent on staying out of the imminent war.

Ireland nevertheless had some anxieties as war loomed. After the 1938 settlement, de Valera reiterated his long-held view that Ireland could never allow itself to be used by foreign powers as a base from which to attack Britain.[19] Since the early 1920s, Ireland, like Afghanistan, had experienced a modest influx of Germans. The state's vast hydroelectric scheme on the River Shannon was built by Siemens, while the drive for industrialization in the 1930s saw German specialists take senior positions in various state enterprises. After 1933, members of the German community in Ireland had come under pressure to demonstrate their loyalty to Hitler through participation in organisations under Nazi control.

The political leader of the German community was an Austrian archaeologist, Dr Adolf Mahr, director of the National Museum of Ireland.

This minor penetration of Germans did not cause London or Dublin any great concern until 1937, when evidence emerged of some espionage involving German residents and the officers of a ship which plied regularly between Dublin and Hamburg. During the Munich crisis in the autumn of 1938 the Irish signalled their concerns to the British government about possible German clandestine activities (although not about German contacts with the IRA, which were only uncovered in 1940). On the advice of MI5, a counter-espionage section was established within Irish military intelligence, and from this small start developed what became a very close relationship with MI5, 'the Dublin link' as it is described in British records.[20]

No comparable pre-war security link was forged between India and Afghanistan, although it is clear that Delhi did have some sources inside the country: in January 1940 MI5's Guy Liddell noted that 'the War Office are thinking of taking over the Police Intelligence organisation which is ready made in Afghanistan. I should feel that this might be unwise.'[21]

Reviewing the situation in Afghanistan since 1939, early in 1943 a British official wrote that

> from the first, the Afghans had a strong anti-British and anti-Soviet bias, and the Germans were easily able to put this fact to good profit. Many Afghans, such as Governors and police officials in the provinces, and Cabinet Ministers and civil and military officials in government departments at Kabul render the Germans services of one sort and another from time to time; and many more preach the German propaganda gospel in the bazaars and elsewhere. Very few of the above can, however, properly be regarded as part of the regular espionage apparatus itself.[22]

The same could not be said of Ireland where, small groups such as the eccentric 'Irish Friends of Germany' aside, public sentiment was firmly pro-neutral and the private sympathies of the majority of people were pro-Ally (particularly after the summer of 1940). The imposition of a remarkably strict system of press censorship also had a dampening effect on the dissemination of propaganda by both Germany and Britain.[23]

The advent of war immediately brought into focus the problem of German civilians in both Ireland and Afghanistan. The Irish had a lucky break, because about fifty of the most active Nazis, including Dr Mahr, were attending a party function in Germany and had to remain in Europe. Shortly afterwards, Dublin arranged with MI5 for the safe conduct through Britain to the Netherlands of a further 100 Germans including most of the remaining active Nazis. Both the British and the German governments thanked the Irish for their help. A few Germans also moved from Britain to Ireland just before war was declared, including one man later arrested as a German agent.[24]

The main security difficulties which the Irish faced during the war came not from German residents but from three inter-related problems. These were the activities of German agents sent to Ireland in 1940, 1941 and 1943 on various clandestine missions directed primarily against Britain. With one exception, these agents were detected and detained very quickly. The second problem was the IRA, which developed its pre-war contacts with Germany and which threatened to act as a potential fifth column should Germany decide to invade. Although the organisation seemed a major threat in the summer of 1940 – London received wildly exaggerated accounts of its size and capacity – by June 1941 the Irish government had it firmly under control and it was clearly incapable of any sustained pro-German activity.[25]

The third problem was the presence of Axis diplomatic missions. Of these, the Italian did little, and until 1943, when it attempted to set up links with the IRA which the Irish police soon uncovered, the two man Japanese consulate did even less.[26] The great worry was the German legation. Here the Irish had both difficulties and advantages. The legation, its personnel and their associates were watched, but its communications with Berlin could not be decoded. Furthermore, while Germany was in the ascendant in 1940-41 the Irish had to tread very carefully: it was only in 1941 that the British learned through decoding hitherto unbreakable German messages that Dublin had adroitly resisted a German plan to fly in three additional staff from France in December 1940, supposedly civilians but in fact army personnel tasked to collect intelligence on bomb damage in Britain, despite very menacing pressure from Berlin.[27] It was in this period that the Irish and the British separately determined that the German legation had a clandestine transmitter. This was to prove a problem second only to neutrality itself in Anglo-Irish relations.

The position in Afghanistan was very different. Central government was extremely weak and power was divided amongst ministers with their own followings and tribal allegiances. Whereas in Ireland there were only two groups on the margins which might attempt to act in the Axis interest – the IRA and the vestiges of General O'Duffy's crypto-Fascist Blueshirt movement–Afghanistan was home not only to a range of diverse ethnic groups and tribes but to large numbers of exiles from Turkestan, Uzbekistan and other Soviet territories. Among these were to be found people who, for reasons of kinship, religion, ideology, or money, would be prepared to make trouble along Afghanistan's Soviet and Indian borders (German propaganda played on Muslim sentiment, and was probably responsible for an outbreak of anti-Jewish feeling in Kabul in 1941, although Pilger later reported that the only Jews in Afghanistan were impoverished hucksters in the bazaars).[28]

With the Soviet Union neutral but in a benign relationship with Germany, the Afghans could not afford to antagonize either the Germans or the Russians by imposing special restrictions on their respective citizens and supporters. Nevertheless, early in 1940, the British minister was instructed to urge the Afghans to reduce the number of German residents because of 'dangers of German-cum-Soviet intrigue'. He was to remind them 'of the methods of treachery and intrigue, now commonly associated with the name of Quisling': two months earlier London had received intelligence that 'a plot is being hatched in Berlin for a rising in favour of Amanullah in Afghanistan'.[29] There are clear parallels with the British warning to Ireland of 1 June 1940 that 'an invasion is not only seriously planned and prepared with the help of the IRA, but is *imminent'*.[30]

The Afghans did take some steps to hamper Axis contacts with tribes along the Indian frontier, as it was a fairly open secret by 1940 that the Italians were paying a subsidy to the Fakir of Ipi in Waziristan to mount operations against British interests: in December 1940, in a cable decoded by the British, the Italian minister said the Fakir was carrying out 'the usual attacks upon military posts and traffic... The Fakir talks of 900 British soldiers killed, but this is certainly an exaggeration.' Even though the Fakir never delivered the widespread tribal revolt of which the Axis powers dreamed, he certainly tied down a lot of British forces: at one point 40,000 troops were said to be involved trying to catch him.[31] Events took a dramatic turn in July 1940, when two recently arrived German armed civilians disguised in Afghan dress had a confused encounter with an Afghan patrol, resulting in one of the men being shot dead, and the other wounded.[32] It was an important demonstration of resolve by the Afghans, whether or not, as one writer suggests, Britain had played a secret hand in arranging it.[33]

In the first years of the war Britain could decode Italian and Japanese diplomatic traffic to and from both Afghanistan and Ireland, but not German. The latter proved impenetrable until the start of 1943, when it was broken and given the cover name Pandora. In the case of Afghanistan, Pandora confirmed other intelligence showing that from early 1941 the German legation had taken over from the Italians as the mainspring of large-scale espionage and subversion directed against India, the Soviet Union and Persia; in the Irish case, it showed that Hempel, while not collecting war intelligence systematically, was increasingly willing to risk his mission if he obtained vital information relating to Allied plans to invade Europe. Britain's inability to read German traffic until 1943 was partly compensated in respect of both Ireland and Afghanistan by material in Italian messages.

In both neutral states the Germans had clandestine transmitters; the Italians, on the other hand, had to rely entirely on the security of their codes as their messages travelled by cable. Decodes of cables between Rome and Dublin showed clearly that, other than passing on vague gossip gleaned from Irish people sympathetic to the Italian cause, the Italian mission in Dublin was not engaged in orchestrating espionage or subversion against British interests (whereas Italian diplomats were so involved in the Middle East and in parts of Asia), and that Dublin was not a significant listening post for

Rome. The most important Italian message which the British decoded was a cable from the Italian embassy in Washington to the Italian legation in Dublin dated 28 December 1940. Although somewhat garbled, enough of this cable was decoded to make out its meaning. It began: ' – has obtained facilities for a connection by wireless telegraph with Dublin via Berlin', and instructed the Italian minister to ask his German colleague if he could use this link for important communications.[34] This was the first clear evidence Britain had obtained that the German mission in Dublin had a clandestine transmitter, a discovery which dominated Anglo-Irish security relations until the set was finally handed over to the Irish in December 1943.[35]

Exchanges between Rome and Kabul yielded a great deal of material on the extensive intrigues of both the Italians and the Germans in Afghanistan and along the Indian frontier. They also threw light on Axis efforts to use Afghanistan as a base from which to collect intelligence and to promote subversion in the southern Soviet Union. After June 1941, the latter problem acquired new significance in London and Delhi, since the Soviet Union had become an ally where it had previously been seen as a major threat: in the immediate aftermath of the attack, the India secretary Leo Amery feared that the Germans might soon be in a position to 'attack us via Persia and Iraq as well as to stir up the Afghans'.[36]

Two months after Barbarossa, it was decided to send a SOE representative to Kabul. This was W.R. Connor-Green, who 'has made a long study of Russia and the language'.[37] Britain already had an intelligence officer in Afghanistan, Major Fletcher, an old Kabul hand who had returned to the Afghan capital as military attaché in July 1940 to establish an intelligence organisation directed against Axis intrigue. After some debate, the British minister prevailed in his argument that it was better not to advise the Afghan government of 'real reasons for this appointment. I do not think that they would object to us organizing counter [measures?] to German and Italian influence here but would be afraid of such measures exciting Russian suspicions.'

Fletcher only lasted a year, attracting complaints from the Afghans about both his 'personal foibles' and his clandestine activities. The British refused to accede to Afghan requests to withdraw him, but privately acknowledged that he had some 'disreputable friends' and was believed to let young men drink alcohol in his home. The British minister complained that he had also made an indiscreet approach to the Soviet embassy shortly after Barbarossa, although he had received permission and the Russians were receptive – 'they have a good deal of information about Germans employed by the Afghan Government, [but] they know little of German activities generally as there is very little contact between Germans and Russians'. A face-saving solution emerged when the British army in Persia issued an urgent call for a Persian-speaking officer, which provided 'a very useful opportunity of settling this unfortunate incident to the satisfaction of all parties'.[38]

Thereafter intelligence work was left solely to SOE's Connor-Green, who was assisted by a Pole and two Afghans employed by the legation. However, their activities were initially greatly hampered by the British minister's disapproval of intelligence activities. Within a year SOE asked for Connor-Green's withdrawal as he was unable to discharge his allotted duties because 'he did not appear to hold the confidence' of the minister. Wylie's unsympathetic attitude arose from his fear that any intelligence activities might antagonise the Afghans – so cautious was he that, shortly after arriving in Kabul early in 1941, he had put an end to contact with the Italian commercial attaché who had 'had secret dealings with us'.[39]

Various plans of Connor-Green, including a 'Northern Informant Scheme' aimed at obtaining information on Soviet Turkestan, had to 'be shelved in deference to the Minister's view that even the smallest risk of being caught out by our [Soviet] allies would not be justified by the potential results'. In Afghanistan, SOE's man outlasted his diplomatic critic. Wylie retired in the summer of 1943, though not before he had embarrassed Soviet intelligence by mentioning their co-operation with SOE in Kabul to the Soviet ambassador, who had been unaware of it.[40] His successor H.C. Squire, like Connor-Green a Russian speaker, was less inclined to fret about intelligence activities. Connor-Green departed, to the plaudits even of the Delhi authorities, towards the end of 1944.[41]

There is some parallel here with circumstances in Ireland, where SOE's agent Roddy Keith was withdrawn in June 1941 after only three months following bitter complaints from the secret intelligence service (SIS) and MI5 about the damage which he might do to Anglo-Irish security relations.[42] The two agencies which forced SOE's departure, however, did themselves operate in Ireland with the blessing of the British representative Sir John Maffey, who was kept informed of their activities generally and who, in May 1943, was even admitted to the ultra-sensitive secret of Pandora.[43] Although the Irish penetrated SIS's clandestine Irish operations, they did not close them down because these were directed primarily at investigating pro-Axis activities and were not a threat to the Irish state, and also because the British would certainly have started up again and the Irish might not have succeeded in penetrating their new operations as effectively as they had the existing ones.[44]

In Kabul Connor-Green secured an early success, enlisting the secret help of one Vichy French diplomat in the summer of 1942. This man won over the French minister to the Allied cause and 'acting in concert with the Minister, [contrived] to gain the confidence of one or more of the enemy Legations'. The result was that the British received 'about a hundred items of information from the enemy' over the following year.[45] This was very much in contrast to Dublin, where relations between the Vichy minister and the Axis legations were minimal, and where most French officials appear from British and Irish intelligence records to have done little beyond feuding.[46] Even the naval attaché Albertas, a diehard *Petainiste* in whose household SIS briefly managed to plant a French-speaking maid in 1941, lived a disappointingly prosaic life until his reluctant and much delayed return to France in the autumn of 1944.[47]

The higher up the chain of command the question of the Axis presence in neutral states was considered, the more drastic were the remedies proposed. The first two years of the war had provided plenty of evidence of Hitler's contempt for the neutrality of small European states; in 1941, Britain took her turn to show disdain for the niceties of international law and the principles of national sovereignty among the newly emerging states of the Middle East. Under the Anglo-Iraqi treaty of 1930 in which Britain recognised Iraqi independence, she had retained defence rights; in 1941 this enabled her to move Indian and other troops into the Basra region after decodes of Italian diplomatic traffic and other intelligence confirmed that a pro-Axis coup was planned. These forces were then employed to expel the nationalist leader Rashid Ali El Gailiani shortly after he seized power with Italian and German encouragement. As the Italian minister in Baghdad put it, after staging the coup Rashid Ali was 'very much vexed by the fact that at this delicate moment...we have as yet given him no reply about support by Axis air forces', which in fact the Axis attempted only to a very limited extent (the imminent attack on the Soviet Union being of more significance to Hitler).

Like the Grand Mufti of Jerusalem, who had settled in Baghdad after fleeing from Palestine and who was closely involved in Axis plans for Middle East subversion, Rashid Ali fled Iraq and sat out the rest of the war in Rome and Berlin. SOE were instructed to kill both fugitives en route but could not do so. In exile he still impressed the Italian foreign minister as 'a vivacious and resolute man, who has great influence upon his people', but he was no longer in a position to influence affairs in the Middle East.[48] The British installed a compliant Iraqi administration which did exactly as it was told until the war ended.

The British success in Iraq appeared to vindicate a robust approach to awkward neutral powers. It was shortly followed by the attack on Vichy-controlled Syria, where the German airforce had been allowed to operate from a number of airfields. The next neutral for attention was Persia, which the British and their new Soviet allies jointly occupied on the largely specious grounds that Tehran had been dilatory in taking action to round up and expel Axis civilians who were regarded as a threat to British and Soviet interests. Whereas the Iraq intervention was reasonably justified in that the main aim was to oust an Axis-sponsored coup – the details of which had been known in advance to the British from decoded Italian cables in which Rome offered reassurance and promises of support – the stated reason for occupying Persia was little more than a pretext for an exercise in *force majeure*.[49]

Within a year the Persian police were reported to be doing well in tracking down Axis agents, and the British minister indicated some sympathy for the Prime Minister's argument that to hand over such prisoners directly to the

British 'would be damaging to [the] prestige of Persian Government', and various ploys were worked out to avoid any embarrassment. The British and Russians also made unilateral searches and arrests in their respective areas of occupation.[50] For the rest of the war both Persia and Iraq operated under the sufferance of the occupying powers, and the Soviets took their time in leaving Persia after the conflict had ended.

The success of these Middle Eastern interventions may well have influenced British Prime Minister Winston Churchill in his increasingly robust approach to other neutrals. In September 1941 he directed that pressure be applied in Kabul to obtain the expulsion of Axis civilians. Such an approach was possible because the Soviet Union was now an ally. He personally overruled the reservations of Wylie about the wisdom of seeming to bully the Afghans in concert with the Russians and, although resented in Kabul, the initiative produced results within weeks.[51] It is reasonable to wonder whether this precedent came into Churchill's mind in 1943, when he began again to press the Dominions Office for strong action to force the hand of the Irish government on the issue of the Axis legations in Dublin.[52]

After the Italian surrender, Quaroni, the Italian minister in Kabul, gave Connor-Green a lengthy though self-serving account of his activities. He particularly criticised the attitude taken by the British and the Soviets at the time of the discovery of the Tirazi plot. This scheme was eerily reminiscent of the centrepiece of John Buchan's First World War adventure *Greenmantle*. Devised with Axis encouragement by Bokharan and Uzbek exiles in India and northern Afghanistan, the plan was that 10,000 horseman would sweep across the Soviet border to coincide with a German breakthrough in the Caucausus, and make for Bokhara and Tashkent. Discovery of the scheme left the German legation in a 'peculiarly delicate' situation, which might have led to its closure.[53] Quaroni, who claimed to have warned his German colleagues that the scheme was 'not only dangerous but futile', said that in this crisis both he and the German minister Pilger found that

> our greatest ally in this matter was Sir Francis Wylie. The terms and method of the Joint Demarche with the Soviets so angered the Afghan Government as almost to neutralize their fury against the Germans. You will forgive me if I say that in this affair you made a great mistake in not taking into account the touchiness of the Afghans on the question of their independence.[54]

Wylie's report of his meeting with the Afghan prime minister Zahir Shah bears out the impression of Afghan resentment:

> Tone of conversation was unfriendly but Prime Minister controlled his temper – sometimes apparently with difficulty – and attempted no

fireworks... After this interview I am strongly reinforced in my previous view viz that it was high time that Government here was pulled up short. Whether it is (? their) hatred of Russians – and indeed of ourselves – or whatever cause may be, their present relations with Axis seem to me to constitute real danger to Allied cause in this part of the world.[55]

Extraordinarily, this confrontation in Kabul caused an Anglo-American row: on 7 June an American diplomat in London told the Foreign Office that 'any show of compulsion by the British and the Russians throughout Afghanistan that any benefits which might otherwise accrue would be outweighed'. If the Afghan authorities took all the action demanded, 'the very stability of the present regime might be endangered by the resultant resentment amongst the tribes'. Coming from an ally with little experience of, and no strategic interest in, Afghanistan, this produced near apoplexy in the Foreign Office. The Foreign Secretary sent Washington a stiff aide memoire on the issue, emphasising that the United States had no right of prior consultation on matters relating to Afghanistan. In Kabul Wylie taxed his American opposite number with furnishing an 'exquisitely wrong' picture of affairs.[56]

In July further Anglo-Soviet pressure for a general round-up of Afghan conspirators and émigrés was applied. The Soviet government, 'while acknowledging the efforts taken... for suppressing the harmful activities of white-emigrés, considers such measures inadequate', and the ambassador provided a list of alleged subversives for detention. Wylie made similar representations a few days later.[57] Such concerted pressure might have backfired, but in fact it achieved its main objects. The Afghans asked for the withdrawal of two German officials, along with one Italian, who were mainly involved in espionage. To avoid loss of face, the Germans and Italians treated these as recalls. The Afghans secured safe passage for the Germans from the British, who were delighted to facilitate their departure, and they reached Germany safely.[58]

The parallel between the Kabul representations and the 'American note' delivered in Dublin in February 1944 is obvious, although the roles of the Allied states involved were reversed. The American note was a clumsy attempt by the US government to force de Valera to close the Axis legations or to risk having Ireland portrayed as indifferent to the security of Overlord, the imminent Allied invasion of Europe.[59] The Americans were egged on by Churchill, despite the 'great misgivings' of MI5 officers, who feared the demarche would jeopardise Anglo-Irish security co-operation just as preparations for Overlord came to fruition, and despite the war cabinet's conclusions that Allied security interests were best met by leaving the legations in place, because their communications were completely controlled.

The American note met with a furious reaction from Dublin, who saw it as a threat to sovereignty and feared that it might be the preamble to armed occupation, as had happened in somewhat similar circumstances in Persia in 1941. British officials privately conveyed to the Irish the point that the impetus for the demand had come from the US minister in Dublin, an indiscreet alarmist who had been told almost nothing of the workings of Anglo-Irish security co-operation since 1940. Controls on communications and movement between Ireland and the outside world were tightened up further by agreement, and security co-operation was not jeopardised. Ireland, however, maintained its diplomatic links with the remaining Axis powers until the end of the war.[60]

The issue of the Axis missions in Dublin and Kabul threw up another commonality. Even when the pressure on the Irish and the Afghans to close them was at its most intense in 1943 and 1944, intelligence officials in London and Delhi dealing with the question took a rather different view. This was for three main reasons. First, all cable traffic to and from Kabul, and to and from Dublin, was routinely delayed by a number of days as a standard security measure. Furthermore, from 1943 all the communications of Axis missions could be decoded. In Dublin, the problem of the uncontrolled radio link with Berlin was resolved in December 1943 when the German minister entrusted his set to the Irish for safekeeping.

In Kabul the German legation retained its clandestine set, but the enforced departures of the staff most involved in espionage, along with the exposure of German intrigues, meant that Pilger and his one remaining subordinate were in no position to continue clandestine activities or to send intelligence. Instead Pilger handed over the German networks in Afghanistan and India to his Japanese colleague. When, in May 1944, the Soviets brought up the question of forcing the closure of the Japanese legation, Delhi told London that 'Security and Intelligence officials here ... regard continued presence of Japanese Legation in Kabul as most desirable'.[61] This was because the Japanese were running the mercurial double agent 'RK', Bhaghat Ram Talwar, whose British codename was Silver.

Silver was a committed communist, who at Soviet behest had been working for the British since November 1942. He was the main link between the exiled Indian political leader, Subhas Chandra Bose, and the nationalist underground in India, which also gathered intelligence for the Axis. Working under British control, from 1942 to 1945 he systematically deceived both Bose and the Axis about the nature and extent of Indian resistance to British rule, and about Allied military dispositions and intentions.[62] Since the British were providing Silver with his material, and since they could read the relevant Japanese traffic, they had every incentive to let the Japanese mission in Kabul remain, and it did. MI5's Guy Liddell, who also dealt extensively with Ireland, remarked

if there are no Jap embassies there will be no channels through which to pass deception ... we might therefore ... leave the one in Afghanistan which from the deception point of view was the most important since it controlled the Silver case.[63]

Dublin was never so significant a base for Axis espionage or for Allied deception as was Kabul, but officials in London argued on similar lines for keeping the enemy missions open. Their key arguments were first that the legations' communications were under British control, thanks to code-breakers and to the cable system (all cables to and from Ireland were routed through London for the duration of the war); and second, that to bring about the expulsion of Axis diplomats might cause the enemy to send more agents 'with means of communication which it would take some time to discover', and who might obtain and radio back crucial war information.[64]

CONCLUSIONS

There are clear parallels in British diplomacy towards both of these small and irritating neutral states with which it shared land borders during the Second World War. This is particularly so in terms of an initial tendency to underestimate the strength of national feeling and *amour propre*, and an unwillingness to comprehend the historical and political factors underpinning the reluctance of these neutrals to be forced to take sides in a conflict from which neither state could expect anything save certain pain and probable civil war. British actions in the Middle East in 1941 demonstrated that they would openly violate other states' neutrality when it suited. The Anglo-Soviet occupation of Persia, in particular, must have sent a chill down Afghan spines. As well as the threat of a German attack in 1940–41, as preamble to, or an element of, an invasion of Britain, Ireland also faced the threat of such unilateral action by the British, particularly in the summer of 1940, and by US troops in Northern Ireland in the spring of 1944.

British management of relations with the two neutrals was characterised at the official level by a growing degree of appreciation of the factors influencing the responses of the respective governments to the diplomatic and security demands made of them. Calculations about the threats posed by the Axis diplomatic missions became increasingly complex as the war progressed, code-breaking improved, and opportunities were recognised for feeding the enemy disinformation through their diplomats. Such nuances were largely lost at the political level in London, where time and again Churchill attempted to short-circuit his officials and to bring matters to a head by threats and, if necessary, by action.

Both of these very different neutral neighbours of Britain managed to stay out of the war despite the temptations of lost lands restored dangled by the Axis, and the pressures exerted by Britain and her allies. The Axis made an unconscious contribution to this outcome through the inadequacy of their codes, which revealed to the British both the extent and the limits of their clandestine activities in, and intentions towards, both Afghanistan and Ireland. But the major credit for the success of Irish and Afghan neutrality plainly lies with the two states themselves. Despite the geographic, cultural, political and historical differences which separated them, they had very similar dealings with the belligerents, and they successfully coped with the crisis confronting them in very similar ways.

ACKNOWLEDGEMENTS

The research on which this article is based was funded partly by grants from the Trinity College, Dublin Arts Humanities Benefactions Fund and the Institute for International Integration Studies.

NOTES

1 William Carlgren, *Swedish Foreign Policy during the Second World War*, London, 1977; Robert Fisk, *In Time of War: Ireland, Ulster and the Price of Neutrality 1939–45*, London, 1983; Christian Leitz, *Nazi Germany and Neutral Europe during the Second World War*, Manchester, 2000; Neville Wylie, *Britain, Switzerland and the Second World War*, Oxford, 2003 and idem (ed.), *European Neutrals and Non-Belligerents in the Second World War*, Cambridge, 2003.
2 Ludwig W. Adamec, *Historical Dictionary of Afghanistan*, Metuchen, NJ, 1991, pp. 66–7.
3 Patrick Beesly, *Room 40: British Naval Intelligence, 1914–18*, London, 1982, p. 216.
4 Milan Hauner, *India in Axis Strategy: Germany, Japan and Indian Nationalists in the Second World War*, Stuttgart, 1981; Eunan O'Halpin (ed.), *MI5 and Ireland, 1939–1945: The Official History*, Dublin, 2003, p. 31.
5 Henderson (Berlin) to Foreign Office, 6 July 1937, British Library, India Office Records and Library (hereafter, IOR), L/PS/12/1878.
6 DIB to London, 22 May, and India Office minute, 27 June 1945, and minute by Baker, Foreign Office, 15 March 1946, IOR, L/PS/12/1878.
7 Berlin to Pilger, 29 November 1943, The National Archives (TNA), HW12/295.
8 William Magan, *Middle Eastern Approaches: Memoirs of an Intelligence Officer*, London, 2001, pp. 17–18; interviews with Brigadier Magan, 2000 and 2001.
9 Francis R. Nicosia, '"Drang nach Osten" continued? Germany and Afghanistan during the Weimar Republic', *Journal of Contemporary History*, 32, 2, (1997) pp. 238–9; SOE war diary, 9, 17, 22, 24, 26 and 29 January, 4 and 5 February, 19 March, 4 April 1941, TNA, HS7/212, 213, 214 and 215; Adamec, *Historical Dictionary of Afghanistan*, pp. 108–9.
10 Nicosia, '"Drang nach Osten" continued?', p. 238.
11 Ibid., pp. 235–6.
12 Lorraine to Foreign Office, 19 December 1923, quoting the German minister; Wassmuss (in Tehran) to Lorraine, 15 February 1924, IOR, L/PS/11/246.
13 Milan Hauner, 'Afghanistan between the Great Powers, 1938–1945', *International Journal of Middle Eastern Studies*, 14 (1982), pp. 481–2.
14 Ibid., p. 482.
15 Adamec, *Historical Dictionary of Afghanistan*, p. 29.
16 Milan Hauner, 'The Soviet threat to Afghanistan and India 1938-1940', *Modern Asian Studies*, 15, 2 (1981), pp. 288–9.
17 Hauner, 'Afghanistan between the great powers', p. 485.
18 John Cudady, US Minister, Dublin, to J.C. Walsh, 25 May 1938, New York Public Library, J.C. Walsh papers, box 3; de Valera to Roosevelt, 22 April 1938, in Catriona Crowe, Ronan Fanning, Michael Kennedy, Dermot Keogh and Eunan O'Halpin (eds), *Documents in Irish*

Foreign Policy, Vol. 5, *1937–1939*, Dublin, 2006), p. 274.
19 O'Halpin (ed.), *MI5 and Ireland*, pp.28–9.
20 O'Halpin (ed.), *MI5 and Ireland*, pp. 18–22.
21 Liddell diary, 10 January 1940, TNA, KV4/185.
22 Connor-Green to ? [probably Vickery of IPI], 4 January 1943, IOR, L/PS/12/1933.
23 Eunan O'Halpin, *Defending Ireland: The Irish State and its Enemies since 1922*, Oxford, 1999, pp. 210–13, 222–3.
24 O'Halpin (ed.), *MI5 and Ireland*, p. 51.
25 Mark Hull, *Irish Secrets: German Espionage in Wartime Ireland 1939–1945*, Dublin, 2003, is the best study of this question.
26 Walshe (External Affairs) to taoiseach, 27 May and 1 June 1944, National Archives of Ireland (NAI), DFA A2.
27 Reports by Walshe (External Affairs, Dublin) of discussions with Hempel, 19 December 1940 and 6 January 1941, NAI, DFA A21; undated extract from decode of Berlin to Hempel, and extract from decode of Berlin to Hempel, 18 December 1940, given under 'Researches into Earlier Material', in 'Summary of Most Secret Information from Dublin 8–22 January 1944', TNA, DO121/87.
28 Military attaché's diary, 22 February 1941, IOR, L/PS/12/1844; Pilger to Berlin, 18 May 1943, TNA, HW12/288.
29 Liddell diary, 18 February 1940, TNA, KV4/185; draft India Office message for Kabul, 24 April 1940, IOR, L/PS/12/1774.
30 Antrobus (British Representative's Office, Dublin) to External Affairs, 1 June 1940, NAI, DFA, A3.
31 Japanese minister, Kabul, to Tokyo, 11 July 1940, TNA, HW12/54; Italian minister, Kabul, to Rome, 2 January 1941, TNA, HW12/260; Milan Hauner, 'One Man against the Empire: the Faqir of Ipi and the British in Central Asia on the Eve of and during the Second World War', *Journal of Contemporary History*, 16 (1981), p. 183; Charles Chenevix Trench, *The Frontier Scouts*, Oxford, 1985, pp. 221–60.
32 Military attaché's diary, 4 and 25 July 1941, IOR, L/PS/12/1844.
33 Richard Aldrich, *Intelligence and the War against Japan: Britain, America and the Politics of Secret Service*, Cambridge, 2000, p. 165.
34 Italian embassy, Washington, to Italian legation, Dublin, 28 December 1940, TNA, HW12/260.
35 O'Halpin (ed.), *MI5 and Ireland*, pp. 68–70, 78–82.
36 Amery diary, 22 June 1941, Churchill College Cambridge Archives (CCCA), AMEL7/35.
37 Mallet (Foreign Office) to Clauson (India Office), 12 August 1941, IOR, L/PS/12/699.
38 Military attaché's diary, 27 June 1941, IOR, L/PS/12/1844; British minister, Kabul, to Foreign Office, 7 July, Delhi to London, 11 July, and India Office minute, 9 September 1941, IOR, L/PS/12/1932.
39 Wylie to Foreign Office, 13 February [1943], and 19 November 1942, IOR, L/PS/12/699 and 1882.
40 Hill (SOE, Moscow) to SOE London, and reply, 1 and 7 June 1943, TNA, HS1/191.
41 Pilditch (head of IB, Delhi) to Mackenzie (head of SOE in India), 13 December 1944, TNA, HS1/191.
42 Foreign Office to India Office, 2 June 1942, IOR, L/PS/12/699; SOE war diary, undated [late May 1942], TNA, HS7/233; Eunan O'Halpin, '"Toys" and "Whispers" in 16-land: SOE and Ireland, 1940–1942', *Intelligence and National Security*, 15, 4 (Winter 2000), pp. 1–16.
43 O'Halpin (ed.), *MI5 and Ireland*, p. 77.
44 Ibid., p. 7.
45 Kabul to Delhi, 11 June 1942, and Connor-Green to ?[probably Vickery of IPI], 21 January 1943, IOR, L/PS/12/1933.
46 See Irish intelligence reports on the Vichy legation in NAI, DFA A8 and 8/1 and P70.
47 Unsigned m.s. reports [by Moore, an Irish intelligence informer within an MI6 network], 5 October 1941, and undated, Military Archives of Ireland, G2/X/1091; the saga of Albertas's eventual departure is dealt with in decodes of the French minister, Dublin, to Paris , 22 October 4 and 8 December 1944, TNA, HW12/305 and 307.
48 Italian minister, Baghdad, to Rome, 22 and 30 January, 5, 14 February, 5 and 12 March, 3, 4, 8, 14, 17 and 23 April 1941, TNA, HW12/260, 261, 262 and 263. Rashid Ali is referred to in these messages as 'Gailiani', an Italianised version of the suffix; Amery diary, 8 and 18 April

1941, CCCA, AMEL7/35; Malcolm Muggeridge (ed.), *Ciano's Diaries, 1939–1943*, London, 1947, p. 432, entry for 10 February 1942.

49 Joan Beaumont, 'Great Britain and the Rights of Neutral Countries: The Case of Persia, 1941', *Journal of Contemporary History*, 6 (1981), p. 217.

50 Bullard (Tehran) to Foreign Office, 22 April, 4 May and 9 June 1942, British Library India Office Library and Records (IOR), L/PS/12/656. Magan, *Middle Eastern Approaches*, pp. 66–8.

51 Churchill to Eden, 11 September, and to Wylie (British minister in Kabul), 19 October 1941, in Martin Gilbert (ed.), *The Churchill War Papers*, Vol 3, *The Ever-widening War*, London, 2000, pp. 1173 and 1350; Llewellyn Woodwar, *British Foreign Policy in the Second World War*, 5 vols, London, 1970–76, Vol. 2 (1971), p. 58.

52 O'Halpin (ed.), *MI5 and Ireland*, p. 78.

53 Vickery (IPI) to Silver (India Office), 16 November 1943, British Library, IOR, L/PS/12/1805.

54 Connor-Green's note of talk with Quaroni, 2 October 1943, IOR, L/PS/12/1805.

55 British minister, Kabul, to Delhi, 27 May 1943, IOR, L/PS/12/1798.

56 Gillman (US embassy, London) to Foreign Office, 7 June, and British minister, Kabul, to Foreign Office, 26 July 1943, IOR, L/PS/12/1798.

57 Text of Soviet foreign minister to British ambassador, Moscow, 10 July 1943, IOR, L/PS/12/1798.

58 Chargé d'affaires, Kabul, to Foreign Office, 25 July 1943, IOR, L/PS/12/1798; German minister, Kabul, to Berlin, 6 April and 5 August, and Italian minister, Kabul, to Rome, 8 August; Berlin to German minister, Kabul, 4 December 1943, TNA, HW12/287, 290 and 294. In 1971 Professor Milan Hauner met one of the Germans concerned, Witzel, at a conference in Calcutta commemorating Subhas Chandra Bose. Witzel was disconcerted to learn that his wartime reports from Kabul were open to research and that his cover had been blown. Information from Milan Hauner, April 2006.

59 Eunan O'Halpin, 'Irish-Allied Security Relations and the 'American Note' Crisis: New Evidence from British Records', *Irish Studies in International Affairs*, 11 (2000), pp. 71–83.

60 O'Halpin (ed.), *MI5 and Ireland*, pp. 82–4.

61 Delhi to London, 16 May 1944, IOR, L/PS/12/1798.

62 F.H. Hinsley and C.A.G. Simkins, *British Intelligence in the Second World War*, Vol. 4, *Security and Counter-Intelligence*, London, 1990, pp. 232–4.

63 Guy Liddell diary, 26 September 1944, TNA, KV4/195.

64 O'Halpin (ed.), *MI5 and Ireland*, p. 83.

The birth of the idea of revolt: the Irish example and the Irgun Tzvai Leumi

Jonathan Spyer

The steady transformation of British policy towards the Middle East and the Zionist project in the course of the 1930s presented the organisations of Revisionist Zionism, or the 'Herzlian' movement, as it called itself at that time[1] – the Irgun Tsvai Leumi (IZL), the Betar youth movement and the New Zionist Organisation (NZO), with a dilemma. Since its inception, Revisionism had been the most consistently pro-British of all Zionist streams. Movement leader Ze'ev Jabotinsky's central political achievement, often recalled by his followers, was the creation of the Jewish Legion within the British army of General Edmund Allenby which conquered the area that became Mandatory Palestine from the Turks.

Revisionism's pro-British stance derived from the movement's greater focus on, and clarity regarding, political and diplomatic matters when compared to other elements within Zionism.[2] Revisionism, in contrast to other Zionist streams, had a clear goal (a Jewish sovereign state). It also possessed perhaps the most fully realised conception of international affairs of any Zionist element. In his writings, Jabotinsky articulated a 'realist", dispassionate understanding of the process whereby Zionism would realise itself. This understanding assumed the inevitability of Arab opposition to Zionism, and overtly depicted Zionism as a pro-Western movement.

Jabotinsky combined a profound sympathy for British methods and institutions with militant activity in the defence of what he perceived as the Jewish interest in the British–Jewish–Arab triangle around which politics in Mandate Palestine revolved. As he expressed it during the partition debate in 1937:

We may have a number of grievances against England but the English government is, and will be, the government of a well-disposed mother. We must have patience. We shall finally achieve our aim of a Palestine on both sides of the Jordan. This will be achieved with the aid of England who always puts obstacles in our way and always helps us.[3]

In the course of the 1930s, however, and particularly from 1937 onward, a younger, more militant, generation of individuals came to political maturity within the organs of the movement founded by Jabotinsky, and most importantly, within the IZL and Betar, both in Mandatory Palestine and in the Diaspora. These younger men were influenced by the 'maximalist' school within the Revisionist movement of the early 1930s – led by Abba Ahimeir, Y.H. Yeivin and the poet Uri Zvi Greenberg.[4] The maximalist school represented a significant departure from traditional Revisionism. It replaced Jabotinsky's pro-Western orientation and realist view of international affairs with a stark, social Darwinist type outlook, which stressed the role of force in the creation of sovereignty. This was combined with a fervent nationalism with a mystical flavour – best exemplified in Greenberg's poetry.[5]

The young militants on the rise in Betar and the IZL in the 1930s were organisationally independent from, though influenced by, maximalist Revisionism. They despaired of what they perceived as the increasing British abandonment of the Balfour Declaration. They had come to political maturity in the 1930s, with no memory of earlier days of British–Jewish co-operation. The idea which they began to develop represented a new departure for Revisionist Zionism – namely, that of open military revolt against British rule.

No precedents existed in modern Jewish history for the idea of military revolt. The Zionist experience itself offered little guidance – the main focus of the IZL up to that point, and indeed the reason for its emergence, had been the organisation of more active opposition to Arab attacks against Jews in Mandatory Palestine. Jabotinsky had from the outset placed great stress on the need for Jews to rediscover the ability to defend themselves. He had himself been jailed by the British for organising Jewish self-defence in Jerusalem in 1920. But Jabotinsky in the 1930s continued to see an independent Jewish military organisation as a way to pressure the British to honour their commitments made in the Balfour Declaration.[6]

The young radicals, by contrast, were not merely arguing for a more vigorous implementation of existing policy. They were suggesting a new paradigm. The young men who began to formulate the idea of revolt therefore looked back to earlier examples and traditions of insurrection, both for inspiration and, more concretely, as models for the productive employment of irregular military force as a strategy in a national struggle. They were able to draw on ancient Jewish history for inspiration – from the Maccabees to Bar-Kochba. But observation of the writings and recorded discussions of the central early advocates of the idea of revolt show that they also drew on models of the national struggles of other peoples. The three main sources of inspiration in this regard were the experiences of Poland, Italy and Ireland.[7] This chapter will explore the influence of the Irish model on the formulation and development of policy within the Revisionist movement, from the first stirrings of the idea of revolt against British rule, in the 1930s, until the declaration and outbreak of the IZL revolt in 1944.

THE 'IRISH MODEL' AND ITS USE BY THE IZL

The focus here on Ireland should not be understood as implying that the Irish model was the most central or significant of the three. On the contrary, in many ways it may well have been the most marginal. But it also remains the least explored by serious research.[8] I intend in a sense to commence two separate tasks here. The first is to look at the role played by the Irish example as a model and inspiration for IZL and Betar members formulating a strategy of insurgency in the late 1930s and 1940s. The second is to examine from a historical point of view whether useful comparisons may be drawn from the two experiences – whether points of similarity in fact exist, whether they cast light on the specific experiences of each, and whether any general lessons may be learned for the study of insurgent movements and nationalist ideologies by making this comparison.

Let us then examine the historical record. First, it is important to note the key reasons why Ireland might have been of interest as an example to a group of Jewish nationalist revolutionaries, born mainly in eastern Europe or the Middle East, planning revolt and seeking examples on which to draw. Ireland represented at that time the only example of successful insurrection against the British Empire in the twentieth century, and the twentieth century's first example of a successful national liberation struggle. Further points of comparison existed between the two national movements – such as the role of language and religious tradition in both Zionism and Irish nationalism, and the transition from cultural to political nationalism in the last years of the nineteenth century.

But these were not the elements of the Irish experience that primarily interested those activists of the NZO, Betar and the IZL as they began to plan revolt in the last years of the 1930s. Rather, they were particularly interested in the example the Irish experience seemed to offer of how a small, determined group of people could light the spark of revolt, transforming the situation through determined activism, although they represented only a minority trend in the national movement of which they were a part. It was this aspect, and this version, of the Irish achievement of independence that interested these young Zionist radicals.

Who were the individuals, among the early pioneers of the idea of revolt in the late 1930s, in whose writings and statements we may find evidence of the influence of the Irish example? Among the most significant was Avraham Yair Stern, the leading IZL militant who later broke from the organisation to found a separate group – the 'Lohamei Herut Yisrael' or Lehi (Israel Freedom Fighters) – known by their British opponents as the 'Stern Group' or gang.

Stern, in the 1930s, translated 'The Victory of Sinn Fein' by Patrick Sarsfield O'Hegarty into Hebrew.[9] This book deals with the Irish insurrectionary period between 1916 and 1921. Its author was a member of the Irish Republican Brotherhood (IRB), the secret, conspiratorial group of which both Michael Collins and the leader of the Easter Rising of 1916, Padraig Pearse, were also members. The book is written very much from an IRB perspective. The importance of self-sacrifice, and of the role of the revolutionary elite are stressed in it. These elements – of the blood sacrifice, the elite few willing to act without the consent of the majority and, notably, the actions of a small, conspiratorial group operating within the larger body of the revolutionary movement, were of practical interest to Stern.

The standard version of the Easter Rising, according to which a group of idealists offered themselves for sacrifice in an act of armed defiance that was doomed from the outset has been subject to much subsequent historical revision. It was this version of events, however, which would have been familiar to Stern and his cohorts, and it was to this idea that Stern himself repeatedly returned. O'Hegarty, certainly, in common with Irish nationalist writing of the time, held to the view that the British execution of the leaders of the Rising, and the perception of them as martyrs, was the springboard for the much larger and successful Irish rebellion which broke out in 1919.[10]

The resemblance between this version of Easter 1916, and the conception of the Revolt as first imagined by Stern and others in the late 1930s is clear. Let us consider here the planned nature of the actual revolt which Stern and his cohorts were promoting in the 1930s. The idea that was spreading in the secret cells of the IZL in Poland and in Mandatory Palestine was for a dramatic act of rebellion which, it was hoped, would transform the situation. This idea, to which Jabotinsky may also have become, at least partially, converted in the period immediately preceding the war, envisaged the landing of 40,000 armed Jewish fighters in Eretz Yisrael.[11] They would seize Government House in Jerusalem and other important installations, proclaim a Jewish state and a provisional government, and hold out for as long as possible. This idea was first openly formulated by Uriel Halperin, following the publication of the 1937 Royal Commission on Palestine (Peel) report.

Some historians, including Yaacov Shavit, have suggested that it was merely a fanciful idea, emanating from despair.[12] This is by no means certain. Stern and the secret cells of the IZL in Poland had links to high levels in the Polish government,[13] as well as training camps in the Carpathian mountains, where Polish officers trained IZL fighters in methods of insurgency.[14] The activities of Stern and the 'secret cells' were kept secret from the leadership of Betar and Jabotinsky, and the Polish Betar leadership was apparently unaware of them. But support for a dramatic military gesture on the model of Easter 1916, a gesture undertaken without much hope of military victory, but as an attempt to give the world and the Yishuv the memory of a proclaimed Jewish state, was not confined to Stern and his immediate cohorts. Influential support for it also existed among senior members of the NZO.[15]

In this regard, it is important here to specifically recall three supporters of the NZO and Jabotinsky, two Irishmen and one Englishman, only one of the three a Jew, who were active in promoting the idea of a revolt against Britain in this period – the three are Robert Briscoe, Colonel John Patterson and Colonel Josiah Wedgwood.

Wedgwood was a former officer of the Jewish Legion, which Patterson, an Irish Protestant, had commanded. Briscoe, a Jew from Dublin, and later mayor of that city, had held high rank in the IRA during its war against Britain in the period 1919–21. Working under the pseudonym of 'Captain Swift', he was a leading figure in IRA arms-purchasing efforts in Europe. The arms he purchased in Germany, and transported to Ireland, were vital to the success of the Irish insurrection, and he remains a noted figure in the history of the Irish Republic.[16]

In the Irish Civil war that followed the rebellion, Briscoe was one of the leaders of the Republican side, who rejected partition of Ireland and the treaty which created the Irish Free State. Briscoe also became a member of the NZO on its foundation, and was a personal friend of Jabotinsky's.[17] In 1938, he hosted Jabotinsky on the latter's first and only visit to Ireland, during which Jabotinsky met with Irish president and former IRA leader Eamon de Valera. In his memoirs, which have never been translated into Hebrew, Briscoe describes the reason for Jabotinsky's visit to 'learn all he could in order to form a physical force movement in Palestine on the same lines as the IRA'.[18]

It is worthwhile treating Briscoe's remarks regarding Jabotinsky's desire to create an IRA-style movement with scepticism. Jabotinsky never makes such an allusion himself, and Briscoe has a clear interest in playing up the similarities and parallels between the two movements. Nevertheless, Jabotinsky's visit to Ireland and association with Briscoe is a matter of record, and undoubtedly represents a significant shift in the Revisionist leader's attitude towards Britain. From a position of overt identification with Britain which exceeded that of any other Zionist leader, Jabotinsky had moved by the 1930s to a point whereby association with de Valera and his lieutenants seemed natural and desirable.[19]

After Jabotinsky's visit, Briscoe worked for a time for the NZO, making trips to the United States to raise funds and support. He describes himself as being involved in 'organizing Irgun on the lines of the IRA'.[20] Briscoe and Patterson, together with the Irgun officers Chaim Lubinsky and Yitzhak Ben-Ami, headed the IZL fundraising mission in the United States in the period immediately preceding the Second World War.[21] Briscoe had headed a similar mission on behalf of the IRA in the early 1920s. He used his connections with prominent Irish-Americans to try to gain access to senior US policymakers in order to enlist their support for the cause of Zionist activism. Among the Irish-Americans who came to Briscoe's assistance were William O'Dwyer, the Brooklyn District Attorney and later mayor of New York, and James J. Farley, Postmaster-General under Franklin Roosevelt.[22]

Briscoe's mission was a failure, however. He failed to gain an audience with the president, or to make headway in the Jewish community, where his past as an Irish revolutionary tended to work against him. It was suspected that far from being a true Zionist, his main intention was simply to damage British interests. Briscoe returned to Ireland in April 1939 to re-commence his duties as a member of parliament for the Fianna Fáil party. Before his departure, he was instrumental in the founding of the American Friends of Jewish Palestine. He continued his association with the NZO, and after 1945 became associated with the Lehi, basing himself in Cairo for a period and aiding the Lehi in their fight against Britain.[23]

Briscoe and his cohorts deliberately stressed the parallel with the Irish experience while in America, where the Irish cause had a great deal of support. In the *New York World Telegram* of 13 July 1939, for example, there is an article entitled 'Jewish IRA fights for sovereign Palestine'.[24] The article, by Morris Gilbert, contains an interview with an un-named IZL member, who draws a direct parallel between the two situations. The interviewee, most probably Briscoe himself, points out that numbers are unimportant when one considers that, in Ireland in the 1919–21 period, 1,800 IRA members had successfully fought a British garrison of 80,000.[25]

Josiah Wedgwood, then a Member of Parliament for the British Labour Party, was one of the earliest advocates of Jewish armed resistance, and indeed some sources credit Wedgwood with the original idea of the 'invasion from the sea' mentioned above. As a member of the British Labour Party, but a supporter of the NZO rather than Mapai, Labour's sister party of the Socialist International, Wedgwood was in a somewhat anomalous position. He clashed with the leadership of the Jewish Agency on more than one occasion because of his outspoken support for the NZO and the IZL.

After he wrote that 'I want to see in Palestine once again a fighting nation, free and courageous like the Maccabees...An army of forty thousand fit to defend what is dear to them and to me,'[26] David Ben-Gurion cabled the Jewish Agency in London, instructing them to contact the Labour Party in order to investigate Wedgwood and his views.[27] Wedgwood was outspoken in his call for the Jews to use guerrilla tactics, which, he also claimed, would win the respect and attention of the British. As he put it 'I hear all sorts of excellent ideas about blowing up the pipeline, blowing up bridges, bombing, and doing all that the IRA are doing.'

This comment was made by Wedgwood in a debate in the House of

Commons in 1937. Together with John Patterson, he was the staunchest and most prominent of Jabotinsky's advocates in Britain. Wedgwood claimed to base his support for Jabotinsky's movement on what he regarded as his acute understanding of the British mentality. Wedgwood stressed the British respect and understanding for those who were prepared to use force in support of their cause, and their contempt for those who were content merely with petitioning. The above quote is taken from a context in which he contrasted the Irish approach with that of mainstream Zionism, and encouraged his Jewish friends to learn from the Irish tradition of insurrection.[28]

THE DEVELOPMENT OF IZL STRATEGY: TOWARDS THE DECLARATION OF THE REVOLT OF 1944

The clash between the maximalist view within Revisionism, as supporters of revolt were known, and those who wished to continue the movement's traditional orientation dominated Revisionist discussions in the years immediately preceding the outbreak of war in 1939. The debate came out into the open at the Third Conference of World Betar in Warsaw in 1938. This was the scene of a famous exchange between Jabotinsky and Begin which encapsulated the clash between traditional Revisionism and the new, militant younger generation.

Menachem Begin's position in the dispute should be clarified here. He was not a member of the 'secret cells' of the IZL in Poland, nor was he aware of all the details of the paramilitary activity being undertaken in Poland. He was, and remained, a loyal follower of Jabotinsky. He was not among the advocates of the 'invasion from the sea'. But he shared with the radicals the view that military struggle must now take precedence over the diplomatic approach favoured by traditional Revisionism. At the 1938 Conference, Begin tabled a motion expressing support in principle for a future war of liberation, and calling for the establishment of an independent military force.

It is interesting to note that in refuting Begin, Jabotinsky specifically rejected the attempt to apply examples of other national liberation movements to the Zionist case. In his speech, Begin referred directly to the Italian experience of the *risorgimento*, stressing the important role of Garibaldi and military pressure in the achievement of Italian unification. This may be seen as an attempt to stress his underlying loyalty to Jabotinsky, who was known for his great affection for Italy, where he had studied, and for the influence of the Italian experience on his thought.

Jabotinsky, in his response, referred to the Italian and to the Irish examples. 'Not a single strategist in the world', he said, 'would claim that under present circumstances, we could do what Garibaldi and De Valera have done. Our situation bears no resemblance to that of the Italians and the Irish.'

The key difference, in Jabotinsky's view, was that Zionism was a movement of immigration and settlement, which had not yet achieved a majority within the borders of Mandatory Palestine. As such, talk of a military rising was premature and misleading.[29]

It is outside the scope of this chapter to enter into detail regarding the nature and extent of the change in Jabotinsky's position towards support for the idea of an armed rising and seizure of government buildings, on the model of the 1916 Easter Rising. As he became increasingly aware of the desperation of the situation, it appears that he began to look more favourably on the idea of an 'armed demonstration' of this sort.[30] Whether or not such an act would have taken place, and what its effect would have been is of course a matter for speculation only. The outbreak of war in September 1939 removed the possibility of such action.

We will now turn to look at the resumption of Jewish underground activity, with the IZL's declaration of its 'Revolt' in early 1944. I will not deal here with the subsequent very different trajectory of the Lohamei Herut Yisrael (Lehi, or 'Stern Group') after the split in the IZL in July, 1940. This is not because there is nothing to say on this subject. Indeed, the Lehi, far more than the IZL under Begin's leadership, sought very much to define itself as one insurgent movement among many others fighting British imperialism.

Lehi Operations Officer Yitzhak Shamir's chosen nom de guerre – 'Michael', in honour of Michael Collins, is only the most famous example of this, and Stern's own deep interest in, and influence by, Irish republicanism is detailed above. Lehi, however, developed a very different political and military orientation of its own in the years 1942–49, (and to some extent into the 1950s, since remnants of Lehi, alone of the Zionist undergrounds, continued with paramilitary activity after Israel's War of Independence). This organisation thus deserves separate treatment in a study of its own. This chapter is concerned with the IZL, and for this reason Lehi's place in this discussion will not be further explored here.

The revolt proclaimed by the IZL, under the leadership of Menachem Begin, in February 1944, involved the use of limited guerrilla warfare, and was intended to place maximum political pressure on the British authorities, making optimal use of limited resources and personnel. It represented a far more sophisticated approach than that of those in the IZL who had first raised the idea of revolt in the late 1930s, and with whom we have been concerned above. The revolt was neither a gesture, nor a symbolic act of defiance, but was rather a campaign of urban guerrilla warfare, combining sporadic military actions with propaganda.

What is of interest to note is that this trajectory – from notions of an almost suicidal act of defiance, to a more sophisticated and effective conception of guerrilla warfare, closely resembles that taken by Irish nationalism – from Pearse and Connolly's all-out rising of Easter 1916, to the very effective and ultimately victorious guerrilla campaign waged by the

IRA under Michael Collins, in the period 1919–21.[31] Begin himself acknowledges this. Begin's rhetoric, unlike that of his predecessors, tended to avoid concrete comparisons and parallels with other modern cases of revolt. *The Revolt*, for example, Begin's account of the paramilitary campaign of the IZL, contains no references to Ireland, and precious few to other examples from modern history. Begin preferred to anchor the revolt within a specifically Jewish context.

Elsewhere, however, in discussions of tactics and strategy, Begin does make reference to the Irish experience. Where he refers to Ireland, it is in order to praise the effectiveness of the methods of Michael Collins, who succeeded in creating a feared and ultimately victorious underground movement, involving the participation of a far smaller number of individuals than the scope of its activities suggested. Only on a couple of occasions in his writings does Begin refer directly to the 'Irish model', and he embarks on a detailed discussion of it only once. To my knowledge, none of these references has previously been translated from the Hebrew.

On both occasions, Begin uses the Irish example to explore the important role of British public opinion in bringing about a change of policy. Learning from Wedgwood, whom he cites on several occasions, Begin stresses that the use of force would not have a detrimental effect on that section of British public opinion inclined to sympathise. As such, says Begin,

> The Irish example is particularly striking in this regard. The Irish war for independence became, as is well known, a central aspect of internal debate in England, which decided the results of elections to parliament, and this was despite the fact that the Irish made no special effort to find out what would, or would not, find favour in the eyes of the English.[32]

Elsewhere, in an article written prior to the declaration of the revolt, Begin compares in detail the situation facing the Irish in the 1919–21 period (i.e. the period of their successful struggle for independence) with the situation facing the Jews in Eretz Israel/Mandatory Palestine at the time of writing. Begin once again stresses the ability of the Irish to make an impact on British public opinion through their actions, thereby forcing pressure on the British policymaking echelon. Given the situation, Begin observes, 'we have a far greater chance of putting the English nation into a state of spiritual embarassment and confusion, into the same unpleasant state, as that which caused the beginnings of negotiation between the strong Lloyd George and the weak Collins'.[33] Here, Begin cites Wedgwood in the following terms,

> It is worth being reminded of the words of one of our real friends, the late Wedgwood... that the friends of Zionism in England are unable to help until the Yishuv itself launches a real war against the policy of

betrayal...Wedgwood demanded of us that we begin a war of masses, his whole proposal boiled down to a single short sentence – 'go to jail'.[34]

Begin continues: 'To return to the Irish rebellion. The writer of the survey proves that only 75–100 men, from a camp consisting of thousands, carried out all the military operations which brought about negotiations between the British Prime Minister and the leader of the rebels. 75–100 men, remember the number.'[35]

Begin goes on to compare in detail the military conditions facing the Irish with that which the Yishuv faced on the eve of the revolt. He then returns to the issue with which he had clashed with Jabotinsky in 1938 in Warsaw – that of the absence of a Jewish majority in Mandatory Palestine, whereas the Irish rebels had been able to move in territory favourable to them. In a long discourse, Begin observes the central role of cities in modern revolution. He observes that a modern administration requires control of the urban centres of a country in order to be able to govern. The cities, he concludes, are precisely where the core of support for the IZL lies. Thus this aspect, the only area, says Begin, where the conditions facing the Irish were clearly more favourable than those facing the Jews, need not be decisive.[36] The greater sophistication of Begin's thinking is clear. The Irish revolt that interests him is the one that forced the British to talk, through a combination of military action and propaganda. Armed demonstrations and gestures of defiance are already part of the past.

Whether he succeeded in solving by this the dilemma to which Jabotinsky had pointed to in 1938 is of course a different matter. Begin here, as elsewhere in his writings and in a way typical of the IZL tradition, tends to ignore the Arab population of the country. His perspective is one in which the struggle between the Jews and the British is the paramount historical process taking place. The Arabs are regarded primarily as spectators, and their own attempts at political and military organisation tend to be downplayed or dismissed as evidence of British manipulation and agitation. It could be argued that only from such a perspective could the sense of a direct parallel between the Zionist and Irish Republican experiences be made.

The Jabotinsky tradition, in direct contradiction to its rivals in the Zionist labour movement, had never made the process of settlement and creating the Jewish infrastructure in the country a matter of primary concern. The matter at hand for Revisionism had always been over who held the official title deeds to the country. Since in the 1940s this was Britain, the British were either the natural ally, or the natural opponent, depending on their own actions regarding Zionism. The logic of Begin's campaign derived from this. Hence Revisionism's shift from being the most pro-British Zionist faction to being the Zionist stream most open to identifying with Britain's enemies (including Irish Republicanism) was quite logical in terms of the movement's own terms of reference, and took place within this context.

CONCLUSIONS

The 'Irish example' constituted an important, though not paramount, historical model for the individuals within the organisations of Revisionist Zionism (primarily Betar and the Irgun Zvai Leumi) who first began to conceive of the idea of rebellion against British rule in Eretz Yisrael/ Mandatory Palestine. Some similarities may also be drawn on the process by which the strategy and tactics of Irish and Jewish insurgents developed and grew more sophisticated and effective. In his short history of Zionism, written just after the birth of the State of Israel, Arthur Koestler called his chapter on the growth of the Irgun and resistance to British rule in Mandatory Palestine 'John Bull's other Ireland',[37] and the similarities were not lost on other correspondents covering the conflict, as the *New York World Telegram* article mentioned earlier indicates.

There is considerable scope for further research on this subject – both for students of insurgency and low-intensity conflicts, for whom the similar strategic trajectories followed by Irish Republicanism and militant Zionism offer a point of interest, and for researchers interested in comparing and contrasting nationalist ideologies. However, it already seems apparent that the points of similarity between the Zionist militancy of the IZL and the physical force tradition of Irish republicanism are striking. And while the nature of Zionism as a movement of immigration and settlement, as well as of national liberation prevents direct comparisons between the experience of the two movements, the influence of the latter on the former, as detailed above, is worthy of further investigation.[38]

NOTES

1   This term was used by the Revisionists as part of their view of themselves as the inheritors of the tradition of 'political' Zionism, as represented by Theodor Herzl, in contrast with the settlement-oriented Zionism of the Labour and General Zionist alliance that controlled the movement. 'Political' Zionism in this context relates to the notion that only the clear statement of the eventual goal of Zionism – a Jewish state – and diplomatic action toward that goal would lead the movement to success.
2   See Yaacov Shavit, *Jabotinsky and the Revisionist Movement, 1925–1948*, London, 1988.
3   Colin Shindler, 'Militarism and the new Jewish identity: Vladimir Jabotinsky and the politics of inspiration, 1900–1940', Lecture given at the School of Oriental and African Studies, 11 December, 2002. www.arts.monash.edu.au/history/ events/genidwar/papers/shindler.
4   Greenberg, one of the giants of modern Hebrew literature, was a former adherent of Labour Zionism, whose views were transformed by the events of the 1920s and 1930s. Some of his poetry was deeply topical, and harshly critical, of the official leadership of Zionism. His book 'sefer hakitrug ve ha emuna' (*The Book of Denunciation and Faith*) achieved canonic status in the circles of the IZL and Lehi. In the book, the sacrifices of the underground fighters were linked to stories of the ancient Jewish past, and the official leaders of Zionism were held up to bitter reproach.
5   For a discussion of the emergence of radical Revisionism in the 1930s see Joseph Heller, *The Stern Gang: Ideology, Politics and Terror, 1940–49*, London, 1995, pp. 11–29.
6   See Zeev Jabotinsky, *The War and the Jew*, New York, 1987, pp. 169–80. See also Joseph B. Schechtman, *Fighter and Prophet: The Last Years*, New York, 1961, p. 297. Jabotinsky is here

quoted, from a conversation with Leopold Amery, in the following terms: 'critical as I am and shall probably have to remain, for me – so long as the Balfour Declaration stands – it is England, right or wrong'.

7   Jabotinsky's fascination with Italy in general, and the period of the *risorgimento*, 1848 and the figures of Mazzini and Garibaldi is well known, and well documented. Regarding Poland, Jabotinsky expressed his views in *The War and the Jew*, pp. 65–95, where his admiration for the figure of Marshal Pilsudski is apparent, and wherein he makes the famous, somewhat tortuous separation between the 'antisemitism of men' and the 'antisemitism of things.' For the (mainly Polish-born or of east European descent) Betarim who formed the leadership of the IZL, the reference to Polish nationalism was natural, and its influence on their outlook oft-remarked upon. See Sasson Sofer, *Zionism and the Foundations of Israeli Diplomacy*, Cambridge, 1998, p. 203 for a discussion of the general attitude of Revisionist Zionism to Poland. Of course, a *de facto* alliance with Poland in the 1937–39 period was the main feature of the foreign relations of IZL, and a central factor in the policy of insurrection planned by the organisation at that time. For further discussion of this aspect, see John Bowyer-Bell, *Terror Out of Zion*, New York, 1977, pp. 27–9, also Heller, *The Stern Gang*, pp. 45–7.

8   To my knowledge, this article is among the first to deal exclusively with the influence of the Irish experience on the IZL and militant Revisionism. A recent article in an Israeli newspaper by an expert on Revisionist Zionism focused on the links, similarities and differences between Revisionist Zionism and Irish Republicanism. See Colin Shindler, 'Jabotinsky and the Troubles', *Jerusalem Post*, 20 April 2006. The subject has also been dealt with in passing by a number of scholars.

9   Patrick Sarsfield O'Hegarty, *The Victory of Sinn Fein*, Dublin, 1998.

10 For a solid historical account of the events of the Rising, see Tim Pat Coogan, *1916: The Easter Rising*, New Delhi, 2002. For a work challenging the consensus on the origins of the Rising, see Brian Barton and Michael Foy, *The Easter Rising*, Stroud, 2004. See also Alan J. Ward, *The Easter Rising: Revolution and Irish Nationalism*, Wheeling, IL, 2003. I think a comparison of the poetry of Avraham Stern with that written by Irish nationalist leaders such as Padraig Pearse would be a fascinating project –not necessarily from an aesthetic point of view, but from the point of view of what one might learn regarding the core ideas driving these individuals. Stern's surviving written works are suffused with ideas of martyrdom, purity and self-sacrifice, unmistakably comparable in tone to some of Pearse's rhetoric.

11 Natan Yellin-Mor, *Fighters for the Freedom of Israel. People, Ideas, Deeds*, Haifa, 1974, pp. 45–7, (Hebrew).

12 Shavit, *Jabotinsky and the Revisionist Movement*.

13 Although exactly how high is a matter of dispute. While Stern's followers have sought to create the impression of links and access to ministers, Joseph Heller considers that Stern's Polish government links were at a 'bureaucratic' rather than 'ministerial' level. See Joseph Heller, 'The Zionist Right and National Liberation', in Robert Wistrich and David Ohana (eds), *The Shaping of Israeli Identity: Myth, Memory and Trauma*, London, 1995, pp. 85–109, p. 95.

14 Yitzhak Ben Ami, *Years of Wrath, Days of Glory*, New York, 1982, p. 192.

15 Ibid., pp. 199–201 for a discussion of the debates within the movement on this matter.

16 Robert Briscoe, *For the Life of Me*, Toronto, 1958, pp. 79–91.

17 Ibid., pp. 258–70.

18 Ibid., p. 264.

19 See Shindler, 'Jabotinsky and the Troubles', for examples of Jabotinsky's earlier, unsympathetic statements on the Easter Rising.

20 Briscoe, *For the Life of Me*, p. 265.

21 Ben-Ami, *Years of Wrath*, p. 214.

22 Ibid., p. 220.

23 Briscoe, *For the Life of Me*, p. 297.

24 Morris Gilbert, 'Jewish IRA fights for sovereign Palestine', *New York World Telegram*, 13 July 1939. In Golomb Archives, File 11.

25 Ibid.

26 Ben-Ami, *Years of Wrath*, p.202.

27 Ibid., p.203.

28 For a further examination of Wedgwood's position see Menachem Begin, *In the Underground: Writings and Documents*, Tel Aviv, 1978, pp.181–81.

29 Sofer, *Zionism and the foundations of Israeli Diplomacy*, p. 227.
30 See Ben-Ami, *Years of Wrath*, pp. 200–1, and Joseph Schechtman, *Fighter and Prophet: the Last years*, London, 1961, pp 482–5 for Jabotinsky's possible partial conversion to the idea of the invasion from the sea in the period immediately preceding the outbreak of the Second World War.
31 See Tim Pat Coogan, *De Valera: Long Fellow, Long Shadow*, London, 1995, for a detailed description of the development of Irish paramilitary strategy in the period 1916–21. Coogan is particularly sympathetic to the role played by Michael Collins in this period, and has been accused of bias in this regard. However, the book is reliable in terms of the broad picture painted of development and change in Irish guerrilla tactics and strategy, if more questionable in terms of the depiction of the particular roles of particular individuals.
32 Begin, *In the Underground*, p. 181.
33 Ibid., p.89–90.
34 Ibid., p. 90.
35 Ibid.
36 Ibid., p. 91.
37 See Arthur Koestler, *Promise and Fulfilment: Palestine, 1917–49*, London, 1949, especially ch. 12.
38 It would be impossible to write on this subject without touching on the much-observed phenomenon that in the Northern Ireland conflict of the later twentieth century, Irish Republicanism began to openly identify with Palestinian nationalism, as part of the larger location of the leaders of the IRA of the 1970s of their campaign with broader 'national liberation' struggles in the decolonised world. This, in turn, provoked the counter-phenomenon of Ulster loyalist hardliners identifying with Israel. This process is interesting in itself, and forms an element of the 're-branding' of Israel in the eyes of much of the European Left in the 1960s and 1970s from a developing country, to a country associated with colonialism. This later development is of no direct relevance, however, to the subject under discussion here. Both the IZL men of the 1930s and 1940s, and the particular Irish nationalist insurgents who interested them, were non-socialist nationalists of a conservative, traditional bent.

Myths of massacre and nationalist mobilisation: Ireland and Algeria in comparative perspective

Jonathan Githens-Mazer

The Irish Easter Rising of 1916 and the Philippeville Massacre of 1955 are examples of specific events in history which subsequently triggered the radicalisation of previously moderate nationalist movements. These 'tipping points' appear to have possessed a potency beyond their immediate and tangible impact – leading to popular violent and confrontational agitation for what was previously considered to have been achievable by constitutional and moderate strategies. The task at hand is to understand why radical nationalism had the most appeal at these specific moments – why, in Tilly's words, there was 'a rapid increase in the number of people accepting those [radical] claims and/or rapid expansion of [its] coalition'.[1]

This chapter will analyse the symbolic potency of the Philippeville Massacre of 1955 in Algeria, and the Easter Rising in Ireland, 1916, in terms of the way they were popularly understood during these moments of 'crisis' to correspond to the repression of the Irish and Algerian nations and nationalisms in history. These tipping points are salient, significant and potent because they were closely, and popularly, associated with Irish and Algerian national myths, memories and symbols of disasters, defeats and massacres.[2] It is argued here that the Easter Rising and Philippeville Massacre are significant, not solely because the British and French authorities, and Unionist and *Colons* communities, pursued a policy of torture, execution, repression and internment, but because these actions were understood by Irish and Algerian members of the nation through the prism of the preceding colonial/inter-nation relationship.

THE EASTER RISING, IRELAND 1916

The Easter Rising and its aftermath triggered the popular resonance of Irish national myths, memories and symbols and spoke to an Irish national perception of the preceding Anglo-Irish and Protestant–Catholic relationships.[3] Myths, memories and symbols of the Anglo-Irish relationship, especially those of the Famine of the 1840s and 1850s informed individual interpretations of, and reactions to, the Rising, and provided the basis for, and language through which, grassroots radical nationalism emerged in the political vacuum of legitimate parties and leaders in the wake of the Rising. Did these myths, memories and symbols simply emerge from the ether in a time of crisis? Were they present before the Rising? If so, why did they not matter ante-Rising?

The troubled relationship between England and Ireland, Protestant and Catholic, in terms of the disestablishment of the Catholic Church and the Penal Era determined the course of the Irish nationalist experience from the sixteenth to the early nineteenth century and fundamentally shaped the Irish nation. The Famine, especially as it was 'remembered' in the repertoire of Irish national myths, memories and symbols, transposed these experiences to become contemporarily relevant and popularly accessible to individuals at the time of the Rising. It bridged divides between cultural, political and religious nationalisms, unifying past with present and healing various splits in the nation itself. Irish nationalism sought to advance the nation through a fundamental moral regeneration of the 'corrupted' and 'tainted' contemporary Irish nation to a pre-Famine status quo, thereby restoring it to a mythical 'pre-English' golden age.

Around the time of the Rising, the Famine was understood as being the cause of 'all joy [leaving] the people...a hatred of England and Lords [sinking] deeper than ever into their souls'.[4] From the Famine onwards, commentators such as Mitchel laid the foundations for these interpretations, perceiving the Anglo-Irish relationship to be inherently exploitative.[5] These ideas were crystallised and disseminated in nationalist histories, stories, plays and poems written in the latter half of the nineteenth century and the beginning of the twentieth century.[6] The myths and memories of the Anglo-Protestant other, of the plantations, Penal Laws, hedge schools and exile, had been kept alive in the glowing emotional embers of the Famine; kept alive in newspapers, ballads and book covers.[7] Its recounting provided a repertoire of meaning by which survivors could apportion blame for the devastation of the Famine, and explain the vast repertoire of myths, memories and symbols of Irish historical suffering.

The Famine was highly relevant to nationalists at the time of the Rising. Descriptions of the Anglo-Hibernian relationship were full of references to Irish cultural and political nationalism, evidenced in contemporary nationalist descriptions of the formation of the Ulster Volunteers in 1912 which cited the lack of reaction by the British authorities to Loyalist gun-running at Larne, and later culminating in the refusal of British Army officers to disarm the Ulster Volunteers during the Curragh Mutiny.[8] In the wake of the Famine, there was a drive for tangible political gains, but now nationalism had an added role – to prevent the recurrence of the past. Sectarian tensions – reflected in concepts of the Famine, appeared to observers to have been exacerbated by the formation of the Ulster Volunteers such that these feelings were 'heightened and made manifest by the close relationship between the Ulster Volunteers and the Orange Order'.[9]

Despite the presence of these national myths, memories and symbols of sectarian difference, they had yet to create the basis for popular support for radical nationalism, and violence remained checked despite the presence of this resonant repertoire of myths. Various events – massacres even – had occurred without creating the basis for popular reaction, such as the killing of three and wounding of thirty-two, during the march of the Irish Volunteers, following their arming just outside of Dublin (the Bachelors Walk Incident).

The Rising was one of four elite-led insurgencies which took place over 'the long nineteenth century', all of which failed to excite popular sympathy and the Rising itself failed in its bid to unite the nation behind its mixed banner of Catholic–Socialist nationalism. Commencing, as it did, with the proclamation of an Irish Republic, and concluding in the utter devastation of central Dublin after its shelling by British gunships and the destruction caused by the fighting, its tactical objectives appeared foolhardy and ridiculous. Its extreme idealism, ranging from religious to Gaelic to socialist did little to inspire moderate nationalists. Its messages were mixed, and those that seemed obvious to observers appeared to reinforce the notion of its leaders and participants as extremists. In a majority of personal accounts of the events by non-participants, the leaders of the Rising were initially demonised, its participants and supporters labelled 'fools', and blamed for the destruction of central Dublin.

The significance of the Rising lay in its broader context, which included, but also extended beyond, the preceding and subsequent political realities, such as the stresses and strains of the First World War including a looming threat of the potential extension of conscription to Ireland.[10] In this way fears about the British–Irish relationship were apparent in concerns that conscription was to be implemented as a punitive measure against Catholic-Nationalist and now 'disloyal' Ireland. The Rising left a political vacuum in its wake, as Redmond and the Irish Party misjudged the shifting mood among members of the Irish nation – initially expressing a popular condemnation of the leaders of the Rising, but subsequently unable to stop the increasingly unpopular executions as they began to build to a crescendo.

To this extent, the summary execution of the vegetarian pacifist journalist, Francis Sheehy-Skeffington (and the subsequent persecution of his wife) by an officer later determined to have been suffering from 'mental exhaustion' following his service in the trenches; the execution of Patrick Pearse's brother Willy – who was deemed to have had no leading role in the Rising; the execution of a seriously wounded James Connolly (so seriously wounded that he had to be tied to a chair in order to be shot); the refusal to release the remains of those executed; and the implementation of a severe form of martial law and system of courts-martial were all viewed through the popular repertoire of understandings of the British-Irish relationship. When Asquith signalled his willingness to work for a solution to the Irish problem along the lines of Home Rule – something for which Parnell, Redmond and the Irish Party had been agitating for since the 1870s – the impotence of moderate constitutional nationalism was placed into even greater relief and the success of radical and violent 'physical force' nationalism in Ireland was apparent for all to see.

This was the context in which the Rising was transformed from an act of misguided fools into an event which was described by the moderate nationalist John Dillon as 'letting loose a river of blood... between two races who, after three hundred years of hatred and strife we nearly had succeeded in bringing together'.[11] The Catholic Church, which had been conservative in its dealings with Irish nationalism as a whole, let alone radical nationalism, was now forced to accommodate this grassroots change in their parishes, with one Bishop refusing a request by the British authorities to discipline two priests because the pleas for mercy on behalf of 'those poor young fellows who surrendered to you in Dublin' had gone unheeded and because the actions of the authorities had been 'as fatuous as arbitrary' and had served only to 'outrage the conscience of the country'.[12]

During several by-elections in the wake of the Rising, regular reference was made to the heroism of the '1500 Volunteers who had saved you from conscription'.[13] Bishop O'Dwyer also pronounced in the wake of the Rising that these events had 'galvanised the dead bones in Ireland and created the spirit with which England now has to reckon'.[14] During the South Longford by-election one prelate summed up the radicalising power of the Rising, when he proclaimed on the stump for Sinn Féin that his party 'will see that the crops which you planted to feed yourselves and your children will not be taken away from the country as they were in [18]46 and [18]47'.[15]

In reaction to these events, and in a context whereby moderate constitutional nationalism appeared at first to be out of touch, and later to be a complete failure, the national myths, memories and symbols that spoke of the persecution of the Irish nation at the hands of the Anglo-Protestant 'Other' were unleashed. From the British point of view there was a belief that the Rising had not been 'an *Irish* rebellion... it would be a pity if *ex post facto* it becomes one'.[16] Yeats' 'sixteen dead men' were stirring the boiling pot of cultural imagery, and through a combination of cultural and religious myths and symbols, these men would come to be rehabilitated and resurrected, as saints and martyrs for the Irish nation. The process of their 'beatification' in the pantheon of Irish heroes was a grassroots one – in the immediate aftermath of the Rising there were no radical institutions or organisations to propel this process, as they had been destroyed or broken up after the Rising by internment and martial law.

THE PHILIPPEVILLE MASSACRE, ALGERIA 1955

The Algerian case both mirrors and deviates from the Irish example. The role played by traumatic myths, memories and symbols of massacre and perceived ethnocidal intentions on the part of an 'anti-national' other is apparent in the recounting of, and reliance on, older memories of what is construed as a national past. These included myths, memories and symbols of events such as the crusades; the expulsion of Muslims from Spain at the end of the sixteenth century; the Ottoman legacy and the Dey and Bey system in Algeria and, more generally, the wider Maghreb; the rise and fall of the Barbary States; and the bloody and protracted war of French colonisation.

This repertoire of national myths, memories and symbols was disseminated through a variety of formats including, but not limited to, religion and the media. It was made contemporarily tangible and manifest broadly in the colonial experience, and specifically in events such as the Sétif Massacre of 1945, the Philippeville Massacre of 1955, as well as being constantly reinforced in the Algerian War through the deployment of torture as a French Army counterinsurgency tactic post-1954.[17] These sentiments reflected the Algerian characterisation of their colonisation as being typified by 'a degree of violence rare in the history of modern colonisation'.[18] The process of subjugation included a 'scorched earth policy' to quell rural unrest, with vivid descriptions of the levelling of villages, orchards, etc., the pillaging of valuables, the mass execution of thousands in religious grottos, and the capture of Algerian women – some kept as sexual hostages others 'auctioned to the troops like animals'.[19]

As in Ireland, the Algerian nation was typified by differing 'strands' – religious, ethnic, cultural, etc. During the inter-war period, four strands were most prominent – the Ulama, the Jeune Algérien movement, the communists and the radical Étoile Nord-Africaine (ENA).[20] All strands emphasised the differences in experiences and material living conditions between the *Colons* and the indigenous population, and the severity of the treatment of the latter group at the hands of Europeans.[21] Political frustration was largely based on the different treatment of Algerians compared to that of their European counterparts, with Algerians serving twenty-four months of military service compared to ten months for Europeans; receiving considerably lower salaries inside and outside of the military; not receiving the same bonuses if a government employee; and, perhaps most significantly, being denied the franchise.[22]

The economic discrepancies were obvious. The population of the slums of Algiers had grown twenty-six-fold between 1938 and 1954, from 4,800 to 125,000, and there were half the number of schools (699) for Muslims compared with their European counterparts, despite their much larger population, and only 150 Muslim students at the University of Algiers out of a student body of some 4,000.[23] Through the process of colonisation, the indigenous population was stripped of its lands and rights, so that by 1930, 20 per cent of French *Colons* owned some 74 per cent of the land, including over 90 per cent of the best farming land.[24] The transformation of Algeria under colonisation also resulted in the decay and failure of traditional social structures, so that various 'safety-nets' such as religious charities were eradicated, due to the French expropriation of the properties of the *habbous*.[25] Political structures also suffered, when complex and evolved structures of political legitimacy, in terms of institutions, practices and offices which had evolved in post-Ottoman Algeria were thrown into complete disarray.[26]

During the inter-war period, nationalists emphasised the role of Islam, contextualising their modern 'nation' within the broader narrative of the Arab conquest, and through a focus on pre-French independent Islamic states in Algeria.[27] Defining the Algerian 'nation' in terms of religion, highlighted Algerian differences from *Colons* and the French authorities, and explained away historical splits between the Berber and Ottoman traditions as momentary cultural misunderstandings of intent in the face of the 'longevity' of the nation thus creating a basis for national unity.[28] Religion had previously provided foundations for agitation against, and resistance to, colonisation prior to the inter-war period, as religious confraternities had provided mechanisms for the expression of violent dissatisfaction with French colonisation.[29] These confraternities, such as the Tijaniya, Sennusiya and Rahmaniya all had different traditions and foci for their preaching and practice, but all included ideas of independence and resistance – to Ottoman as well as French rule.[30]

There was also a secular construction of an Algerian, as opposed to French, historiography of Algeria, and the Maghreb more generally. This mirrored the cultural nationalist projects that lay at the heart of the Gaelic revivals in Ireland over the course of the eighteenth and nineteenth centuries.[31] Algerian history was attached to a concern with a specifically Algerian set of traumas, in particular the 'loss of cultural identity due to [its] long and particularly intensive [process of] colonisation'.[32] Algerian perceptions of their Arabic heritage became increasingly crucial, overcoming other ethnic, tribal and regional considerations, especially in the period that coincided with the outbreak of the Algerian War up to the time of the Philippeville Massacre.[33]

This heritage was contextualised through the prism of twelve centuries of Islamic history, with particular emphasis placed on its role as a centre of civilisation in the Middle Ages.[34] For the Ulamas, this historiography indicated the importance of Islam in the Algerian nation, and its distinction from the infidel coloniser; for communists it demonstrated how colonisation had knocked Algeria off of its course of development; and for nationalists it demonstrated the unique and organic character of the Algerian people and their political legitimacy as a nation.[35]

The changes in Algerian nationalism caused a hardening in the nationalist position during the inter-war period, including the rejection of assimilationist and integrationist conceptions of the Franco-Algerian relationship. This was typified by the political transformation of figures such as Ferhat Abbas, whose stance evolved from one of integration with France to a call for greater Algerian independence by 1943. In particular the failure of the inter-war Blum-Violette plan to address moderate Algerian nationalist demands led to the emergence of the hard-line and pro-independence Parti du Peuple Algérien (PPA).[36]

During the Second World War, the formation of the Amis du Manifeste et de la Liberté (AML), a political entity where nationalists came together to push for increasing independence for Algeria, reflected this shift in moderate nationalism.[37] In this context, and in recognition of France's dependence on the colony, De Gaulle was forced to concede some reforms. These wartime concessions reached their apotheosis in the post-war Algerian Statutes, which were part of the foundation of the French Fourth Republic.

Nationalist hopes of reform were relatively short-lived. On 8 May 1945, the day that the armistice was signed, Algerian nationalists initially marched peacefully into urban centres throughout Algeria demanding an end to Fascism and colonialism. Their marches were not welcomed by the *Colons* and French authorities, who attempted to ban them, and suppress the carrying of nationalist banners and flags. The size, and popular resonance, of these marches took the French authorities and *Colons* by surprise, and some *Colons* believed that this was the opening act of a full blown nationalist uprising. It is reported that in some places riots broke out in response to the *Colons* confiscation of Algerian nationalist flags and banners.

The French response took the form of the Sétif Massacre – in which an estimated 15,000 to 45,000 Algerians were killed and mass arrests and detention occurred – in order to quell nationalist aspirations. The personal experience of such horrors, and the subsequent retelling of events which were recounted as myth, symbol and memory, coloured perceptions of the Islamic–Christian and Franco-Algerian relationship, and underpinned the Algerian popular political transformation from moderate-constitutional/ integrationist to radical, violent, and independence-based nationalism. Fanon suggests that the Algerian nationalist reliance on violence and terrorism was a function of the bloody colonial legacy, in so far as 'The violence of the colonial regime and the counter-violence of the native balance[d] each other and respond[ed] to each other in an extraordinary reciprocal homogeneity'.[38]

For a decade following the Sétif Massacre reform measures foundered and nationalist demands did not disappear. Radical nationalists regrouped themselves into the Front de Libération Nationale (FLN), and its emergence represented a change from past Algerian political agitation. It broke with the 'cult of personality' that had driven followers of Hadj and Abbas, and represented 'a Muslim effort to wipe the slate clean'.[39] This call for a purer political nationalism fell within broader Algerian Islamic cultural traditions where there was a regular, almost cyclical, emergence of calls for a simpler and purer Islam.[40] The FLN announced its arrival with a series of bombings on 1 November 1954, killing several Europeans. In the immediate aftermath of the November 1954 bombings, French Prime Minister Pierre Mèndes-France proposed another set of reforms to address the problems in Algeria, in order to assuage moderate constitutional demands for reform and to draw the sting from the FLN's radical programme.

Whatever the reformist intentions of the French political elite had been, the moment had passed and, by late August, 1955, the door was permanently shut on reform in Algeria. On 20 August, thousands of peasants – *fellaghs* – revolted and attacked urban centres throughout Algeria, especially those in the North Constantinois region. This area had always been subject to high degrees of sectarianism – competition between settlers and the indigenous population ran rife over land issues, and this region bore the brunt of the repression following the events of the Sétif Uprising in May 1945.[41] The choice of this date was not accidental – it had a great deal of resonance as it was the second anniversary of the overthrow of the Sultan of Morocco by the French. The *fellaghs* moved into thirty cities and villages and, organised by uniformed members of the Armée de Libération Nationale (ALN), proceeded to attack police stations and public buildings. Over 100 were killed in scenes of terrifying violence – and yet there was a real sense that the situation had not unalterably changed.

In the immediate aftermath of the rising, private militias formed under the auspices of the *Colons*, the *Gendarmerie* and the Army. These went on to kill between 1,273 and 12,000 Algerians. In Philippeville, hundreds of Algerian men were summarily executed in the stadium.[42] French soldiers were ordered 'to shoot every Arab met'.[43] The French military, it was reported, was 'on the rampage...more than 20,000 Arabs have been killed in the aftermath of 20 August'.[44] On the ground French reactions were perceived as 'a re-enactment of the events which surrounded the Sétif Uprising of 1945...leaving an indelible impression on Europeans and Muslims alike', and it was felt that the brutality of the French authorities and *Colons* 'confirme les appréhensions de ceux qui redouaient qu'un nouveau fossé fût creusé entre les deux communautés'.[45]

The radicalising impact of these actions was 'identique à celui de Mai 1945, tuerais et répression devaient rendre le conflit irréversible et contraindre chacun à choisir son camp'.[46] Ageron, from a French academic perspective, wrote that the Philippeville massacre of 20 August 'provoked the desired split between Muslims and Europeans... the latter regarding all Muslims as rebels, while Muslims themselves came to regard... the ALN as mujahadin'.[47] As Algerian Muslims took to the mountains for refuge from repression, many joined the ALN, making it virtually 'impossible to distinguish rebels from the general population' and thereby increasing the repression on non-participants, itself fuelling the increase in membership in the ALN.[48]

At the same time, moderate nationalism seemed to have utterly failed, as sixty-one Muslim deputies in the Algerian Assembly, who had been moderate constitutional nationalists, declared in reaction that 'the great majority of the population is now won over to the Algerian national idea'.[49] These moderates now feared that 'some Europeans are thinking in terms of the extermination of the Muslims' and French officials feared that the conflict had 'reached the point of holy war'.[50] Looming behind such comments were regular references not only to the recent past, in the form of the Sétif Massacre, but also more historical events, such as the process of colonisation, jihad and the Crusades, all of which fuelled radicalisation amongst Algerians.

In the context of the repertoire of Algerian national myths, memories and symbols this event became a tipping point for the rise in popularity of radical nationalism – further reinforced by the 'Battle of the Kasbah' and the deployment of determined and severe counter-insurgency tactics, including torture, extra-judicial killings and the forced relocation and interment that continued throughout the Algerian War. The Philippeville Massacre and the violent and bloody repression of Algerian nationalism would come to resonate with personal experiences and conceptions of nationhood for Algerians that had existed from the time of the Sétif Massacre.[51] The way that the Algerian nation reacted to the events of August 1955 was based in no small part on the memories of colonisation, made more tangible and focused on the massacre which had followed the Sétif Rising of 1945.

Radicalisation seemed natural in light of the apparent evidence that moderate nationalism achieved little or nothing when dealing with the French colonial establishment. Members of the FLN believed that they themselves were not to blame for terror tactics, but that terror had its origins in French actions in May 1945 reflecting Fanon's assertion of the equilibrium of colonial violence and the insurgents' counter-violence.[52] For the French, the experience of the Second World War had been turned on its head – with members of the army who had been in the Resistance, and subsequently interned and tortured in Buchenwald and Dachau, now deploying these same techniques to quell the Algerian insurgents.

For Algerians torture reified at the individual level what was becoming ever more apparent at a communal and political one – that there could be no accommodation for Algerian independence under a French regime sympathetic to the *Colons*. Torture and vigorous and extreme counter-insurgency tactics 'accelerated' the decline of traditional politics. They also made the population 'increasingly receptive' to new radical and violent forms of direct political action.[53] In such a context, it seemed reasonable that a permanent [and popular] cultural change should result from this conflagration.[54]

In the wake of the events of August 1955, the popular national interpretation of these events led to a belief that survival was dependent on the radical 'terrorist' tactics of the FLN/ALN – a situation in which, as Fanon noted, the stress of ethnocidal fears create the basis for the deployment of violence.[55] Moderate Algerian nationalism had been split over the role of direct action, as well as the definitional questions of the Algerian nation, and so was not poised to harness a radicalised Algerian nation in the same way as the FLN.[56] The FLN/ALN was able to claim a new political legitimacy, in part because its leaders reflected a new generation of nationalists, all of whom were radicalised after the massacres of May 1945.[57]

To further this process, the FLN couched their demands in secular and religious myths, memories and symbols which were sure to resonate with the entire Algerian nation – French civic rights, anti-colonialism and anti-colonial exploitation and, in cultural and religious terms, demanding 'la restauration de l'État Algérien souverain, démocratique et social dans le cadre des principes islamiques' and considering itself first and foremost a sacred union of Algerians.[58]

Post-1955, and especially after the initial success of French counter-insurgency tactics, the FLN underwent a transformation, not unlike Sinn Fein in the post-Rising environment, emerging from a 'Jacobin organisation of closely knit conspirators' to become a popular and wide-reaching political movement, a heterogeneous umbrella alliance, embracing and uniting the various and disparate strands of Algerian nationalism in a moment of crisis.[59] Such a development represented the full emergence of the FLN as a political movement that reflected the popular voice of the Algerian people – not just the radical nationalist vanguard and elites. Underpinning this transformation was the reliance on all that made Algeria a nation – and the interpretation of these events in light of the repertoire of national myth, memory and symbol that was so heavily shaped by the negative experience of French colonisation. In a moment of national crisis the FLN was able to provide a nationalist agenda which united Algeria and provided a way forward for the nation.[60]

LESSONS FROM IRELAND AND ALGERIA

The Irish case is marked by established 'national repertoires' subject to high degrees of popular resonance, thanks in no small part to the immediately preceding sixty-five plus years of struggle and the legacy of the Great Famine. The Algerian case, while perhaps less marked by a prototypical nation, with a 'long established' or 'deeply held' national repertoire, was clearly defined and delimited in terms of religion, distinguished from the European 'other', thanks to 120 years of colonial experience. This 'difference' was reified by the consistent denial of those rights accorded to French citizens.

In both of these cases initial unpopular acts of insurgency by members of the elite countenanced an 'opening act'. This led to what subsequently appeared to be disproportionate and extreme reactions by the British and French authorities. The scales of the reactions are not similar – the execution of those who participated in the Rising, and the internment of several thousand not being comparable to the massacre of over 12,000. Both cases saw the introduction of extra-judicial powers, in the case of Ireland the suspension of the Defence of the Realm Act, in the French case the *Assemblée Nationale*'s vote to re-implement even more draconian special powers in March 1956.

However, in both these cases retrenchment increased sympathy for radical nationalism. Internment, extra-judicial executions, and general repression seemed to make the myths, memories and symbols espoused by the radical nationalists come alive. However, beyond the numbers, both reactions were symbolically potent – unleashing pent-up frustrations with moderate constitutional nationalism, and apparently emphasising the ability of radical nationalism to gain nationalist aims and objectives which moderate and constitutional agitation had failed to deliver, i.e. forcing the authorities to address a nationalist agenda.

The accomplishment of this initial political *volte face* when combined with real fears about the 'ethnocidal' intentions of the British and French authorities, and *Colons* and Unionist communities, meant that these specific actions – on the part of Pearse and his comrades in the General Post Office, and of the ALN on 20 August 1955, and especially the reactions of the British/French authorities to their actions, were potent within the respective national memories (among all parties – the British and French, as well as the Anglo-Irish, the Pieds Noirs, the Irish-Catholics and Algerian Muslims).

In both cases, the existence of an 'Other' – by which to contrast the nation and against which to cast the nation's traumas and disasters – is particularly significant. In both cases the nation was engaged in a conflict for survival with both internal and external forces of 'otherness' – so that the opponent of the nationalist movement was both within the borders of the nation (i.e. the *Colons* and Anglo-Protestants) and imposing on these borders (the British authorities and the French Army).

In both the Irish and Algerian cases, this sense of otherness was shaped in no small part by the experience of the loss of land and later by the demand for land reform. This experience was enshrined in national memory. In both of these cases, this sense of otherness was also largely defined through the ethno-national boundary-markers of religion and language, which helped to distinguish the nations from their opponents, and defined their repertoire of myths, memories and symbols.[61] In this way, religion and linguistic myths, memories and symbols represented accessible, popular and resonant forms of the national repertoire which reverberated in the national memory. This was not least apparent in the fact that Ireland's opponents were portrayed as being exclusively non-Catholic, and Algeria's were portrayed as being non-Muslim.

In Ireland such sentiment was popularly expressed in the unofficial beatification of Pearse and others in the wake of the Rising; in Algeria this was seen in the fact that the FLN newspaper was named *El-Moudjahid*.[62] In both cases, these 'others' blocked moderate constitutional reforms proposed by the state to address nationalist demands, and in both cases they managed to do this through the implied threat of violence – in terms of the *Ultras* and Ulster Volunteers.

For these nations, senses of organic distinction and injustice became ever more apparent, the failure of integration and/or assimilation ever more apparent, and it seemed as though the systems of political manipulation and control had been constantly stacked in favour of the Unionists/*Colons*. In both of these cases, the aftermath of these risings led to repression and war. Torture, in the Algerian context was an issue which resonated down to the very core of French national identity in the wake of the German occupation and the experience of the Vichy regime; while in Ireland the employment of unsettled ex-soldiers returning home from the trenches, in the guise of the auxiliary 'Black and Tans' would only begin to harden and consolidate nationalism and nationalist ambitions on the ground. Both also undermined elements of support amongst British and French domestic political audiences. As states, neither France nor Britain could afford to be seen as losing a war of secession – and much was at stake domestically and internationally. Even after both of these nationalist movements achieved their relative aims, there followed more civil war – as the visions and rhetoric which were espoused as the message behind these movements were perceived as not equating with the actual achievements of the movements, something which has plagued Northern Ireland and Algeria up to the present day.

NOTES

1 Charles Tilly, *From Mobilization to Revolution*, New York, 1978, pp. 216–19.
2 Jonathan Githens-Mazer, *Myths and Memories of the Easter Rising: Cultural and Political Nationalism in Ireland*, Dublin, 2006; Anthony D. Smith, *The Ethnic Origins of Nations*, London, 1988.
3 Popular resonance of a nation's repertoire of myths, memories and symbols is dependent on this repertoire having a collective meaning for individual members of the nation. See Githens-Mazer, *Myths and Memories*, p. 27.
4 Louis F.A. Paul-Dubois, *Contemporary Ireland*, Dublin, 1911, p. 73.
5 John Mitchel, *Jail Journal: with an Introductory Narrative of Transactions in Ireland* [1854],

London, 1983.
6 Chris Morash and Richard Hayes (eds), *Fearful Realities: New Perspectives on the Famine*, Dublin, 1996, p. 115.
7 Eileen Reilly, 'Beyond the Gilt Shamrock: Symbolism and Realism in the Cover Art of Irish Historical and Political Fiction, 1880–1914' in Lawrence W. McBride (ed.), *Images and Icons and the Irish Nationalist Imagination*, Dublin, 1999.
8 Githens-Mazer, *Myths and Memories*, pp. 49–56.
9 County Inspectors Reports, Public Records Office (hereafter, PRO) CO 903/8, September 1913; Githens-Mazer, *Myths and Memories*, p. 53.
10 See especially Githens-Mazer, *Myths and Memories*, ch. 6.
11 John Dillon speech to House of Commons 11 May 1916 is cited in William H. Kautt, *The Anglo-Irish War, 1916–1921: A People's War*, London, 1999, p. 50.
12 Letters of Correspondence between General Sir John Maxwell and Bishop O'Dwyer, MS. 32695 National Library of Ireland (hereafter, NLI); David W. Miller, 'The Roman Catholic Church in Ireland, 1865–1914' in Alan O'Day (ed.), *Reactions to Irish Nationalism, 1865-1914*, London, 1987, p. 198; Thomas Hennessey, *Dividing Ireland: World War I and Partition*, London, 1998, p. 142.
13 Githens-Mazer, *Myths and Memories*, p. 194, 198–9; Report on Speech in Elphin, 13 February, 1917, PRO CO 903/23 PRO Kew; see also citation in Robert Kee, *The Green Flag*, Vol. 3: *Ourselves Alone*, London, 1982, p. 28.
14 Proclamation of Bishop O'Dwyer, 30 April 1917, Archbishop Walsh Papers/Special Papers.
15 Githens-Mazer, *Myths and Memories*, p. 196; Report on Speech of Mr. F. O'Connor, Meeting at Ballymahon, 6 May 1917, PRO CO 903/23.
16 Augustine Birrell cited in Robert Kee, *The Green Flag, Volume 3*, p. 1
17 Abdelmajid Hannoum, 'Historiography, Mythology and Memory in Modern North Africa: The Story of the Kahina', *Studia Islamica*, 85 (1997) pp. 85–130; see also Tal Shuval, 'The Ottoman Algerian Elite and its Ideology', in *International Journal of Middle East Studies*, 32, 3 (2000), pp. 323–44 for a discussion of Ottoman North Africa.
18 Douglas Johnson 'Algeria: some Problems of Modern History', *Journal of African History*, 5, 2 (1964), pp. 221–42, p. 223; Paul Silverstein 'Realizing Myth: Berbers in France and Algeria', *Middle East Report*, No. 200 (Minorities in the Middle East: Power and Politics of Difference, 1996) pp. 11–15, p. 12; Mahfoud Bennoune, 'The Origins of the Algerian Proletariat', *MERIP Reports*, 94 (Origins of the Working Class in the Middle East, 1981) pp. 5–13, p. 5; Nevill Barbour, 'The Significance of the Conflict in Algeria', *African Affairs*, 56, 222 (1957), pp. 20–31, p. 20.
19 General Saint Arnaud, 1846 cited in Bennoune, 'The Origins of the Algerian Proletariat', p. 7
20 Benjamin Stora, *Algeria 1830–2000: A Short History*, Ithaca, NY, 2001, p. 16.
21 Jacques Frémeaux *La France et L'Algérie en Guerre: 1830–1870, 1954–1962*, Paris, 2002, pp. 30–1.
22 Stora, *Algeria 1830–2000*, p. 18.
23 Ibid., pp. 23–5.
24 Ibid., pp. 10–15.
25 Michael Clark, *Algeria in Turmoil: A History of the Rebellion*, New York, 1959, p. 49; Stora, *Algeria: 1830–2000*, pp. 10–15.
26 G.F. Andrews, 'Islam and the Confraternities in North Africa', *Geographical Journal*, 47, 2 (1916), pp. 116–30, p. 117; Peter von Sivers, 'Insurrection and Accommodation: Indigenous Leadership in Eastern Algeria, 1840–1900', *International Journal of Middle Eastern Studies*, 6, 3 (1975) pp. 259–75.
27 Mahfoud Hannoum, 'Historiography, Mythology and Memory in Modern North Africa: The Story of the Kahina', pp. 86–7; Ulrike Freitag, 'Writing Arab History: The Search for the Nation', *British Journal of Middle Eastern Studies*, 21, 1 (1994), pp. 19–37, p. 27.
28 Mahfoud Hannoum, 'Historiography, Mythology and Memory in Modern North Africa: The Story of the Kahina', pp. 89, 129; G. E Von Grunenbaum, 'Nationalism and Cultural Trends in the Arab Near East', *Studia Islamica*, 14 (1961), pp. 121–153, p. 123
29 Andrews, 'Islam and the Confraternities in North Africa', p. 120.
30 Ibid., p. 122.
31 John Hutchinson *The Dynamics of Cultural Nationalism: The Gaelic Revival and the Creation of the Irish Nation State*, London, 1987 see especially chs 3 and 4.; John Hutchinson 'Archaeology and the Irish Rediscovery of the Celtic Past', *Nations and Nationalism*, 7, 4

(October 2001), pp. 505–19; Mahfoud Hannoum, 'Historiography, Mythology and Memory in Modern North Africa', p. 91.

32 Freitag, 'Writing Arab History: The Search for the Nation', p. 26.

33 Barbour, 'The Significance of the Conflict in Algeria', p. 20.

34 Benjamin Rivlin, 'Context and Sources of Political Tensions in French North Africa', *Annals of the American Academy of Political and Social Science*, 298 (1955), pp. 109–16, p. 109.

35 B. Marie Perrinbam, 'Fanon and the Revolutionary Peasantry – the Algerian Case', *Journal of Modern African Studies*, 11, 3 (1973), pp. 427–45.

36 Hassan Remaoun, 'La Politique coloniale française et la structuration du projet nationalitaire en Algérie: à propos de l'idéologie du FLN, puis de l'État national' in Charles R. Ageron (ed.), *La Guerre d'Algérie au Miroir des Décolonisations Françaises* Paris, 2000, p. 270; Phillip C. Naylor, *France and Algeria: A History of Decolonisation and Transformation*, Gainesville, FL, 2000, pp. 18–20.

37 Stora, *Algeria 1830–2000*, p. 21.

38 Frantz Fanon *The Wretched of the Earth*, New York, 2004, p. 46.

39 William H. Lewis, 'Algeria: The Cycle of Reciprocal Fear', *African Studies Bulletin*, 12, 3 (1969), pp. 323–37, p. 324.

40 Andrews, 'Islam and the Confraternities in North Africa', p. 117.

41 Sylvie Thénault, *Histoire de la Guerre d'Indépendence Algérienne*, Paris, 2005, p. 50.

42 Ibid., p. 48.

43 Matthew Connelly, *A Diplomatic Revolution: Algeria's Fight for Independence and the Origins of the Post-Cold War Era*, Oxford, 2002, p. 86.

44 Guy Calvet to American Diplomat, cited in Connelly, *A Diplomatic Revolution*, p. 86.

45 Edward Behr, *The Algerian Problem*, London, 1961, pp. 83–4; Philippe Bourdrel, *Le Livre Noir de la Guerre d'Algérie: Français et Algérians 1945–1962*, Paris, 2003, p. 60.

46 Thénault, *Histoire de la Guerre d'Indépendence Algérienne*, p. 51.

47 Charles R. Ageron, *Modern Algeria: A History from 1830 to the Present*, London, 1991, p. 111.

48 Connelly, *A Diplomatic Revolution*, p. 87.

49 *L'Année Politique*, *1955*, p. 278 cited in Connelly, *A Diplomatic Revolution*, p. 87; Ageron, *Modern Algeria*, p. 111.

50 See Connelly, *A Diplomatic Revolution*, p. 87.

51 Stora, *Algeria 1830-2000*, p. 44; Remaoun, 'La Politique coloniale française et la structuration du projet nationalitaire en Algérie: à propos de l'idéologie du FLN, puis de l'État national', p. 271.

52 Joan and Richard Brace, *Algerian Voices*, New York, 1965, p. 116.

53 Johnson, 'Algeria: some Problems of Modern History', p. 241.

54 Paul Beckett, 'Algeria vs. Fanon: The Theory of Revolutionary Decolonization and the Algerian Experience', *Western Political Quarterly*, 26, 1 (1973), pp. 5–27, p. 18.

55 Perrinbam, 'Fanon and the Revolutionary Peasantry, the Algerian Case', p. 432.

56 Thénault, *Histoire de la Guerre d'Indépendence Algérienne*, p. 43

57 Mohammed Bedjaoui, *La Révolution Algérienne et Le Droit*, Brussels, 1961, p. 48.

58 Remaoun, 'La Politique coloniale française et la structuration du projet nationalitaire en Algérie', p. 274; Bedjaoui, *La Révolution Algérienne et Le Droit*, pp. 85–6.

59 Lewis, 'Algeria: The Cycle of Reciprocal Fear', p. 325 ; Mahfoud Bennoune, 'Algerian Peasants and National Politics', *MERIP Reports*, 48 (1976), pp. 3–24, p. 5.

60 Bedjaoui, *La Révolution Algérienne et Le Droit*, p. 86.

61 Frémeaux, *La France et L'Algérie en Guerre : 1830–1870, 1954–1962*, p. 68.

62 Githens-Mazer, *Myths and Memories*, pp. 142–6; Frémeaux, *La France et L'Algérie en Guerre: 1830–1870, 1954–1962*, p. 66.

La Siesta del Hidalgo:
Territoriality in Irish, Israeli and Palestinian Novels

John Maher

The essential images of the irredentist and the invader are very much one and the same: a man or woman clambering furtively over a fence at dead of night. Land won and lost, peoples moving in and out and borders planted/supplanted are features of both perspectives. In this respect, land is to life as language is to literature. We cannot have one without the other. The spelling out of primordial chaos, the creation of order and the occupation of the land are the mainstays, of course, of the tribal ur-narrative of place and possession. *B'reshit bara Elohim et ha-Shamaim V'et HaAretz*, in the patriarchal narratives, starts the whole story. God takes the liberty of making order out of chaos before making man, who then makes (fresh) order out of chaos. As in Babylon, so in Belfast, Beirut and Jerusalem.

It is the keykeeper, however, the one who has built the fence and keeps the gate, who must forever fret in the shadow of the 'Other' until such time, if ever, that peace, or at least benign indifference, ultimately arrives. Until, in the wise weasel words of one secretary of state for Northern Ireland, we reach 'an acceptable level of violence'. In the light of territorial squabbles, underpinned by ideological or religious tenets, this is the only rational hope, in the short term. The lamb may lie down with the lion, but the lamb, if he has any sense at all, will always sleep with one eye open: *la siesta del Hidalgo* – the uneasy sleep of the keykeeper, ever conscious of the fact that a fence, at one remove, is simply a physical representation of the fantasy of eternal occupation.

THE SPECIFIC PICTURE

In the early 1970s, special maps of Belfast city were provided for the British army, the Royal Ulster Constabulary, social services and other 'interested parties' which showed, down to street level, the sectarian distribution of the city's population. It was possible for a visitor, of whatever purpose or hue, to know into which religious fiefdom they were travelling by reference to the colour-coded map – orange for Protestant, green for Catholic and a neutral colour for the more middle-class areas. Similar maps, naturally enough, exist in the Israeli–Palestinian theatre of unease.

The trouble with such maps, of course, is twofold: populations move and land is won and lost. Doubtless, the electronic version of the Belfast and Jerusalem sectarian maps of the future will track population movements as they happen, on a daily basis. It must be pointed out here, of course, that land is as much about place as it is about actual territory. Although, in the annals of the Irish (northern and southern), Israeli and Palestinian novels, the realities of both physical location and possession of the land are played out in different ways, the essential realities stay the same: the who we are is very much based on the where we are – ideology is subservient to the realpolitik of possession.

LINGUISTIC LIMBO DANCING IN THE WESTERN GALILEE

Language itself is land, in the Israeli writer A.B. Yehoshua's novel *The Liberated Bride* (2001). Both the internal mappings of the State of Israel and the realities of the 1967 Green Line are mirrored in the nexus represented in the lives of the novel's central characters. It could hardly be otherwise, for Haifa and its hinterland, as both the cultural cockpit of the Arab Galilee and the greatest symbol of its fall, in 1948, represent the metropole subtended by the coencentric circles of both communal languages.[1] In this respect, Yehoshua's novel, published in the first flush of the al-Aqsa intifada, lies on the same continuum as earlier works – *Facing the Forest* (1966), *The Lover* (1977) and *Mr. Mani* (1990).

By the time we reach *The Liberated Bride*, A.B. Yehoshua has come full circle. From admitting to the presence of the Palestinian in the short story, *Facing the Forests*, to puzzling over the vexed relationship of majority to minority, during the 1973 Yom Kippur War, in *The Lover*, to allowing Palestinian *'ammiyya* sidle into the Hebrew prose of *The Liberated Bride*.[2] In *Facing the Forests*, pre-1967 war, the Palestinian has an ephemeral presence but no voice; by the time we reach the period of the al-Aqsa Intifada and *The Liberated Bride*, the Palestinian, within Israel, is speaking in his own language, dialect and register. That is to say, language now predicates presence – language is land is language. The fact that Yehoshua's latest novel, *A Woman*

of Jerusalem (2006), written at the height of the new intifada, centres on a
foreign worker killed in a suicide bombing, but almost totally omits any
mention of the Palestinian cohort of Israeli society, is almost a commentary by
exclusion.

The linguistic osmosis played out in the interface between majority/
minority languages is crucial to the understanding of realities in the State of
Israel. The majority of Palestinian–Israelis, particularly younger ones, will
understand both street Hebrew and officialese quite well; the majority of
Jewish–Israelis, particularly those of Ashkenazi origin, are unlikely to understand, at any significant level, either Arabic *fusha* or *'ammiyya*.[3] This reality
is adumbrated in *The Liberated Bride*, at many levels.

Yehoshua's protagonist, Rivlin, a Jewish Israeli professor of Arabic at Haifa
university is, that most despised of things, an orientalist.[4] Rivlin himself is
supervising the thesis of a young Palestinian–Israeli woman, Samaher, from a
Galilee village who, seemingly, is suffering from a psychosomatic illness. At
the same time, he is pursuing his own academic hunt-the-thimble in trying to
pin down the causes of the rise in Islamic extremism in Algeria in the light of
written 'warnings' from previous generations. Overshadowing the story is the
half-completed research of another Israeli–Jewish orientalist, Suissa, killed in
a suicide bombing and the peregrinations of an elderly couple of oriental
scholars, the Tedeschis. Rivlin's engagement with the Arab world may be
academic but, as he is drawn into both the realities of village life in the Galilee
hinterland and the Occupied Territories, he floats and flits between these
borders with the good grace of the perplexed. In the Galilee village of
Mansura, he is an object of somewhat suppressed amusement:

> He was led to a spacious bedroom, in which stood a black lacquered chest,
> a closet, a large table, several smaller ones, and some chairs. Half-lying and
> half-leaning on pillows in a big bed, his student of many years looked pale
> and thin. Her hair was gathered in a net and traces of red polish from the
> wedding were still on her fingernails and toenails, which stuck out from
> beneath the blanket. He gave her a suspicious, pitying look. Expecting a
> child, he told himself, as though he had lately become an expert on false
> pregnancies, she was not. It looked more like a case of depression.
> 'You really came.' She blushed and smiled wanly. 'Thank you. Thank
> you, Professor, for coming to your village.'
> '*Sad'uni*', he said, addressing not only Afifa and the grandmother, who
> had followed him into the room, but the women outside in the hallway.
> 'I've been teaching at the university for thirty years and this is my first
> house call. *Bil sitta ow marid.*'
> '*Tiwafakt bil'aml es-saleh.*'
> '*Allah yibarek fik.*'

The souterrain of A.B. Yehoshua's novel conceals a further sombre twist: a tale of incest concealed, even at the end of the novel, from Rivlin, and presided over by the scion of a Palestinian–Israeli family. Deep in the bowels of a Jerusalem hotel, a long-running family secret destroys the marriage of Rivlin's son, Ofer. Like the Palestinian–Israelis, we are privileged to know what Rivlin's caste may not: the secret, subterranean underbelly of the state. Rivlin's son, Ofer, will never reveal the sordid secret of his in-law's family, out of fidelity to his ex-wife, and Rivlin will never know the true cause of his son's failed marriage; any more than he will learn the true causes of the rise in Islamic extremism in Algeria from abstract accounts of events by earlier generations.

Rivlin, the orientalist, despite his linguistic competency and his ability to segue into the society of the Arab villages of the Haifa hinterland, will always remain just outside the loop. At the end of the day, as in *The Lover*, the Palestinian–Israelis will withdraw to their villages, their day's labour done in the towns and cities of the majority community, far from the eyes of the Mediterranean metropole of Haifa. Internal *Gastarbeiter*, they will know more about their overseers' towns and cities than their overseers will know about the winding streets and shuttered windows of their own towns.

A.B. Yehoshua, whose agonised exposition of the conflict between nationality and identity have led him into a certain conceptual cul-de-sac, has expressed artistically what it may be too early to express politically: Palestinian–Israelis, at one-fifth of the population, are an ethnic minority and, inevitably, will become full citizens of an emergent Israeli state that will be unable to assign citizenship/nationality on the basis of religion alone. After the events of October 2001, in the Galilee, at the outbreak of the al-Aqsa intifada, and the 'summer war' in Lebanon, in 2006, the position of Palestinians within Israel is even more prescient.

PUSSY BRADEN COCKS A SNOOK AT THE BORDER

> I have lived in important place, times
> When great events were decided, who owned
> That half a rood of rock, a no-man's land
> Surrounded by our pitchfork-armed claims.
> I heard the Duffys shouting 'Damn your soul!'
> And old McCabe stripped to the waist, seen
> Step the plot defying blue cast-steel-
> 'Here is the march along these iron stones.'
> That was the year of the Munich bother. Which
> Was more important? I inclined
> To lose my faith in Ballyrush and Gortin
> Till Homer's ghost came whispering to my mind.
> He said: 'I made the Iliad from such
> A local row. Gods make their own importance.'

Iliad, Patrick Kavanagh.[5]

The skewed hinterland of Pat McCabe's *Breakfast on Pluto* is an intimate, rural one. The gentleman driving the red Massey Ferguson tractor by day, may well be the same person 'taking out' a British army patrol with a land mine or killing an Ulster Defence Regiment reservist or policeman by night. And there is no mistaking the sectarian sentiment involved: the 'settlers', attacked on the northern side of the border, for the most part, will be Protestant, while their attackers will be Catholics. Close readers of recent Irish history will find plenty of resonances in the murders McCabe glosses.

As was plainly evident only some nights later (not long after the young McCarville fellow came sailing down the river roped to a mattress with a six-inch nail hammered into his head and it had been decided something needed to be done) when the Horse Kinnane and Jackie Timlin called for him and they drove off to stiff old Anderson and his son. Who both conveniently happened to be in the library spraying food onto some exotic plant or other when the three masked desperadoes burst in. Nutting the old chap proved no problem but his son (albeit he was fifty years of age) fought tooth and nail. Almost escaped, indeed, before the Horse managed to get between him and the door, knocking him to his knees and shouting: 'Do him! Do him, Kerr, you bollocks you!'

As Irwin stood there pissing himself – he really did, as anyone with an eye in their head could see from the gathering map on the crotch of his trousers, and being so far away in some other place that eventually Jackie had to push him out of the way, snatch the gun from his hand and put three in your man's head. 'You stupid fucker, Kerr! You stupid dithering little fuck! What do you think this is? What do you think this is?'[6]

The war, at a local level, seems even dirtier because it is more intimate. The sort of bog-road ambush, with the false police/army checkpoint favoured by Protestant paramilitaries, gets an airing too. We are in the same tough, sectarian territory as another borderlands writer, Eugene McCabe, who, writing contemporaneously – and locally – in the mid-1970s, in his short story *Cancer*, has an uncle and son, both Catholics, crossing into the North to visit a relative in hospital. On the back-roads of Fermanagh, they stop by a local 'Protestant' pub, where an off-duty police reservist is in his cups.

Dinny nudged Boyle and winked up at a notice pinned to a
pillar. Boyle read:
Lisnaskea and District Development Association
Extermination of Vermin
1/- for each magpie killed
2/- for each grey crow killed.
10/ for each grey squirrel killed.
1 pound for each fox killed

Underneath, someone had printed with a biro:

For every Fenian Fucker: one old penny.

As the woman measured the whiskies a glass smashed in the snug at the counter end. A voice jumped the frosted glass: 'Wilson was a fly boy, and the Heath man's no better, all them Tories is tricky whores, dale with Micks and Papes and lave us here to rot. Well, by Christ, they'll come no Pope to the townland of Invercloon, I'll not be blown up or burned out, I'll fight to the last ditch.'

All listening in the outer bar, faces, secret and serious, uncomfortable now, as other voices joined: 'You're right, George.'

'Sit down man, you'll toss the table.'

'Let him say out what's in his head.'

'They'll not blow me across the bog; if it's blood they want then, by Jasus they'll get it, all they want of it, gallons of it, wagons, shiploads.'

'Now you're talking, George.'

This is bog-bitterness, the Orange mirror image of the IRA's own campaign to de-Protestantise rural areas of South Ulster by assassination and intimidation. It is a long way from the lofty rhetoric of Republican and Loyalist ideologues. Because it is about land, dispossession and repossession. The Joycean strategies of silence, exile and cunning seem seriously deficient in such a setting. So Patrick 'Pussy' Braden, a post-Padraig Pearse transvestite, decides to sashay past the ambient realities in fishnet tights.

BUILDING BORDERS

Yahyia Yakhlif's *al-Nakba* novel *A Lake Beyond the Wind* (1999) is tinged with melancholia, foreboding, betrayal and, ultimately, dispossession.[7] It is a novelised account of the setting of borders by military means and the establishment of contiguous settlements within those same borders. The railway town of Samakh, on the southern shores of the Sea of Galilee and at the base of the Golan Heights, forms the geocentre of the novel.

In what might be called a *retrospektiver Roman*, we watch the world of Palestinian towns and villages collapse, in microcosm, through the eyes of the young Palestinian, Radi, and the roman-a-clef device of an Iraqi volunteer in the Arab Liberation Army, Abd al-Rahman. The pastoral image of Samakh depicted in the novel tallies with shots taken before its eventual fall and destruction.[8] Mill, station house – apparently all still standing – and houses all sitting lakeside in the southern Galilee. When the real fighting starts it will, inevitably given the situation obtaining in the Galilee, pit Palestinian town and village against Jewish settlement – a war of land. The attack on the settlement of Tirat Zevi represents the first serious military encounter in the novel.

The attack is a disaster for the Palestinian forces; by the end of April 1948, the town of Samakh itself will be abandoned.[9] The chaos, lack of leadership and military incompetence on the Palestinian–Arab side, referred to by later Palestinian historians,[10] is evident in the build-up to the battle. Also evident is the hubris engendered by such leaders as the Circassian Ahmed Bey. This, coupled with the almost mystical belief in the properties of an armoured vest inherited from the British (a tidy little political trope) ensures a rout, when siege is laid to the Jewish settlement of Tirat Zevi. Asad al-Shahba, a Syrian volunteer, relates the grim news.

'The attack on Tirat Zevi', he said, 'started at three in the morning. We encircled it from three directions. It's a fortification, not just a settlement – it's surrounded by watch towers, barbed wire and trenches.'
    'When the Jews sensed we were getting ready for the attack, they opened their water pipes and flooded the fields, so they turned into a swamp. We didn't have the tanks to get across... it was eight-thirty in the morning when the failed attack ended. With my own eyes, I saw the corpses strewn all over the swamp, in all directions. And with my own eyes I saw Ahmed Bey withdraw before we did, running off after his car had got stuck in the mud. I saw Samih Haddad swimming in his own blood. I saw Salim al-Bishtawi disembowelled. I saw Zain al-Saidi take a direct hit from a shell and get blown to bits.'[11]

Criticism of the leadership sidles into the narrative. This is contrasted with the more positive references to Palestinian military leaders such as al-Qawuqji – active in the area of the Galilee – al-Husseini, killed in battle near Qastel, on the Tel Aviv–Jerusalem road, and Fawzi al-Qutub. The sense of a people abandoned, to a very great extent, by its leaders is palpable. The Iraqi fighter, Abd al-Rahman, voices his criticisms in a secret diary.

Oh, Abd al-Rahman bin Kazam, how utterly tired I am of all those discussions, going on all year long, between the intellectuals, the gentlemen and the educated people in the cafes of al-Rashid Street, and between the two underground parties with their burning support for the nationalist struggle. Newspapers, broadcasts, debates – newspaper talk. Night talk wiped out by the day. Could anything possibly mean more than what I've done?[12]

Night talk wiped out by the day. The reality of the Palestinian rout at Kibbutz Tirat Zevi, under the Palestinian leader al-Qawuqji leading the 1st Yarmuk Battallion, is well documented on the Israeli side.[13] Two contrasting campaigns are evident here: the Palestinian one to isolate the Jewish settlements and the Israeli one to unite the settlements into one, contiguous, defensible homeland. The issue of external borders, when seen in the light

of the demographics of pre-1948 Galilee, is almost secondary to the main
thrust of providing internal cohesion. A later attack, under al-Qawuqji, on
Mishmar ha-Emek, fails and, with it, the attempt to isolate Haifa.

Haifa, the 'headland' of the Galilee, is now under direct threat from the
Zionist forces. Jaffa, Safad, Beisan, Acre, Tiberias and other large Palestinian-
populated centres are now also under threat. The conflict continues in
earnest and Samakh, along with other towns in the path of the juggernaut of
the Hagannah, falls in the melée. With the fall of Tiberias, further along the
Sea of Galilee, the fate of Samakh itself is sealed.

> 'People are leaving the town', Hafiza said. 'What are you going to do?'
> Haj Hussein thought for a moment.
> 'If things get much worse', he said, 'we could move the women and
> children, and the old people, to the outlying areas. To al-Hawi, maybe, or
> Tellat al-Duweir, or al-Tawafiq, or even al-Hammeh.'
> Then, looking up at her, he said:
> 'We must hold out for another two weeks, Hafiza, until the Arab armies
> come.'
> Hafiza was brave and stout-hearted, but she knew well enough that,
> with Tiberias fallen, the road to Samakh was open...the refugees who
> hads come to Samakh from Tiberias had started moving on to al-Hammeh
> and al-Adsiyyeh, even east to Jordan. The cows and other animals roamed
> about among the houses, because the shepherds and herdsmen hadn't
> come to take them out to pasture.[14]

The pastoral idyll that is Samakh is no more. The flight has started. When
the refugees halt, for a night or a lifetime, the retrospection begins. Towns,
villages and lands, now vacated. The remembering will start now: towns,
villages and lands. The refugees, from the far side of the new border, look
back at the half-promised land. For them, and their companions still
remaining within the new State of Israel, all is changed. All is the same. The
land will stay the same but now name and nation will be changed.

> Scholars of Israeli society have long argued that the project of making
> place was a central element of the new Hebrew culture that emerged in
> Palestine and that came to dominate Israeli society, particularly in the first
> two decades of statehood. It was, in large part, through this 'territorial
> ethos' that the new national culture would distinguish itself from the
> 'exilic' culture of Diaspora Jews.[15]

The question of those left behind – *al-baqiin*, in the somewhat scathing
Arabic term, 'internal refugees', those displaced from their towns and villages
who remained in the state – is a question that must wait for another day and
another writer, in the mode of Emil Habibi and his hapless collaborating

klutz of an anti-hero, Said, in *The Pessoptimist.*[16] In the meantime, maps, censuses and museums will be used to establish the identity of the victors, after the fashion of *Imagined Communities.*[17]

THE ANOMIE WITHIN

Anton Shammas, the Palestinian–Israeli writer, is clear about the connection between language and territoriality:

> I think the main achievement of Zionism...the greatest achievement and the only one, is the reterritorializing of the Hebrew language. The rest of the Zionist enterprise is a mute question. But I think its only achievement was to reterritorialize Hebrew to this particular territory...and reinvent the language...by reterritorializing the Palestinian vernacular of Palestine...what happened in 1948 was to deterritorialize the Palestinian vernacular...so the problem is that for Palestinians in Israel, identity is not constructed by the people themselves, it is imposed on them.[18]

The Palestinian writer, Ghassan Kanafani, in his *Literature of Resistance in Occupied Palestine, 1948–1966*, also acknowledges the centrality of language in both the creation of identity and, subsequently, literature.[19] This continuity is further indicated to by current commentators, viewing the development of the Palestinian novel up to the late 1990s.[20] The question of which language a Palestinian writer should use, and its answer – Arabic – seem obvious enough. And such is the case, by and large, for the majority of Palestinian writers within Israel. Nevertheless, a minority have chosen to write in Arabic and Hebrew. A smaller group still, have chosen to write in Hebrew alone. Ami Elad-Bouskilla considers these issues in 'The Other Face: The Language Choice of Arab Writers in Israel' and comes to the conclusion that societal, artistic, political and purely linguistic reasons can all be cited.[21]

In the case of the Palestinian–Israeli writer, Said Kashua, the reasons lie buried deep within his first novel, *Dancing Arabs*,[22] an ironic *Bildungsroman* in the tradition of *The Pessoptimist* and *The Good Soldier Schweik*. Inasmuch as Palestinian–Israelis writing in Arabic are writing a minor literature within the majority literature of Arabic, Palestinian–Israelis, such as Kashua, are doing the same, but within the relatively new majority language of Hebrew. In this respect, Palestinian–Israelis writing in Hebrew, subscribe to the three cornerstones of Deleuze and Guattari's description of minor literatures: they exhibit a high coefficient of deterritorialisation, 'everything in them is political' and a collective value is ascribed to everything in the novels of the minor literature.[23] From the opening bars of *Dancing Arabs*, we realise we are knee-deep in nuanced nod-and-wink.

I was always looking for the keys to the cupboard. I looked for them every time Grandma went to visit the home of another old woman in the village who had died. The old brown cupboard was like a locked trunk with a treasure inside – diamonds and royal jewels. One morning, after another night when I'd sneaked into her bed because I was too scared to fall asleep, I saw her take the key out of a hidden pocket she'd sewn in one of her pillows. Grandma handed me the key and asked me to take her prayer rug out of the cupboard for her. I leaped out of bed at once. What had come over her? Was she really letting me open the cupboard? I took the key, and as soon as I put it in the lock, Grandma said, 'Turn it gently. Everything is rusty by now.'[24]

The trope of the key to the lost house in Palestine immediately resonates with the reader, as does the grandmother's statement, later on that 'al-Ard zai al-ird' – land is honour. But Kashua's narrative is not one of translation across borders, in 1948. It is rather one of internal exile, if not refugee status. The internal exile starts, not with the memory of displacement from one village to another during the period of *al-Nakba*, but in an accommodation to the new language of power: Hebrew. What has empowered one group has disempowered the other. The narrator realises early on that to gain access to information and the greater world outside the village, he must engage with the majority language. He learns about his father's imprisonment for a terrorist offence through Hebrew; his middle and higher education will take place through Hebrew; but he will always be an 'inside outsider'. Reading a novel by the Druze writer, Salman Natour, Kashua's *unter*-hero wishes himself into its milieu.

Sometimes, when I am at home, I steal a few of my father's books. I hate reading Arabic, but I owe it to myself to look at those books. To understand why Mahmoud Darwish is considered great, and why Emil Habibi was awarded the Israel Prize. The last book I stole was Hamarat al-Balad by Salman Natour. This young Arab – a poet, maybe, or an author – writes about life in a Tel Aviv pub. He describes all the left-wing Jews, who are really very nice to him. They listen to him with great interest and introduce him to new friends. Pretty young girls sit beside him and sometimes even kiss him. He recalls how at one stage he thought he could blend in completely. I feel like an idiot for even thinking I could blend in too.[25]

There is a poignancy to the narrative that betrays the hurt of a nobody's child, stuck between two cultures. This is not the confident narrative voice of Anton Shammas' *Arabesques*, a subversive take on the Israeli state and its myths.[26] Kashua's central character is more akin to Amos Oz's eponymous Fima, in the novel of the same name,[27] who has internalised the complexities of the Palestinian–Israeli debâcle to the extent that his thought process is

scrambled and he is semi-delusional. The first overt statement of identity in
Dancing Arabs is conveyed by the history teacher, in the local school, in al-
Tira. It is couched in customary *Habibi-esque* irony.

> Once, our history teacher in Tira asked if anyone in the class knew what
> Palestine was, and nobody did, including me. Then he asked
> contemptuously if any of us had ever seen a Palestinian, and Mohammed
> the Fatso, who was afraid of having his knuckles rapped, said he'd once
> been driving with his father in the dark and they'd seen two Palestinians.
> That day, the history teacher rapped every single one of us on the
> knuckles, launching his attack with Mohammad the Fatso. He whacked us
> with his ruler, ranting, 'We are Palestinians, you are Palestinians, I'm a
> Palestinian! You nincompoops, you animals, I'll teach you who you are!'[28]

But self-awareness is still a long way down the road. The narrator must first
go out into the 'real' world of work. He gains employment as an assistant in
a home for disabled children – a job commonly held either by migrant Asian
workers or Palestinians – marries and finds himself beached in the south of
Jerusalem as the al-Aqsa intifada breaks out. Torn between hatred of his
father, for insisting that his place is on 'the land' and the desire to flee,
Kashua's narrator takes off on the sort of flight-of-political-fancy typical of
Oz's *Fima*.

> I'll be a candidate selected by consensus. I'll be a member of the Knesset.
> The media will love me. They'll find it hard to believe that a Moslem MK
> can talk like that, without a trace of fanaticism, gently, almost without an
> accent. I'll express myself well, and I'll represent the views of an entire
> community. Even the Jews will consider me an honest man. I'll get along
> very well with the right-wing parties and the ultra-orthodox. I'll become
> prime minister – the first Arab in the Islamic Movement to be made prime
> minister. I'll bring peace and love to the region. The economy will
> flourish. There will be no war on the horizon.[29]

By the end of the novel, assimilation, religion or *wasta* are in evidence.[30]
Some of the narrator's friends turn to Islam, having forsaken the sunny
uplands of nationalist sentiment, while his father, by stealth and cunning, is
co-opted into the Israeli civil establishment as a minor functionary, while
keeping well in with the Palestinian Authority, on the far side of the Green
Line, and managing to be all things to all people: a hero, a quasi-loyal Israeli
citizen and a go-between, exercising *wasta* for the benefit of his Palestinian
friends. The narrator assimilates into the majority community, after a fashion.
In a nod to the biblical shibboleth, he can pronounce a 'p' correctly, has
almost no accent in Hebrew and can fool the soldiers at roadblocks. He does
not, in a phrase, aspirate where he should not. His father, locked up in the

late 1960s for his involvement in a bombing at the Hebrew University, loses faith not only in his dead hero, Nasser, but in the whole of the Arab world, after a visit to Egypt.

> The trip left both of them depressed, especially my father, who's lost faith in the Arab world. He says they're too busy dealing with hunger and don't have the energy to deal with Zionism, pan-Arabism and war... my father says the best thing would be for our cousins in Tulkarm, Ramallah, Nablus and Bakat al-Hatab to receive the same blue ID cards that we have. Let them become seventh-class citizens in the Zionist state. He says it's better than being third-class citizens in an Arab state. My father hates Arabs. He says it's better to be the slave of your enemy than to be the slave of a leader from within your own people.[31]

The hurt is palpable – the sense of abandonment, loss and disenchantment with the once-revered leadership. All is tawdry now. The gilt and glory of nationalist rhetoric has not delivered, either in the Arab states or in the Palestinian Authority. The novel ends, as it opens, with the question of the key, the perennial Palestinian motif. The narrator's grandmother has also been worn down by realities on the ground.

> 'What's the matter, Grandma?' I ask.
> 'Go back to sleep, habibi. It's nothing. It's like this every day.'
> ...She says the only reason she's crying is that she used to think she'd be buried in her own land. 'Do you remember where the key to the cupboard is?'
> And we both cry together.[32]

A PROTESTANT PICTURE-POSTCARD OF POST-CONFLICT CRIMINALITY

> I have no sense of myself as Protestant. I do though have some sense of Northern Irishness of which I am proud – Northern Irishness free of political and constitutional absolutes – Northern Irishness in the way that I had of Northern Englishness when I lived in Manchester.[33]

The Northern Irish writer Glen Patterson has written in, about and through the 'troubles' in Ulster. Although issues of identity, in the majority Protestant (and minority, in the overall context of the island of Ireland) community season his work, there is not as much agonising over who-is-what, as might be expected.[34] Nevertheless, the bulk of his novelistic output, so far, has reflected the conflict, in either its pre-natal form (during the Civil Rights era, in the late 1960s, as in *The International*); its most intense form (from the early

1970s to early 1990s, as in *Burning Your Own* and *Fat Lad*); or the post-conflict era, as in *That Which Was* published in 2005. Patterson's narrative, according to Kennedy-Andrews, 'seeks to undermine fixed positions and uncover internal contradictions…Patterson deconstructs Protestant history, unmasking mythic memory'.[35] It is not so much the Protestant present that is being taken to task here, but the Protestant past. And *That Which Was*, set in the late 1990s, in the first flush of peace process euphoria, is part of the same novelistic palimpsest.

Geography, in Ireland and Israel/Palestine, is history; and history, vis-à-vis land occupation, is geography. Patterson's narrative concerns a Protestant minister, Avery, in predominantly Protestant East Belfast, who is visited by a man called Larry who, bizarrely, 'seems to remember' committing a murder in the centre of Belfast in the 1970s. Avery tasks himself with trawling through the past to find the truth. But the past is a chronotope of a different colour altogether and Avery ends up being targeted by his own side – Loyalist paramilitaries – for attempting to dig too deeply into what may have been, in reality, a Loyalist-Security Forces killing.

As the murky deeds and the alliances of convenience become increasingly apparent, from the dark, dirty days of the 1970s, unsettling truths must surely surface. This urge to bear witness seems to be essential to many post-colonial literatures. Conscience, rather than justice, may come to be the final arbiter of right and wrong. Of evil deeds done in the first flush of Republicanism or Loyalism.

Peter Taylor, in his 1999 book *Loyalists*, details the case of one Protestant paramilitary, Billy Giles who, after being released from jail having served a long sentence for the murder of a Catholic friend – and acquiring a university degree in the process – finally took his own life because the burden of his own guilt was too much to bear. Giles was convicted of the murder of a former Catholic friend, Michael Fay, in retaliation for the tit-for-tat murder of the Protestant leader of the Shankill Butchers' gang, Lenny Murphy, in 1982. However, it is clear that Giles, brought up in a law-abiding, working-class family, was a man caught up in a conflict who was, at one remove, a victim of the conflict himself.

> The split second it happened, I lost part of myself that I'll never get back. You hear the bang and it's too late. Standing over the body, it hits you. I felt that somebody had reached down inside me and ripped my insides out. You've found somewhere you've never been before and it's not a very nice place. You can't stop. It's too late.[36]

The contrasting elements of Loyalist paramilitary killings and those of Republicans have been pointed out by a number of commentators. The sort of solo-run Shankill Butchers' torture and murder described in Eoin McNamee's *Resurrection Man* (1996) was more a feature of Loyalist than

Republican violence. Equally, Republicans, inheritors of a much more 'seamless' political tradition – stretching back to the 1600s and before, at a pinch – were much more likely to see their own individual acts of terror as part of a communal struggle and a token of the validity of their imagined community. Terms such as 'Crown forces', 'legitimate target' and 'forces of occupation' set such thinking in conceptual cement, in the Republican mindset.

The pattern of post-conflict paramilitary criminality varies in both communities too. Post-conflict Protestant/Loyalist paramilitaries tend to be involved in drugs, general racketeering, extortion and the like. The Loyalist 'commander' with the perma-tan, gold medallion, swanning around the slum in a 'Hampstead tractor' may be a figure of fun, but laughter is kept behind closed doors. Post-conflict Catholic/Republican paramilitaries, although some have been involved in the above, tend to prefer a more business-like approach to empire-building centring on money-laundering, fuel-laundering, cross-border smuggling, real estate investments and running semi-legitimate businesses.[37] Embracing the concept of European enlargement, Republican money-launderers have also started venturing into the foreign property market. At a criminal remove, the Republicans are 'buying back Ireland', if only to line their own 'Celtic Tiger' pockets. Nevertheless, Patterson's post-conflict Belfast is host to hundreds of men like Billy Giles.

> For the past two years the prisons of Northern Ireland had been emptying of paramilitary prisoners. Any day now the most famous prison of them all, the Maze–Long Kesh – would close its gates for good. For the past two years, Avery like most members of the clergy, had been attending conferences on issues arising from this early-release scheme. Many of the prisoners had found the Lord while inside, some had even become pastors and in a few cases established their own congregations. It was expected, though, that for the vast majority the enormity of their deeds would only hit home once they were on the outside again away from their comrades, having to cope on their own.
>
> Avery replayed Larry's words. I think I've got blood on my hands. Classic reluctance to accept responsibility.[38]

By the time memory finally filters through in his novel, Patterson's Protestant minister Avery has been falsely set up for the scandal of kerb-crawling in order to stifle the bad smell from decomposing memory. Larry's final, fictional flashback to the 1970s bears a chilling resemblance to that of Taylor's interviewee, Billy Giles.

> I squeezed the trigger, it felt like it was cutting my finger in two, I wouldn't have been surprised if the thing had just toppled out of my hand on to the floor and then...

Then Roisin gave like a little hop. I wondered what she was doing. I was going to shout, Sit down before you get hit – I'd never seen anybody being shot, I'd no idea, no idea at all – then Davy slumped against the wall. I was deafened. It was like I was in a bubble. I kept walking forward with the gun out in front of me. I had to make sure it was done properly. Roisin's friend was lying to one side. I went to move her and that's when I saw the chain with the locket on it. I picked it up and felt it in my hand. Then the bubble burst.[39]

'The bubble burst': the post-killing, post-coital, post-conflict 'caffeine drop' has kicked in. The glitz and glamour of the 'isms' has worn off. Nothing is quite as green or orange or as clear-cut as it once seemed on those colourful maps of Belfast.

Patterson's narrative is of unrequited memory that must be requited, however painfully; of the reality of post-conflict criminality and working-class communities left defenceless from their erstwhile defenders. It is all set against the background of a Belfast not quite convinced, just yet, that the worst is over. A Belfast where, the message is, from paramilitary groupings on both sides, that 'we haven't gone away, you know'.[40] This is the message of the paramilitaries in all such conflicts: we haven't gone away. It may be that a generation of war must be followed by a generation of cleansing before the patriotic scourge of paramilitarism can be eradicated. After the ball is long over, unfortunately, the band still plays on.

If *omnia Hibernia divisa est in tres partes*, two of those parts belong to the confessional 'entities' themselves. The third block of land now belongs to the paramilitaries, as green becomes orange becomes green. Like money, territory has no smell. The third estate of the paramilitaries, in the post-conflict scenario, may last as long as the recent conflict itself unless, that is, the paramilitaries sero-convert into stakeholders in the new Ireland. Similarly, in Israel and Palestine, such solid examples – outliving two intifadas – of Israeli–Palestinian co-operation on the ground, as the car-thieving cabals operating between the Israeli town of Kfar Sava and the refugee camp of Kalkiliya, are likely to outlast both the conflict and all efforts to contain it. If, as Hebrew has it, *shemen medaber* (oil talks), territory talks even louder. But the question of liberation from the liberators may prove to be the most taxing task of all in the new Jerusalems. Like the wary Hidalgo, the populace must sleep with one eye open and jump to attention when the key to the house drops from the hand and clatters to the ground at the feet of the liberators.

NOTES

1   The part played by the fall of Haifa and its effect on Palestinian resistance in general is well illustrated in M. Golani, 'The Haifa Turning Point: The British Administration and the Civil

War in Palestine, December 1947–May 1948', *Middle Eastern Studies*, 37, 2 (April 2001), pp. 93–130.

2 *Facing the Forests* was greeted with dismay in some quarters. The critic Mordechai Shalev's scathing comments were the most trenchant, accusing Yehoshua of shallow, politically motivated artistic charlatanism, 'The Arabs as Literary Solution', *Ha'aretz*, 20 September 1970. As Yehoshua told this author in a private conversation in Dublin in 2006, he sought the help of Palestinian informants for the use of 'real-time' Galilean Arabic for *The Liberated Bride* and was anxious that the reality on the ground was reflected in the dialect.

3 For an overview of the language situation obtaining in Israel, see Bernard Spolsky, 'Multilingualism in Israel', *Annual Review of Applied Linguistics*, 17 (1996).

4 Yehoshua's own father was an orientalist and, being of mixed Sephardic origin, this tendency is clearly as much familial as political. See 'A.B. Yehoshua and the Sephardic Experience.' G. Ramras-Rauch, *World Literature Today*, 65, 1 (1991), pp. 8–15.

5 Patrick Kavanagh, from the same border hinterland as Patrick McCabe and Eugene McCabe, was born in 1904, before the foundation of the new Free State and, living close to the new border with Northern Ireland, was much exercised at the idea of land and borders. In *Iliad*, he sets a certain 'hard won' rural naïveté against the greater issue of the rise of Nazi Germany, coming to the conclusion that land and sovereignty are at the heart of both the local and international conflict.

6 This scene probably relates to the murder of Billy Fox, a Protestant member of the Southern Irish Seanad (upper house) who was killed in a clumsy, brutish attack outside Clones, McCabe's home town, in the early 1970s. A number of local men were later convicted of the killing. It also has connotations of the murder of Sir Norman Stronge and his son, across the border, in Armagh, Northern Ireland, who were the direct descendants of early Protestant planters. Their ancestral home was gutted by fire after they were murdered, in January 1981, as the Republican hunger strike campaigns took off.

7 Yahyia Yakhlif, *A Lake Beyond the Wind*, New York, 1999.

8 *Al-Nakba* (the catastrophe), as the establishment of Israel and the subsequent of defeat of the Arab armies in the 1948 Arab-Israeli war, is termed in Arabic. The website www.Palestineremembered.org provides a useful, if one-sided, account of *al-Nakba*. Photos, documents and, recently, oral narratives in audio file have been added to the site. It is also useful for detailing those Palestinian towns and villages erased from the pre-1948 map.

9 Benny Morris, *The Birth of the Palestinian Refugee Problem*, Cambridge, 2004, 2nd edn, p. 177.

10 Rashid Khalidi, *Palestinian Identity: The Construction of Modern National Consciousness*, New York, 1997, p.189

11 Yakhlif, *A Lake Beyond the Wind*, pp. 36–7.

12 Ibid., p. 55.

13 Chaim Herzog, *The Arab–Israeli Wars*. London, 2004, p. 25.

14 Yakhlif, *A Lake Beyond the Wind*, pp. 199–200.

15 Nadia Abu El-Haj, *Facts on the Ground: Archaeological Practice and Territorial Self-Fashioning in Israeli Society*, Chicago, IL, 2001, pp.16–17

16 Emile Habibi, *The Secret Life of Saeed: the Pessoptimist*, New York, 1982.

17 Benedict Andersen, *Imagined Communities*, New York & London, 1983; Rachel Feldhay Brenner, in *Inextricably Bonded*, Madison, WI, 2003, pp. 153–72 compares *al-Nakba* narratives in Habibi's *Pessoptimist* and the Israeli writer S. Yizhar's (Yizhar Smilansky) novella *Hirbet Hizah*. Written from the perspectives, respectively, of loser and winner, she considers both to be confessional narratives. Nevertheless, the subversive power of Habibi's hapless *Pessoptimist*, Said, resides in the bathetic nature of his 'little man' encounter with his new Israeli overlord. The sort of sarcasm underwritten by the quirky narrative is scarcely possible when coming from the 'overlord' side of the fence.

18 Mishael Mawari Caspi and Jerome David Weltsch, *From Slumber to Awakening: Culture and Identity of Arab Israeli Literati*, New York, 1988, pp. 30–1.

19 Barbara Harlow, *Resistance Literature*, London, 1987, p. 3.

20 Ibrahim Taha, *The Palestinian Novel: A Communication Study*, London, 2002, p. 29.

21 Ami Elad-Bouskilla, *Modern Palestinian Literature and Culture*, London, 1999, pp. 32–63.

22 Said Kashua, *Dancing Arabs*, New York, 2002.

23 Gilles Deleuze and Felix Guattari, *Kafka: Towards a Minor Literature*, Minneapolis, MN, 1999.

24 Kashua, *Dancing Arabs*, p. 3.

25 Ibid., p. 106.

26 Gershon Shaked, *Modern Hebrew Fiction*, Bloomington & Indianapolis, IN, 2000, p. 186.
27 Amos Oz, *Fima*, London, 1994. The original Hebrew title, *ha-Matzav ha-Shlishi*, was dispensed with in translation.
28 Kashua, *Dancing Arabs*, p. 104.
29 Ibid., p. 172.
30 *Wasta* is the Arabic term used to denote go-between services.
31 Kashua, *Dancing Arabs*, p. 224–5.
32 Ibid., p. 226–7.
33 Brian Walker, *Dancing to History's Tune: Myth and Politics in Ireland*, Belfast, 1996, p. 125.
34 See Karen Trew, 'The Northern Irish Identity' in Anne J. Kershen (ed.), *A Question of Identity*, Aldershot, 1998. In this work Trew states that recent surveys suggest that most Northern Irish Protestants tend to identify themselves as British first and Northern Irish second. The same survey shows that Catholics tend to look on themselves as Irish first and Northern Irish second.
35 E. Kennedy-Andrews, *Fiction and the Northern Ireland Troubles since 1969*, Dublin, 2003, p. 104.
36 Peter Taylor, *Loyalists*, London, 1999, p. 5
37 The Criminal Assets Bureau in the Republic of Ireland, set up in the wake of the murder of the journalist Veronica Guerin, in 1996, has recently begun targeting Republican elements in the south, reflecting the official view that the 'turning a blind eye' phase in the peace process is now over. Golden handshake time for ex-revolutionaries is past. This also reflects southern nervousness at the increasing transfer of paramilitaries skills to young criminals, particularly in Dublin and Limerick. At present, gun crime in the Republic of Ireland outpaces that of the North of Ireland.
38 Glenn Patterson, *That Which Was*, London, 2004, pp. 12–13.
39 Ibid., pp. 235–6.
40 At a Republican rally, shortly after the official sealing of the peace process, in the Good Friday Agreement of 1998, Gerry Adams, Sinn Fein leader, former IRA commander in Belfast and member of the IRA's Army Council, used these words to keep dissident elements onside. Nevertheless, they have come to represent the long-term problems with private armies and public unease. It is, as with the heroin epidemics in Dublin in the 1980s, the working-class areas of Northern Ireland that suffer most from the attentions of those liberators living in their midst who, suffering from nostalgia for the power and glory of the past, still choose to exercise their veto over life, death and the spaces in between.

Irish Nationalism and the Israel–Palestine conflict

John Doyle

Political actors in Northern Ireland, like those in most conflict zones, have drawn international comparisons between their situation and those of other high-profile global conflicts. While there have been few formal proposals to directly import solutions from other conflicts, there have been many attempts to use international comparison to explain the origin and nature of the conflict and to seek to gain sympathy by linking the Northern Ireland conflict to one which a targeted audience has more knowledge of and/or strong views on. There have also been attempts to promote other policy objectives via association with international events or organisations.

This chapter seeks to examine the manner in which Irish nationalists have attempted to link their struggle with the Israel–Palestinian conflict. It analyses two separate components of Irish nationalism. The foreign policy of the Republic of Ireland is analysed not only as the official expression of moderate Irish nationalism, but also because it sets a broader ideological context within which even more radical voices are situated. Second, it examines how Sinn Féin, as the largest expression of radical Irish nationalism, and the majority party among the nationalist community in Northern Ireland, has sought to utilise comparison with the Palestinian cause in their political discourse over the period of the recent conflict and peace process.

There are, of course, also lively academic debates around the validity of such international comparisons. While a lot of academic writing on Northern Ireland tried to avoid the inevitable controversies of such comparison by focusing on the specificity of the Northern Ireland case and perhaps weakening its contribution to analysis of the conflict, there were significant debates, in particular, about the impact of settler colonial ideology, the role of consociational theory and, in the 1990s, the utility of a comparative study of peace processes, in particular the cases of Northern Ireland, South Africa and Israel–Palestine.[1] However, as such comparisons have been well articulated elsewhere, this chapter focuses on the particular comparisons and linkages made by political actors.

ULSTER UNIONISTS AND ISRAEL

While the focus of this article is Irish nationalism and its identification with the Palestinian cause this requires some contextualisation and in particular a brief analysis of the mirroring support by Ulster unionists for the State of Israel. Prior to the end of the Cold War, unionists had made limited use of international contacts, having traditionally seen the wider international community as unsympathetic. They have frequently been described as having a 'siege' mentality – and not just by opponents.[2] Such parallels as were drawn tended to be with what were perceived as similar communities under siege such as Israel, the Turkish Cypriots and apartheid South Africa or other 'abandoned' British settlers such as the white community in Rhodesia/Zimbabwe.[3] Ulster unionists have also seen the Northern Ireland conflict as classically 'asymmetric'. Unionist politician Clifford Smyth quotes an Admiral Hugo Hendrik Bierman of the then South African navy: 'in the nature of this protracted war our enemies have the opportunity to attack time and again and to lose, whereas we shall have but one opportunity to lose'.[4] In a similar vein, and of direct relevance to this volume, the Orange Order, comparing Northern Ireland to Israel, said: 'Having been betrayed before they [the Ulster people] are very alert now', for as Louis Gardner wrote, 'Ulster, like Israel, can only lose once.'[5]

Ulster unionists perceived Britain to be under pressure from an international community sympathetic to Irish nationalism and they had an exaggerated sense of the diplomatic pressure flowing from such sympathy. Nonetheless unionists saw successive British governments as being capable of negotiating a United Ireland without any significant threat to their own position, or to the rest of the British state. This view is expressed in various ways but generally emphasises that Northern Ireland is kept at arm's length or is treated differently from England, Scotland or Wales.[6] Unionists regularly drew attention to the record of the British government in 'abandoning' its supporters in settler colonies when it decided to withdraw – again emphasising the identification with 'settlers' under siege.

Independent unionist MP Jim Kilfedder, for example, has argued 'all over the world where Britain has been kicked in the teeth by violence she has surrendered to the terrorists. Northern Ireland...is no exception', and 'Northern Ireland will not be treated as the Khyber Pass and the North-west Frontier of the 1970s, providing reminiscences for Ministers and for military mess dinners.' In response to guarantees from British ministers about the unionist position he retorted: 'were not such assurances given from these Dispatch Boxes to the unfortunate people of Kenya who were humiliated by the Mau-Mau? But subsequently those evil men were welcomed by politicians here who had earlier condemned them.'[7] Again in Kilfedder's eyes the 'people' of Kenya were all settlers.

Ulster Unionists quite unselfconsciously moved between making common cause with traditional 'settler colonial' situations such as Rhodesia and Kenya to identification with isolated Israel, under siege in a hostile region. As white rule became not only discredited but increasingly unstable, it was clear that drawing such parallels did the unionist cause more harm than good and nostalgia for colonialism is rarely heard in their arguments after the 1980s. However, parallels with Israel are still regularly drawn on by main-stream unionist politicians who remain strong supporters of Israel. David Trimble's former press secretary, Stephen King, has referred to 'Unionists' predominant identification with Israel'.[8] While Dean Godson, Trimble's biographer, has claimed that 'Northern Ireland is one of the very few parts of Europe where there is a very wide measure of popular support in the majority community for the State of Israel.'[9]

Indeed, in 2002, Belfast was festooned with Israeli flags in unionist areas – prompting a wave of Palestinian flags in nationalist districts. The Israeli flags were backed up by supportive graffiti such as 'Go on Sharon' and 'The West Bank of the Lagan [a unionist area] backs Ariel Sharon'.[10] Again, after the Israeli invasion of Lebanon in 2006 there was widespread unionist support for Israel.[11]

However, there are signs of one or two cracks in this previous almost universal support. The late David Ervine of the small Progressive Unionist Party attended a protest rally during the Israeli invasion of Lebanon in 2006,[12] and Ulster Unionist MP, John Taylor, a member of the Middle East sub-committee of the Parliamentary Assembly of the Council of Europe, in a statement on the death of Yasser Arafat, said that his legacy was 'the international community's acceptance of the principle of an independent sovereign state of Palestine', and that, 'A great memorial to his life would be the creation of a democratic Palestine.'[13] While Taylor is well known for his maverick views he is still a very rare example of a senior unionist figure supporting the Palestinians.

Support for Israel and the Palestinians by Unionists and nationalists respectively is therefore more than a simple reflection of 'my enemy's enemy is my friend'. Just as many Unionists make common cause with Israel, which they see as an isolated state peopled by settlers and their descendents and surrounded by hostile forces, Irish nationalists view the Palestinian cause through the lens of a nation struggling to achieve statehood and/or within a wider anti-imperialist ideology.

MODERATE NATIONALISM AND ITS SUPPORT FOR PALESTINIAN
STATEHOOD

Moderate Irish nationalism, as represented by the Irish government and Irish foreign policy, has long expressed its support for Palestinian statehood and this inevitably also frames the context within which northern nationalists make common cause with Palestinians.[14] Since 1967, successive Irish governments have supported the 'Land for Peace' formula set out in United Nations Security Council Resolution 242 of November 1967 and they have explicitly called for a full Israeli withdrawal from the Occupied Territories. They have balanced this position with support for Israel's right to exist within secure borders.[15] Ireland recognised Israel de jure in 1963 and was one of the very few countries acceptable to both Israel and Egypt as a troop-provider for UN forces in the region following the 1967 war.[16]

The Irish position on Palestinian self-determination has been maintained by all governments and is the context for regular official statements on the Israel–Palestine conflict. In 2004 then Foreign Minister Brian Cowen made a statement welcoming the Geneva Initiative and the Saudi/Arab League plan and criticised in very strong terms the Israeli security wall.[17] Cowen's successor, Dermot Ahern, intervened during Israel's invasion of Lebanon in 2006 saying, 'I have condemned and I condemn again today the rising toll of death and destruction, the blockade of Lebanon, the desperate conditions under which 1.5 million Palestinians are living under effective siege in Gaza.'[18] This political support is also seen in the Irish official development aid budget. In 2006, the budget included provision for over €4 million to be spent in the Palestinian territories, including support for the United Nations Relief and Works Agency (UNRWA).[19] Previous development aid support has been given to UNRWA, the Palestinian Authority's ministry of education, the United Nations Development Programme (UNDP), Bethlehem University and local civil society organisations.[20]

This level of diplomatic support for Palestinian self-determination, combined with recognition of Israel's right to exist in security, has been consistent over many years. In seeking an explanation for this position it is possible to look at a number of broader themes in Irish foreign policy. It certainly draws on Ireland's own history and reflects a context where Irish foreign policy maintained a broad support for movements for national self-determination.[21] This was true in sub-Saharan Africa in the late 1950s and 1960s. It formed the context for intervention in the Congo in the 1960s, to prevent what was seen as a colonial attempt to divide the country and in addition allowed the Irish state, as a relatively new UN member, to show its support for the emerging concept of peacekeeping. In more recent years it has been reflected in policies towards Cyprus, East Timor and the Western Sahara.

Irish foreign policy on Palestine is also a reflection of, and consistent with, support for other strong themes within modern Irish foreign policy – a concern with conflict resolution and strong support for the UN, international law and human rights. Statements by ministers often refer back to United Nations Security Council (UNSC) Resolutions, as well as the ruling of the International Court of Justice (on the wall) and the humanitarian condition of Palestinian refugees and those living in the Occupied Territories. The 1996 White Paper on Irish foreign policy, while acknowledging the duty of a state to protect its national interests, set out this self-image as follows:

> Ireland's foreign policy is about much more than self-interest. For many of us it is a statement of the kind of people we are. Irish people are committed to the principles set out in Article 29 of the [Irish] Constitution for the conduct of international relations: the ideal of peace and friendly co-operation amongst nations founded on international justice and morality.[22]

In late 2000, just before Ireland joined the UNSC, then Minister for Foreign Affairs Brian Cowen argued against an analysis of foreign policy on the basis of values versus interests. He said it was not an either/or situation because small states could not compete in a power-seeking international system run by realist principles. Ireland, he argued,

> like most small nations, has always known that a multilateral rules-based international order is in our national interest. We would like to think, and I believe with much justification that we have demonstrated this, that our commitment to liberal internationalism is also based on principle.[23]

It is also possible to argue, as Rory Miller has done, that Ireland's position on Palestine has been beneficial to the development of its economic relationships with the wider Arab world.[24] The 1996 White Paper, indeed, acknowledges that 'Ireland is small and hugely dependent on external trade for its well-being'.[25] While it is difficult to separate the importance of different motivating factors in foreign policy some indications can be drawn by comparison with other cases. For example, while Ireland was on the UNSC in 2001–02, Ireland seriously annoyed a stronger trade partner (Morocco) by supporting Polisario on the question of the Western Sahara. Indeed, during its time on the UNSC in 2001–02, Ireland in many respects was the leading supporter of the Polisario position, with no obvious 'realist' benefits.[26]

Clearly, as a small state, Ireland has had limited opportunities to influence politics in the Middle East. It has sought to strengthen EU intervention but in common with its diplomatic approach on all issues of EU Common Foreign and Security Policy (CFSP) it is not the policy of the Irish government to articulate an 'opening position' on EU negotiations on foreign policy statements and the government tends to support loyally CFSP positions once agreed. While it is widely reported that Ireland adopts a position of support for the Palestinians in such talks, there is limited public detail on the degrees of difference between the Irish approach and what is ultimately agreed at EU level. However, in a review of developments in EU foreign policy in the 1980s, former Taoiseach, Garret FitzGerald asserted

> There was a major shift in European foreign policy [in the 1970s] which eventually secured the assent of all the member states although at the start of that period only three countries, France, Italy and Ireland, held the position of seeing the Palestinian problem as one of fundamental importance requiring action to provide the Palestinians with a homeland and a State of their own whereas the majority of States saw it still as a refugee problem. From that position these countries have shifted towards the position which we then held.[27]

A little more detail is revealed by Ireland's most recent period on the UNSC, which provided a context whereby Ireland had some degree of influence at the highest levels of international politics and was also doing so in a much more open forum than the Council of EU foreign ministers. The details of the Irish position was indeed articulated at length over this period. The changes to the Council's membership in January 2001, and Ireland's broad support for the rights of the Palestinian people altered the previous balance on the Council.

The United States had become more wary of using its Security Council veto to block resolutions critical of Israel, being a little more conscious, in the immediate post 9/11 era (if not later) of the negative impact such vetoes have in the Arab world and internationally. In the Security Council term prior to Ireland's membership, a Palestinian-promoted motion proposed in December 2000 calling for a UN Observer Force in the Occupied Territories got only eight votes, and so the United States did not have to use its veto, as nine positive votes from among the 15 members are required to pass a resolution. Ireland's support for the idea of Palestinian statehood meant that a passing majority of nine votes was now more likely – potentially forcing the United States to engage more fully.

The first significant Council discussion on Palestine during Ireland's term was in March 2001. Ireland's statements with regard to the Palestinian issue[28] stressed five key themes: first, the right of the Security Council to concern itself with the Middle East; second, Israel's right to security within recognised borders; third, the legitimate rights of the Palestinian people to a state; fourth, condemnation of terrorism, the counter-productive nature of Palestinian violence, Israel's excessive reaction to such violence and illegal Israeli settlements; and finally Israel's right to defend itself along with its obligation to do so in accordance with international humanitarian law. Ireland abstained on this draft resolution, which sought to deploy UN observers in the occupied Palestinian territories without Israeli agreement, as they believed that no state would deploy troops in such circumstances.

Ireland's support for Palestinian statehood was demonstrated most clearly in December 2001 when Ireland's support for a draft resolution promoted by the Arab states encouraged three other non-permanent Council members to vote in favour, seeing Ireland's lead as giving them diplomatic cover, despite a certain US veto (and obvious British displeasure).[29] The vetoing of this draft resolution and a recognition that there was now a majority on the Council in favour of moderate motions critical of Israel were important factors in pressurising the United States towards supporting the principle of Palestinian statehood. In March 2002, faced with a moderate Arab resolution that it would again have had to veto to defeat, the US introduced its own draft, which endorsed the principle of Palestinian statehood and welcomed the involvement of the International Quartet (made up of Russia, the European Union, the United States and the United Nations), as a mediating group in the Israeli–Palestinian conflict.[30]

The United States also introduced its own drafts of proposed resolutions dealing with the conflict on three occasions in late March/April 2002. These called for an Israeli withdrawal from Palestinian cities and welcomed Secretary-General Kofi Annan's initiative to send a fact-finding mission to Jenin to investigate allegations of an Israeli massacre of civilians in that city.[31] In late 2002, however, following the killing of UN employees by Israeli forces, the US shifted back to a more traditional defence of Israel and vetoed a draft resolution, one that had been supported by Ireland.[32]

Obviously Ireland was not the only, or even the most significant, factor in the changing UN and US approach to the Middle East. However, notwithstanding considerable pressure from the United States, Ireland held a fairly consistently pro-Palestinian position on the UN Security Council and contributed to the existence of a block of nine votes that had some degree of influence over US strategy at this time.

An analysis of Irish foreign policy on the Palestinian question shows therefore that it is maintained even when realist considerations (such as not annoying the United States) were at stake. Therefore while trade links with the Arab world are not irrelevant to Ireland's position on Palestine, the willingness to pursue this policy in the face of considerable pressure from the United States indicates that its roots in Irish foreign policy are deeper and more fundamental and draw on themes other than economic self-interest.

SINN FÉIN AND THE PALESTINIAN QUESTION

An analysis of Sinn Féin's position on the Middle East offers a different perspective to that of the Irish state's foreign policy, given the party's links to the IRA and its espousal of a more militant politics on Irish unity and international affairs. Sinn Féin has elaborated a consistent position in support of the PLO and Palestinian statehood and while its position goes beyond that articulated by the Irish state it is not fundamentally in contradiction with it. There are three key dimensions to Sinn Féin's use of the Palestinian question over the past thirty years, which follow more or less chronologically.

First, there is a linking of the IRA and the PLO as 'equivalent' armed national liberation movements and the use of an internationalist policy on questions such as Palestinian statehood in an effort to defend Sinn Féin from attacks by others on the left who sought to dismiss them as inward-looking conservative nationalists. Second, there were strong links between the Northern Ireland, South African and Oslo peace processes in the early to mid 1990s. Finally, in the aftermath of the 1998 Belfast Agreement, links with radical causes and involvement in international attempts at conflict resolution, have served to strengthen the Sinn Féin leadership's claims to remain 'radical' in their politics, and have also strengthened its claim to be an organisation concerned with conflict resolution in general.

The outbreak of the modern conflict in the late 1960s developed out of a conscious use of 'civil rights' discourse and early international comparisons were inevitably made between the suffering of nationalists in Northern Ireland and African-Americans in the southern states of the US. The movement's name – Northern Ireland Civil Rights Association – as well as the tactics of peaceful marches and the focus on issues such as discrimination in jobs, housing, voting and police behaviour sought to draw international attention and sympathy especially in the United States. This strategy also attempted to improve the international profile of Northern Ireland and embarrass the British government into a programme of reform.

This comparison continued throughout the conflict. Orange Order[33] marches through nationalist areas have been compared to the Klu Klux Klan marching through Harlem and a senior member of the Clinton administration in the 1990s alledgedly compared the then Northern Ireland police force, the Royal Ulster Constabulary (RUC), to the policing of Alabama and Georgia by 'all white cops'.[34] As the conflict developed, Republicans continued this focus but also added a more anti-imperialist and revolutionary rhetoric.

This saw the use of such figures as Che Guevera and expressions of 'solidarity' with leftist movements in Latin America. By far the most common comparison over the ensuing decades was with the African National Congress (ANC) struggle against apartheid. This was regularly seen in publications, on painted murals in nationalist areas and in speeches by senior Sinn Féin leaders. It was in this wider context that comparisons with the Palestinian struggle for statehood and with the PLO itself were made.

In the early years of the conflict, Sinn Féin and the IRA sought to link their campaign for Irish unity to that of the Palestinians for statehood and, in particular, sought to link the IRA and the PLO. This is mostly strongly seen in the 1970s and early 1980s and its most visible manifestation was in murals in nationalist areas. One prominent example in Belfast depicted armed IRA and PLO members under the slogan 'IRA-PLO one struggle'.[35] By linking its wider political strategy to organisations and 'struggles' which were widely supported in Ireland, such as those being carried out by the ANC and PLO, Sinn Féin sought to provide a wider political context for its political action.

This was regularly seen in the weekly Sinn Féin newspaper *An Phoblacht* and became stronger as the organisation moved to the left under the influence of the Gerry Adams' leadership in the 1980s. Interestingly, the comparison with the PLO continued in *An Phoblacht* throughout this period, notwithstanding the reliance of the IRA on fund raising among the Irish diaspora in the United States, where links with Palestinians would hardly have been popular.

During the 1990s there was a widespread academic and public discourse on the interconnections and possible lessons to be learned by a comparative study of the then emerging peace processes in South Africa, Northern Ireland and the Oslo process in the Middle East. This type of comparison went well beyond those who used it for nationalist rhetoric. Some, including Michael Cox, have argued that the previous attempts by Sinn Féin to link themselves to the ANC and PLO created its own pressure in a reverse fashion in the 1990s. If the IRA campaign was in part justified by some comparison to the ANC and PLO then the ANC and PLO involvement in peace processes added to the other pressures on the Sinn Féin leadership to do likewise.[36]

However, the Sinn Féin leadership played up these comparisons and regularly referred to them in their public speeches and publicity.[37] The South African link was the more enduring as its peace process obviously succeeded and was then used after the end of apartheid as both an example and a lever. Nevertheless, links with the Palestinian cause have continued right up to the present day. This helped to cement the Irish process and helped persuade their own supporters that this was a road they could go down given the widespread support for the PLO and ANC among their target voters.

In the post-Belfast Agreement (and post-armed conflict) era in Northern Ireland, Sinn Féin has sought to present an image of a party still committed to its radical tradition, in order to hold onto more militant supporters. But it has also sought to strengthen its image as a 'peace-maker' and international actor by regular engagement in other conflicts. On the question of maintaining a radical political agenda this is obviously primarily reflected in domestic policy and in its continuing campaign on Irish unity.[38]

However, international politics gives a wider context to Sinn Féin's politics and allows it to use international situations to build its domestic support base among key target audiences. Sinn Féin continues to articulate a leftist position, consistent with the 'anti-globalisation' movement in the post-1998 Agreement era. It is highly critical of the global economic system and of the dominant role of the United States, despite the considerable significance which it attaches to a strategic involvement with the United States regarding the peace process. The party was also very active in the anti-war movement on Iraq – providing speakers for all of the major rallies and opposing the use of Shannon airport by the US military. More generally, it has consistently been highly critical of US policy in the Middle East.[39]

More explicit links with the Palestinian cause continued throughout this time period. Sinn Fein has called for an end to Israel's preferential trade access to the European Union until there is an end to the occupation of the West Bank and Gaza.[40] Dr Jamal Zahalka, a member of the Palestinian Authority, spoke at the 'Bloody Sunday' anniversary march in 2005, one of the most high profile republican events of recent times.[41] Gerry Adams condemned Israel's invasion of Lebanon in July 2006,[42] while party spokesperson on foreign affairs Aengus O Snodaigh, TD, attacked the EU over its decision to suspend funds to the Palestinian Authority after the election of Hamas in January of 2006.[43]

Inevitably, these policy positions are used against them in the United States but there is no evidence that the party has sought to distance itself from these policies or to camouflage them. Neither is there any evidence that the party feels itself under pressure to do so from its support base. The domestic importance of their international positions is sometimes lost on Sinn Féin's political opponents and even some of its international supporters. There was, for example, considerable debate about Gerry Adams' visit to Cuba in 2001 and his very public and friendly reception by Fidel Castro. Supporters of the peace process in the US Congress were highy vocal in their attacks on the visit.[44]

Despite this, Sinn Féin not only proceeded with the visit but promoted it heavily via its press office. The 2002 general election manifesto showed no sign that the party was concerned that its position on Cuba was a problem and it explicitly called for an end to the US embargo of Cuba.[45] Likewise, there is little evidence that editorials in conservative newspapers such as the *Daily Telegraph*,[46] attempting to link Sinn Féin to organisations such as the PLO, are regarded as damaging by Sinn Féin in the Irish domestic context.

In the aftermath of the 9/11 attacks there was clearly a much more limited political space for any Republican return to the 'armed struggle'. However, as Western policy makers struggled to come to terms with the threat of al Qaeda, it was contrasted by some commentators with 'old' terrorism – which was perceived (rightly or wrongly) to have more rational political aims around which a government could negotiate. The *Daily Telegraph* attacked what it perceived to be the influence of this sort of logic within the British government in an editorial in 2003:

Mr Blair also appears to believe that clear distinctions can be made between different kinds of terrorism. This holds that terrorism for no discernible, rational purpose (such as September 11) is beyond the pale.

By contrast, terrorism that has clear political purpose (a united Ireland as demanded by the IRA, a Palestinian state as demanded by the PLO and Hamas) can be conciliated.[47]

The domestic impact of links with popular international causes are cemented by the party's high profile involvement in international conflict resolution efforts. There is little doubt that Sinn Féin played a positive role in the Basque Country where it had long-standing ties to Basque militants in Batasuna. The initial forum where supporters of Batasuna and the moderate Basque nationalists discussed the possibilities of a post-ceasefire common strategy was called the 'Irish Forum', such was the level of involvement by Irish nationalists.[48] Senior negotiator Martin McGuinness has also been involved in the Tamil-Sri Lanka conflict with a number of visits to the area. While the involvement of Sinn Féin in the Israel–Palestinian conflict has been marginal compared to these other examples, the 2006 visit by Gerry Adams to the region was presented in this light.[49] A senior Sinn Féin figure, writing in the local press explicitly stated:

At great personal risk Martin McGuinness visited Sri Lanka and spoke to the country's president and the Tiger Tamils about making peace between enemies. Gerry Adams's trip to the Middle East was as perilous. He also recently visited the Basque country and Spain following ETA's decision to ceasefire.[50]

This international involvement serves to heighten the party's profile, to constantly remind Irish voters of the party's involvement in the Northern Ireland peace process and to link it directly to ongoing issues of concern for potential supporters in a manner which is rarely open to opposition politicians. For those with whom they build links, the perceived 'success' of the Irish peace process in the international media allows other groups to use this opportunity to pressurise their own local state actors. For example, Basques welcomed the involvement of Sinn Féin as they could contrast the refusal of the Partido Popular Spanish government to engage in any talks with the willingness of the British to do so in Northern Ireland. It also strengthened the case of those advocating an ETA ceasefire, as the IRA was held in high regard by most ETA members. During Gerry Adams' visit to Palestine in 2006, Sinn Féin compared the attempts to isolate the Hamas-led government with its own isolation prior to the commencement of the peace process, arguing that it would not work and should be abandoned.[51]

Irish nationalism's engagement with the Israel–Palestine conflict, for both the Irish Government and for Sinn Féin have grown out of strong themes which are also visible in other contexts. The Irish state's position in support of Palestinian statehood (as well as Israel's right to live in security) has been consistently expressed over many years, even at times (such as during the most recent Security Council term) when there was considerable pressure from the United States to refrain from doing so.

Given the close links between Ireland and the United States and the high level of US investment in Ireland this might be expected to have had a defining influence on foreign policy decisions. However, ultimately support for the Palestinian right to statehood went beyond the particulars of the Palestinian question and was based on a firm belief that it was vital in the context of both the current international security situation and in order to strengthen the UN system and international law more broadly. As such, the government was willing to risk disagreeing with the United States on the matter.

Sinn Féin, while having a similar position on the fundamentals of the issue, uses a more radical rhetoric, historically supporting the PLO's campaign of violence (unlike the Irish government) and attacking Irish government/EU decisions to suspend funding to the Palestinian Authority after the Hamas victory in the 2006 elections. It also places the Palestinian question in a wider context, within its critique of US foreign policy which draws on both the politics of the anti-globalisation movement and the appeal of continuing to build alliances with Palestinians and other (most notably the Basque) nationalist groups in an age of conflict resolution.

NOTES

1   On this issue see John McGarry *Northern Ireland and the Divided World*, Oxford, 2001; John McGarry & Brendan O'Leary, *Explaining Northern Ireland*, Oxford, 1995; Michael Cox, Adrian Guelke and Fiona Stephen (eds) *A Farewell to Arms?: Beyond the Good Friday Agreement*, Manchester, 2006.

2   See Arthur Aughey, *Under Siege: Ulster Unionism and the Anglo-Irish Agreement*, Belfast, 1989.

3   Pamela Clayton, *Enemies and Passing Friends: Settler Ideologies in Twentieth Century Ulster*, London, 1996, pp. 40–6. For direct examples see also *Combat*, August 1974 and September 1974; Jim Kilfedder, *Parliamentary Debates, House of Commons*, Vol. 945, col. 1003, 6 March 1978.

4   *Protestant Telegraph*, 15 June 1974.

5   See Martin Smyth's introduction to the Orange Order pamphlet *The Twelfth*, 1982.

6   For example, see Arthur Aughey 'The Idea of the Union', in John Wilson Foster (ed.) *The Idea of the Union: Statements and Critiques in Support of the Union of Great Britain and Northern Ireland*, Vancouver, 1995. For some direct examples see Ian Paisley, *Parliamentary Debates, House of Commons*, Vol. 832, col. 1040, 6 March 1972; James Kilfedder, *Parliamentary Debates, House of Commons*, Vol. 882, col. 842, 28 November 1974 and in *Co. Down Spectator*, 6 February 1976; Enoch Powell, *Parliamentary Debates, House of Commons*, Vol. 110, col. 277, 10 February 1987.

7   For this, and other examples, see *Parliamentary Debates, House of Commons*, Vol. 834, col. 283, 28 March 1972; Vol. 929, col. 1390, 7 April 1977; Vol. 945, col. 1003, 6 March 1978.

8   *Belfast Telegraph*, 9 April 2003. See also Stephen King and Bob McCartney, MP, *Belfast Telegraph*, 9 October 2001.

9   Dean Godson, 'Lessons from Northern Ireland For the Arab Israeli Conflict', *Jerusalem Viewpoints*, No. 523, 1–15 October 2004, http://www.jcpa.org/jl/vp523.htm. Godson's biography of Trimble is *Himself Alone: David Trimble & the Ordeal of Unionism*, London, 2004.

10 *The Irish Times*, 6 July 2002.

11 See, for example, Mark Davenport, 'NI–Middle East Parallels Still Drawn', 4 August 2006, http://news.bbc.co.uk/2/hi/uk_news/northern_ireland/5246330.stm.
12 *Belfast Telegraph*, 9 August 2006.
13 *Irish News*, 12 November 2004.
14 This section focuses on Irish state policy but the SDLP in Northern Ireland shares a similar perspective. See its statement in the *Irish News*, 12 November 2004.
15 See, for example, the statement by Minister for Foreign affairs Garret FitzGerald in Dáil Éireann, Vol. 275, col 925, 5 November 1974.
16 Richard E. M. Heaslip, 'Ireland's First Engagement in United Nations Peacekeeping Operations: An Assessment', *Irish Studies in International Affairs*, 17 (2006), pp. 31-42. Ireland had military officers stationed in the region on behalf of the UN since the formation of the UNOGIL observer mission in 1958.
17 Statement to Seanad Éireann by the Minister for Foreign Affairs, Mr Brian Cowen, see Department of Foreign Affairs (hereafter, DFA) Press release, 4 February 2004, www.dfa.ie
18 See DFA press release, 18 July 2004, http://www.dfa.ie/information/display.asp?ID=2118.
19 See DFA press release, http://www.dfa.ie/information/display.asp?ID=2119.
20 See DFA press release, http://www.dfa.ie/information/display.asp?ID=1239.
21 See Patrick Keatinge, *A Place Among the Nations: Issues of Irish Foreign Policy*, Dublin, 1978.
22 See *White Paper on Irish Foreign Policy*, Dublin, 1996, paragraph 1.
23 Brian Cowen, 'Challenges to Liberal Internationalism', *Irish Studies in International Affairs*, 12 (2001), p .2.
24 Rory Miller 'The Politics of Trade and Diplomacy: Ireland's Evolving Relationship with the Muslim Middle East', *Irish Studies in International Affairs*, 15 (2004), pp. 123–45.
25 1996 *White Paper*, paragraph 2.
26 John Doyle, 'Irish Diplomacy on the UN Security Council 2001–2: Foreign Policy-making in the Light of Day', *Irish Studies in International Affairs*, 15 (2004), pp. 73–101.
27 *Dáil Éireann Debates*, Vol. 371, col. 2279, 22 April 1987.
28 For details see, for example, statements and vetoed resolution on 15 and 27 March, 2001, available at http://www.un.org/Docs/sc/.
29 See Security Council Report for 14 December 2001, available at http://www.un.org/Docs/sc/.
30 Ultimately, UNSC Resolution 1397, based on the US draft, was adopted on 12 March 2002.
31 Resolutions 1402, 1403 and 1405, adopted on 29 March, 9 April and 19 April, respectively.
32 See Security Council Reports for 20 December 2002, available at http://www.un.org/Docs/sc/
33 The Orange Order is a sectarian unionist organisation, whose main activity consists of public 'parades'. There are over 3000 such parades each year – about fifty of the most contentious ones going directly through nationalist communities.
34 See John McGarry (ed.) *Northern Ireland and the Divided World: Post Agreement Northern Ireland in Comparative Perspective*, Oxford, 2001, p.4.
35 Reproduced on http://www.bbc.co.uk/history/recent/troubles/gallery/nationalist/gall4.shtml
36 See Michael Cox, 'Bringing in the International: the IRA Cease-fire and the End of the Cold War', *International Affairs*, 73, 4 (1997), and 'Northern Ireland: The War that Came in From the Cold', *Irish Studies in International Affairs*, 9 (1998), pp. 73–84.
37 See *Irish Times*, 22 December 1994 and 28 September 1994 for examples of this relating to the Middle East. There were also 441 references to Palestine on the Sinn Féin website as of September 2006. Links with the ANC were even more prominent in Sinn Fein publicity. See, for example, Adams meeting with Nelson Mandela, 20 June 1995 and Cyril Ramaposa in Belfast, 30 April 1998.
38 For a wider discussion see John Doyle, *After conflict – Placing the Sinn Féin Party in a Comparative Politics Context*, Working Paper in International Studies, Centre for International Studies Dublin City University. http://www.dcu.ie/~cis/publications.htm.
39 See, for example, the Sinn Féin manifesto for the 2002 Irish general election, *Building an Ireland of Equals*, 2002.

40 See Sinn Féin statement of 5 October 2005 http://www.sinnfein.ie/news/detail/6773.
41 *Irish News*, 29 January 2005.
42 *Irish News*, 9 August 2006.
43 For Sinn Féin's full statement on this see its website for 26 April 2006, www.sinnfein.ie.
44 *Belfast News Letter*, 24 December 2001; *Irish News*, 17 December 2001.
45 See, for example, *Building an Ireland of Equals*.
46 For examples of such editorials see the *Daily Telegraph*, 27 February 2001, which attacks Sinn Féin on the grounds that its 'natural allies are other 'national liberation movements', such as ETA, the PLO, the PFLP and the Sandinistas.'
47 *Daily Telegraph*, 7 April 2003.
48 See *The Irish Times*, 17 September 1998.
49 'Sinn Fein president meets Hamas', *BBCNewsOnline*, 6 September 2006, http://news.bbc.co.uk/2/hi/uk_news/northern_ireland/5318978.stm
50 *Irish News*, 7 Sept 2006.
51 Ibid.

Irish Republicanism and the Peace Process: Lessons for Hamas?

Jonathan Moore

On 4 October 2006 the Provisional Irish Republican Army (IRA) officially ceased to be a factor in the Northern Ireland conflict. Although they had been adhering to a ceasefire since July 1997, the commitment of the IRA to totally peaceful means was often questioned. In order to monitor the integrity of the IRA ceasefire, much to the anger of Irish republicans, an Independent Monitoring Commission (IMC) had been set up by the British and Irish governments in 2003. It was this body that made the announcement that they believed that the IRA was not 'now engaged in terrorism'.[1] Most significantly, the IMC argued that the IRA leadership had 'disbanded military structures, including the general headquarters departments responsible for procurement, engineering and training and it has stood down volunteers'.[2]

Political responses to the report reflected the significance of the moment. British Prime Minister Tony Blair concluded that 'The IRA's campaign is over. The IRA has done what we asked it to do.'[3] Even Democratic Unionist Party (DUP) leader Dr Ian Paisley acknowledged that 'progress' had been made and did not attempt to question the conclusions reached by the IMC, choosing instead to move on to the question of Sinn Féin support for policing as the major sticking point for any movement towards the setting up of a DUP/Sinn Féin executive in Belfast.[4]

For republicans there was frustrated relief that the outside world had finally accepted that the IRA was no longer an active organisation. They had been dismayed that obstacles were still being put in the way of the party's participation in a Belfast power-sharing executive. Republicans pointed to the fact that in July 2005, the Army Council of the IRA had put out a statement ordering all IRA units to dump their weapons, and that all members had been 'instructed to assist the development of purely political and democratic programmes through exclusively peaceful means'.[5] The IMC report meant that one major obstacle had been removed for Sinn Féin on the road towards being accepted as a wholly legitimate political party.

The success of the Republican movement in moving from armed conflict to strictly peaceful means has led some to wonder if this transformation could be used as a kind of template for other groups involved in armed struggle across the globe. Certainly Sinn Féin leader Gerry Adams believed that broader lessons could be learnt from the republican journey. In September 2006 Adams visited the Middle East 'to share experiences with those working for peace there and to advocate an alternative to war'.[6] He admitted he did not have 'any magic formula or panacea for any conflict situation' but he stressed that

> the broad principles which apply here after years of conflict – recognition of democratic mandates, dialogue as a means [of going] forward, governments playing a full part – we think some of those certainly could be applied in the Middle East. We'll see how we get on.[7]

Adams was not alone in believing that the success of the Irish peace process could be used as a kind of model of conflict resolution for other global conflicts. Speaking in Washington in June 2006, Tony Blair spoke about the lessons that international conflicts could learn from the Irish peace process. He implied that progress in the Middle East should in fact be easier than in Northern Ireland because in the former, 'we now have agreement as to the basic nature of the settlement: two states'.[8] Three months earlier Father Alec Reid spoke of the advice he had given to the leaders of the Basque group ETA. 'I explained the lessons we learned in Ireland', the Belfast priest explained and went on to explain the common ground shared by the two conflicts.[9]

Gerry Adams, Tony Blair and Alec Reid were more intimate with the minutiae of the Irish peace process than most. Adams was the driving force behind the transformation of the IRA. Blair was the Prime Minister of the United Kingdom at the time of the historic Good Friday Agreement of 1998 and Reid had done a huge amount in bringing about dialogue between Irish republicans and constitutional nationalists. Their Northern Irish peace process credentials are clear, but are they right in arguing that the experience in Northern Ireland in general, and that of the IRA in particular, could be applicable to other global conflicts?

Interest in this question has been greatly heightened since the sensational landslide victory of Hamas in the election for the Palestinian Authority (PA) in January 2006. The party won 74 of the 132 seats. Pundits and polls alike were equally proved wrong, as the ruling Fatah party was swept aside by

Hamas in a dramatic and unexpected result. The dismay shown by many in the international community in this clear move to the extremes was tempered by the hope that maybe the surprise election result would force Hamas to become more political, more accommodating and less militaristic. In other words, perhaps Hamas would now go down the same road as the Irish republican movement.

The argument that the IRA's engagement with the peace process could have lessons for Hamas and its engagement with Israel has been denied by most pro Israeli opinion.[10] The latter have clamed that Hamas had locked the door on its own participation in any meaningful talks by its refusal to moderate its position and with its outright refusal to recognise Israel's right to exist. Israel urged the European Union (EU) to take a firm stance against a Hamas administration, which it called a 'terrorist government'.[11] Hamas leader Mohammed Al-Zahar certainly gave Israel ammunition for refusing to engage with them with statements such as the following made at the time of the January election:

Why should we recognise... Israel's right to exist? In this region we have faced Roman occupation, Persian occupation, Crusader occupation, British occupation, they are all gone. The Israeli enemy does not belong to the region. It does not belong to the region's history, geography or faith.[12]

Such a statement is totally in keeping with the Hamas Charter.[13]

The association of Northern Ireland with political progress, flexibility and transformation is a very recent phenomenon. As one historian of the IRA has commented, the troubles in Northern Ireland had historically been characterised as a conflict 'that no one could really see an end to'.[14] As the old joke goes: 'What do Northern Ireland's politicians do when they see light at the end of the tunnel? Answer: Build more tunnel.'[15] The view of many politicians, pundits and ordinary people was that this was a conflict without resolution, a conflict fuelled by hatred and bigotry, which would continue. At the heart of this pessimism was the view that the IRA would continue indefinitely to fight until it achieved its final aim. Given that this aim, the achievement of Irish unity by violent means, was opposed by a majority of people in Northern Ireland, the conflict would go on ad infinitum.

The provisional IRA had been born in 1969 as the very model of a hard line, uncompromising and militaristic paramilitary group. Their split from the majority of the IRA in that year signalled a rejection of compromise, electoral politics and non-violence. In an early statement, their political wing, Sinn Féin, made it clear where the priorities lay with a rallying call to the nationalist people:

Think again. The road to Westminster, Stormont and Leinster House is paved with the good intentions of erstwhile republicans. Tomorrow may be too late. Give your support now to the republican movement which will last. Do not throw your efforts away on yet another parliamentary debacle.[16]

By dismissing the parliamentary road, the message was clear – the armed struggle was the only way forward.

Angered by the refusal of the IRA to defend the nationalist ghettoes in August 1969, the provisionals now invested all their considerable energies in the armed struggle. Their belief was that this struggle could push the British government into withdrawing from Northern Ireland. The idea of reform was rejected since, as one early 1970s IRA volunteer put it, 'the six county area is irreformable'.[17] In 1971 the IRA military campaign began and in that year they killed fifty-six members of the security forces. Such military success and the apparent inability of the state to respond in any way except through a reckless combination of repression and ineptitude convinced the IRA that military victory was now only a matter of time.

Political thought in the republican movement of this time was very limited. This was not due to the republicans being apolitical, far from it. However, outside the republican dream of forcing Britain out of Ireland, their political programme was less than impressive. The republican programme for Ireland was contained in the 1972 document *Eire Nua*.[18] This programme reflected the distance between the political leadership who looked at life through rural eyes and the conflict in the north which was, at this stage, overwhelmingly an urban one.

As one account of this period notes: 'Within the movement there was disinterest amongst the urban supporters in Belfast and Derry, for whom *Eire Nua's* worthy pronouncements on farming co-operatives were of minimal relevance.'[19] In some ways this did not matter to the average volunteer for whom republicanism was about the armed struggle not broader political policy. *Eire Nua* had the practical lack of relevance to the situation in Northern Ireland in 1972 in much the same way that the Hamas Charter has to the Middle East today.

The limitations of republican political strategy were clearly exposed in July 1972, when, following the military success of the IRA in bringing about the prorogation of Stormont, the British government sat down and met the IRA leadership in London. Accounts from men who were on opposite sides of the table in that extraordinary meeting show the lack of realistic political thinking on the IRA's side. Sean Macstiofoián, the chief of staff of the IRA, called on the British government 'to declare its intention to withdraw all British forces from Irish soil'.[20] As William Whitelaw, who was secretary of state for Northern Ireland, later commented 'Once it was clear that withdrawal was not on the agenda, the IRA had little else to say.'[21]

The belief in the inevitability of British withdrawal was the cornerstone of republican thinking at the time. The problem for republicans was that the

British state had absolutely no intention of withdrawing from Northern Ireland. What they were prepared to do was to convince the IRA that withdrawal was on the cards in order to bring about a cessation of IRA violence. From a British point of view, this latter plan was to be brilliantly executed. During Christmas, 1974, Ruairi O'Bradaigh, the President of Sinn Féin, received a message from an intermediary that the British government wanted to discuss ways of disengaging from Ireland.[22] O'Bradaigh and other senior republicans totally believed this and an IRA truce followed.

This first phase of the IRA campaign showed the limitations of a purely militaristic approach. The failure to make serious constructive demands at the time of the talks with Whitelaw in 1972 was indicative of these limitations. The folly in believing that Britain was planning withdrawal in the mid-1970s showed a lack of basic political analysis. In this period, it is intriguing to note that both hard-line republicans and unionists believed that Britain planned withdrawal, with Ian Paisley famously commenting on the 1973 agreement that 'Dublin is only a Sunningdale away'.[23] The IRA and the DUP were united for once: both being totally wrong in understanding British intentions.

The lessons from this for Hamas are clear. Militarism can produce a response but it is very rarely enough to force a powerful state to surrender. If a group is to make political progress, it needs a sophisticated political strategy and must seriously analyse those that it is in conflict with. The IRA in the 1970s viewed the British government through the prism of green-tinted spectacles. Their analysis was found to be lacking when dealing with the most fundamental of questions, namely what are the true intentions of the British state? Likewise, if Hamas is to move forward, it needs to seriously analyse the state of Israel and work out what is the bottom line in terms of what Israel will, or will not, accept.

The 1970s in Northern Ireland is also illuminating in highlighting another shared aspect with the Israeli–Palestinian conflict. Both conflicts are products of that most basic of disputes, namely the question over land, national self-determination and statehood. Such conflicts have real roots, roots that underpin the ability of the conflict to be sustained over a long time. Ireland and Israel–Palestine can be compared to those conflicts without real roots, where violence is the result of the actions of small totally unrepresentative groups such as the Baader Meinhoff group or the Angry Brigade. In these latter conflicts the state will be able to militarily defeat the paramilitary groups. The important characteristic of conflicts such as Northern Ireland and Palestine–Israel is that whereas it is inconceivable that the paramilitary group can defeat a state, it is also apparent that the state cannot defeat the paramilitary group.

Roy Mason was secretary of state between 1976 and 1979. During his time in the post, the language of British government policy towards Northern Ireland changed. Gone was the rhetoric of men such as Conservative home secretary Reginald Maudling who had spoken infamously in 1971 of seeing violence 'reduced to an acceptable level'.[24] In its place was something far more bullish, with Mason claiming in October 1977 that the IRA 'had waned to the point where they cannot sustain a campaign'.[25] By the end of the year he was claiming that the 'tide had turned against the men of violence'.[26] Mason believed that military victory over the IRA was a real possibility. In 1979 such optimism was to be dealt a heavy blow.

In November 1978, Brigadier J.M. Glover of the Defence Intelligence Staff had produced a report called 'Northern Ireland future terrorist trends'. Its aim was to look at future trends in the IRA. The report was leaked to Sinn Féin in May 1979 and it duly appeared in their weekly newspaper.[27] Sinn Féin's decision to publish the report was due to the fact that its contents flatly contradicted the optimistic view of the government in terms of beating the IRA. One conclusion was that

The Provisionals' campaign of violence is likely to continue while the British remain in Northern Ireland. We see little prospect of political developments of a kind which would seriously undermine the Provisionals' position.[28]

The Glover report remains the clearest army document spelling out the limitations of the British army in attempting to win the war in Northern Ireland. In 1978 the IRA was at its weakest position since its very creation. Ulsterisation, criminilisation and normalisation had hit the organisation hard. Yet the Glover report concluded that the organisation could not be militarily beaten. This led the British state to believe that only negotiations with the political representatives of the IRA could bring peace. Having shown that the exclusion of republicans from meaningful peace talks would make such talks meaningless, republicans had to create circumstances whereby it was possible for the British government to sit down with them. This necessitated a peace strategy. There are plenty of lessons here for both Israel and Hamas.

At the time of the January 2006 election, Mohammed al-Zahar talked of Hamas using 'a bullet and ballot box'[29] strategy. Knowingly or not, he was echoing the words of leading Sinn Féin figure Danny Morrison who in 1981 had proposed that republicans go forward 'with a ballot box in this hand and an armalite in this hand'.[30] The strategy formed the cornerstone of IRA and Sinn Féin policy until 1994. Central to those that supported it was the belief that it was possible to combine electoral politics with the armed struggle without harming either activity. Richard McAuley, Gerry Adams' press officer, argued in 1983 that 'the armed struggle would not stop Sinn Féin overtaking the SDLP as the main nationalist party in Northern Ireland'. He was also confident that there would be electoral success in the Irish Republic.[31]

There were those who disagreed with the strategy. Ivor Bell was a close colleague of Gerry Adams who had been part of the IRA delegation that met with Whitelaw in London in 1972. In 1982 he became IRA Chief of Staff. However Bell viewed Sinn Féin's growing involvement in electoral politics with deep concern especially in Belfast where 'operations had been scaled down to facilitate Adams' bid for the Belfast seat and then for Morrison's European contest'.[32] Bell was later forced to leave the republican movement.

Bell was right that there was an inherent contradiction between the armed struggle and electoral politics. Which takes primacy? Prior to 1982, the primacy of the armed struggle was obvious since there was no electoral strategy, but after the Sinn Féin successes in the elections of 1982 and 1983, the question became hugely relevant. Perhaps the best example of this contradiction was to occur in 1992 when the IRA blew up seven Protestant workmen at Teebane Cross in County Tyrone whose crime had been repairing British army bases. There was widespread condemnation of the killings, including from many within the nationalist community. Sinn Féin was barred from using the Mansion House in Dublin for their Ard Fheis that year because of their support for the armed struggle and there was a general consensus that the party had been damaged by the IRA operation. A senior figure in the IRA at the time described the IRA action rather differently claiming 'it was a first class operation which will have weakened the ability of the Brits to keep army bases operative'.[33] The simple fact was that although Sinn Féin and the IRA shared the same goal, their ways of achieving this were increasingly in sharp contradiction to each other.

Interviewed at the time, Adams was adamant that 'Sinn Féin support would not be affected by responses to any particular IRA operation'.[34] However, the loss of his West Belfast Westminster seat in April of that year to the SDLP's Joe Hendron did much to concentrate the minds of those republicans who wished to see further Sinn Féin electoral growth. Richard McAuley wrote in September of that year, 'We're not going to realise our full potential as long as the war is going on in the north and as long as Sinn Fein is presented the way it is with regard to armed struggle and violence.'[35]

This was the same Richard McAuley who ten years previously had not seen the IRA's armed struggle as an obstacle to Sinn Féin's electoral growth but now the reality of the situation had become apparent to him. For there to be a growth in the Sinn Féin vote on both sides of the border, the armalite and ballot box strategy had to be replaced by a strategy in which the armalite was no longer playing an active role. Another key Adams aide, Jim Gibney, called on republicans in the early 1990s not to be 'deafened by the deadly sound of their own gunfire'.[36] The fact that key aides of Adams could be so public in questioning the efficacy of the armed struggle meant that the republican movement was edging towards an historic decision.

The problems of trying to engage in constitutional politics while at the same time engaging or supporting an armed struggle was a key factor in the IRA's decision to call a ceasefire in 1994. Hamas have found to their cost that the relationship with violence has to be unambiguous. Since 2005 Hamas has observed a ceasefire or *tadiya* and indeed, at the time of its election, had not perpetrated any direct attack on Israel since 2003. However, in April 2006 Islamic Jihad carried out a suicide bombing in Tel Aviv. Eleven were killed, all of them civilians. Importantly Hamas refused to condemn the attack.

Sami Abu Zuhri, the official spokesman for Hamas, said that the attack was 'a natural result of the continued Israeli crimes' against Palestinians, adding that, 'Our people are in a state of self-defence and they have every right to use all means to defend themselves.[37] This refusal to condemn the slaughter may well have been an attempt 'to signal clearly that they would not be Israel's policeman in the territories'.[38]

However, the result was to associate the party running the Palestinian Authority with an act of appalling carnage. Teebane Cross may have been for the republican movement the final nail in the coffin of the ballot box and armalite strategy. The armed struggle was shown to be utterly counter-productive in the furtherance of republican aims. Hamas' refusal to condemn the Tel Aviv bombing made the further international isolation of the Palestinian Authority inevitable. If Hamas wants the world to listen to them, they cannot be quiet when such violence occurs.

Following the realisation that the continuation of the armed struggle was now harming, rather than helping, the republican struggle, the IRA moved towards a non-violent strategy. The decision to call a ceasefire in August 1994 followed three years of talks between republicans and representatives of the British government, which had started in October 1990.

As late as August 1989, the IRA had been claiming that 'At some point in the future, due to the pressure of the continuing and sustained armed struggle, the will of the British government will be broken.'[39] However, such statements were increasingly for internal republican consumption only. As time went on republicans had become aware not only of the problems for Sinn Féin electorally of the IRA remaining active but intriguingly of a British government using very different language in describing the relationship between Britain and Northern Ireland. Since becoming secretary of state in August 1989 Peter Brooke had spoken on various occasions about the circumstances in which open talks could occur between the government and Sinn Féin. Most famously, when asked whether he would speak to Adams and McGuinness, Brooke replied that he would not use the word 'never' and insisted that the government would be 'flexible' in approaching such a question.[40]

In November 1990, a month after secret talks began with republicans, Brooke made a statement which showed how far the British government was prepared to go to get the IRA to stop its violence. Speaking in his Westminster constituency Brooke gave the clearest expression ever as to the neutrality of the British government in approaching Northern Ireland. He declared: 'The British government has no selfish strategic or economic interest in Northern Ireland: our role is to help, enable and encourage.'[41]

Although Britain had granted Northern Ireland the right of self-determination back in 1949 in the so-called constitutional guarantee and this had been a cornerstone of every government paper since the outbreak of the Troubles, the Westminster speech was something very different. Brooke was expressly saying that Britain did not care if Northern Ireland remained part of the United Kingdom or chose to join the Irish Republic. If the IRA's campaign of violence was harming Sinn Féin, and if the British government had moved towards a position of declared neutrality, then what was the point of the armed struggle? From this moment onwards, the question of a ceasefire was about timing, not principle.

The ceasefire moved Sinn Féin to the centre of politics in Northern Ireland and gave it a real chance of an electoral breakthrough in the Republic. However, such a dramatic change of tactics by republicans has inevitably brought about criticism from those who believe that Adams and McGuinness have sold the movement short. The most important of these on the military side were the Real IRA (RIRA) who, rather like the Provisionals back in 1969, had split from the movement in 1997 when they considered that the IRA had turned their back on traditional values and had become seduced by the false gold of electoral politics.

Their relevance was greatly diminished following their bombing of Omagh town centre in August 1998, which resulted in twenty-nine deaths, the highest number of casualties in the whole of the Troubles in Northern Ireland. The bombing cost RIRA what little credibility it had possessed previously. The IRA, in the wake of Omagh, has been greatly helped by the inability of republican critics to mobilise a real alternative to them.

The strength of the 1998 Good Friday Agreement is that the neutrality of the British government has allowed unionists and nationalists to hold power without actually agreeing on the constitutional future of Northern Ireland. Tony Blair argued in June 2006 that 'The problem we had in Northern Ireland is that there has never been agreement on the basic nature of the final outcome, one part wanting union with the UK, the other with the Republic of Ireland.'[42] The disagreement over the future constitutional status of Northern Ireland has, of course, been at the very heart of the Troubles. However, the fact that republicans have never had to commit themselves to the long-term existence of the Northern Irish state made their participation in the peace process and support for the Good Friday agreement much easier. In practical terms the participation of Sinn Féin in the Northern Ireland executive from 1999 meant that it was accepting the constitutional legitimacy of Northern Ireland, yet you will never find a Sinn Fein statement accepting the right of Northern Ireland to exist. The important point to remember is that this is a peace process not based on an agreed outcome and this has made it far easier for republicans to participate in it.

The comparison with the Middle East could hardly be greater. Hamas has been told by Israel, the European Union and the United States that acceptance of a two-state solution is imperative if there is to be dialogue. Hamas has refused to do this. In October 2006 Ismail Haniya, the Palestinian Prime Minister told a large crowd of supporters that: 'We will not recognise Israel, we will not recognise Israel, we will not recognise Israel.'[43]

Hamas must realise that the situation in the Middle East, in this sense, is very different from Northern Ireland. The IRA has not had to recognise publicly Northern Ireland because the British state has accepted that Northern Ireland has the right of self-determination. The Good Friday agreement has recognised 'the legitimacy of whatever choice is freely exercised by a majority of the people of Northern Ireland with regard to its status, whether they prefer to continue to support the Union with Great Britain or a sovereign united Ireland.'[44] Demographically this may well mean that the democratic choice of Northern Ireland by the third decade of this century would be to end partition. For Hamas, there has to be an understanding that, in the context of an Israeli–Palestinian settlement, partition is permanent.

For Irish republicans, the role of the international community was key in pushing forward their peace strategy. The strength of the Irish diaspora in the United States meant that there were few in that country opposed to a united Ireland per se. Republican violence was condemned but the aspiration of a united Ireland was always politically acceptable. Once the IRA was on ceasefire, invites to the White House quickly followed. The strength of the Jewish Diaspora in the United States means that acceptance of a two-state strategy by Hamas is the only way any US government could ever talk to Hamas. This is a lesson which Fatah eventually learnt. Hamas has got to learn it too.

There are lessons that Hamas can learn from the Irish republican experience but they are not straightforward. If Hamas was to attempt to go down the same road as the IRA, the outcome might well not be so rewarding. However, the party must start, as Irish republicans did, with understanding 'the pitfalls of maximalism'.[45] Irish republicans accepted the idea of participation in a partitioned Northern Irish state, thereby rejecting their traditional policy of demanding a British commitment to military and political withdrawal. Hamas needs to refine its programme so that its maximalist demands are replaced by policies, which cannot be so easily rejected by Israel.

For Hamas this will be far more difficult than in the Irish case. From 1990 onwards, Irish republicans were being told that if the armed struggle were to stop, then they would find that major political progress would follow. The Downing Street declaration[46] published by the London and Dublin governments at the end of 1993 was, in essence, a call to Irish republicans to come inside. A ceasefire was called eight months later.

There is little evidence to suggest that Israel would contemplate such a strategy. Their strategy since the Hamas election has been to deny that result and argue that 'there is no Palestinian partner'.[47] Unless Israel is prepared to move, then no progress can be made. Efraim Halevy, a former head of Israel's secret service, has argued that for there to be peace then in the first place Israel should recognise Hamas.[48] That is what the British government did after 1990 with Irish republicans. Israel appears unlikely to do the same with Hamas in the foreseeable future. Hamas must therefore remove the obstacles in the way of such recognition. The lessons from Ireland are that it has no other choice.

NOTES

1 *Twelfth Report of the Independent Monitoring Commission*, 4 October 2006, p. 9.
2 Ibid., p. 8.
3 *Irish Times*, 5 October 2006.
4 Ibid.
5 *Irish Times*, 27 July 2005.
6 *Irish Times*, 5 September 2006.
7 Ibid.
8 Speech by Tony Blair at Georgetown University, 26 May 2006, Downing Street Press Office: www.number-10.gov.uk/output,page9549.asp.
9 *Irish Times*, 23 March 2006.
10 When, for example, this author suggested on a BBC Radio programme in February 2006 that there could be lessons learnt from the IRA experiences for both Hamas and Israel, he was roundly condemned by a number of pro-Israeli academics and writers both during and after the programme, *The Moral Maze*, BBC Radio 4, 2 February 2006.
11 *Irish Times*, 27 January 2006.
12 http://memritv.org/Transcript.asp?P1=1014.
13 http://www.mideastweb.org/hamas.htm.
14 Ed Moloney, *A Secret History of the IRA*, London, 2002, p. xiii.
15 Michael Kerr, *Imposing Power-sharing: Conflict and Coexistence in Northern Ireland and Lebanon*, Dublin, 2005, p. 73.
16 Sinn Féin, *Where Sinn Féin Stands*, Dublin 1970.
17 Richard English, *Armed Struggle: The History of the IRA*, London 2003, p. 125.
18 Sinn Fein, *Eire Nua*, Dublin 1972.
19 Gerard Murray and Jonathan Tonge, *Sinn Fein and the SDLP: From Alienation to Participation*, Dublin, 2005, p.39.
20 Sean MacStiofián, *Memoirs of a Revolutionary*, Dublin, 1975, p. 275.
21 Author interview with William Whitelaw, London, 5 October 1986.
22 Moloney, *A Secret History of the IRA*, p.142.
23 Graham Walker, *A History of the Ulster Unionist Party: Protest, Pragmatism and Pessimism*, Manchester, 2004, p. 219.
24 M. Wallace, *British Government in Northern Ireland: From Devolution to Direct Rule*, London, 1982, p. 54.
25 *Irish Times*, 16 May 1977.
26 *Irish Times*, 30 December 1977.
27 *An Phoblacht/Republican News*, 12 May 1979.
28 Ibid.
29 *Observer*, 22 January 2006.
30 *An Phoblacht/Republican News*, 5 November 1981.
31 Author interview with Richard McAuley, Belfast, 4 September 1983.
32 Moloney, *A Secret History of the IRA*, pp. 242–3.
33 Author interview with IRA member, Dublin, 30 January 1992.
34 Author interview with Gerry Adams, Dublin, 30 January 1992.
35 'Time for Magnanimity' *Fortnight*, No 309, September 1992 p. 5.

36 Murray and Tonge, *Sinn Féin and the SDLP*, p.181.
37 http://news.bbc.co.uk/1/hi/world/middle_east/4915868.stm.
38 Alastair Crooke, 'Talking to Hamas', *Prospect*, June 2006, p. 50.
39 *An Phoblacht/Republican News*, 17 August 1989.
40 Eamonn Mallie and David McKittrick, *The Fight for Peace*, London, 1996, p. 100.
41 Ibid, p.107.
42 Speech by Tony Blair at Georgetown University, 26 May 2006, Downing Street Press Office:
    www.number-10.gov.uk/output,page9549.asp.
43 http://english.aljazeera.net/NR/exeres/5E24D771-2ED1-4368-BCB8-EFDB83584E71.htm
44 *Agreement between the Government of the United Kingdom of Great Britain and Northern Ireland and
    the Government of Ireland*, London, HMSO, 1998, p. 3.
45 D.L. Horowitz, 'The Northern Ireland agreement: Clear, Consociational and Risky', in J.
    McGarry (ed.), *Northern Ireland and the Divided World*, Oxford, 2001, pp. 103–5.
46 *Joint Declaration*, London, HMSO, 1993.
47 *The Economist*, 8 July 2006, p. 12.
48 Crooke, 'Talking to Hamas', p. 50.

Deadly Decisions: Israel's Policy of Targeted Killing

Steven R. David

Israel has openly pursued a policy of targeted killing since the outbreak of the second intifada in September 2000. The Israelis have identified, located and then killed alleged Palestinian terrorists with fighter aircraft, helicopter gunships, tanks, car bombs, booby traps and bullets. Over 200 Palestinian militants (and more than 100 innocent bystanders) have been killed prompting international condemnation, domestic soul searching and bloody retaliation. Given its controversial nature and obvious costs, it is worth considering whether this policy is worth pursuing. Why has Israel embarked on a policy of targeted killings? Has the policy been effective in reducing Palestinian attacks on Israeli civilians? Are targeted killings permitted by Israeli and international law? Is it moral? Most important, is the policy of targeted killing in the Israeli national interest?

The answers to these questions are of critical importance. For Israel, it is necessary to know whether its policy of targeted killings is pragmatically and ethically justified. If it is, it makes sense for Israel to continue, or even expand, upon this approach. If there are serious shortcomings, they need to be highlighted so that the policy can be modified or discarded. For countries outside Israel, and especially the United States, assessing the worth of targeted killings is hardly less significant. Ever since the terror attacks of 11 September 2001, much of the world, with the United States in the lead, has sought ways to counter terrorism. If the Israelis have embarked upon a successful approach, it makes sense to emulate them.

If Israeli policy is fundamentally flawed, however, better to understand that now, especially when voices demanding that terrorists be hunted down and killed have grown so loud. Either way, learning from the Israeli experience is central to those seeking to combat the threat from terrorism.

This chapter argues that the policy of targeted killing is in Israel's interests and, subject to certain guidelines, should be retained. Despite many short-comings, targeted killings have proven to be effective in reducing terrorist attacks while providing a sense of retribution to a population under siege. So long as Israel's adversaries target innocent civilians as a prime goal of its military operations, Jerusalem will have little choice but to continue this practice.

DEFINITION AND HISTORICAL BACKGROUND

Targeted killing is the intentional slaying of a specific individual or group of individuals undertaken with explicit governmental approval. It is not 'assassination' for three reasons. First, assassination typically has a pejorative connotation of 'murder by treacherous means'. Whether the Israeli killing of alleged Palestinian terrorists is 'treacherous' or not is a debatable proposition that should not be assumed a priori by employing loaded terms such as assassination. Second, assassination usually refers to the killing of a politically prominent individual to effect political change. For the most part – though not exclusively – Israel has focused on killing armed combatants and those who plan the actual attacks. Finally, Israel itself does not use the term, 'assassination', and instead prefers 'targeted thwarting' or 'interceptions'.[1]

While it is not necessary to accept Israeli terminology for their actions, neither does it make sense to accept the terminology of their critics. Targeted killing accurately refers to what the Israelis actually do, with a minimum of semantic baggage implying approval or disapproval of their actions.

The practice of targeted killing by Israel is not new. Underground Jewish groups in the period before Israeli independence such as the Hagana, Irgun and Lehi often cited biblical and ancient historical examples to justify their own practices of targeted killing. These groups had little compunction about eliminating individuals who supported the British occupation of Palestine. A few of the victims were prominent figures, such as the mediator, Count Bernadotte. Most, however, were fellow Jews suspected of being informers.[2] Some of the leaders of these groups, such as Menachem Begin and Yitzhak Shamir, later reached the post of Israeli Prime Minister, despite having sanctioned targeted killings in the past and perhaps with the belief that this policy helped them achieve their aims.

From its independence in 1948 to the present, Israel has used the policy of targeted killings to advance its interests. When the intensity of the Arab–Israeli conflict is high, especially if the main antagonist is the Palestinians, the number of targeted killings rise. At times of relative peace, such as just after the signing of the Oslo Peace Accords in 1993, targeted killings drop. While the numbers may fluctuate, this practice has never totally disappeared. Exact figures are difficult to come by, because Israel does not always publicly acknowledge responsibility for a specific killing. Nevertheless, in most cases it is clear who is responsible. Israeli attacks are characterised by their professionalism, efforts to minimise innocent casualties, and (occasionally) the sophistication of the weapons used (such as helicopter gun-ships and F-16 fighters). The identity of the target also provides a strong indication of Israeli responsibility; when an enemy of Israel is killed it is usually not difficult to determine who is behind the operation.

The persistence of the Israeli policy of targeted killing can be seen by a brief historical overview. Examples of targeted killings provided are meant to be illustrative, not exhaustive. In the 1950s, Israel focused its targeted killings on efforts to halt *fedayeen* attacks from Egypt. Two senior Egyptian military intelligence officials in charge of fedayeen operations were killed by mail bombs sent by Israeli intelligence.[3] In the 1960s, Israel's policies of targeted killing had another key success when mail bombs were again sent, this time to German scientists developing missiles capable of reaching Israel from Nasser's Egypt. The bombs, sent to the scientists and their families, convinced the scientists to return to Germany, bringing about an end to the missile programme.[4]

The administration of the territories following Israel's victory in the 1967 war and an increase in Palestinian terror operations dramatically increased the use of targeted killings by Israel. General Ariel Sharon commanded an anti-terror detachment in 1971 that attempted to eliminate Palestinian militants from Gaza. Often posing as Arab civilians or guerrillas, Sharon's unit killed 104 Palestinians and arrested 742 others.[5] The slaughter of eleven Israeli athletes at the Munich Olympics galvanized the policy of targeted killing as no previous event had done. Israel established 'Committee X' chaired by Prime Minister Golda Meir and Defence Minister Moshe Dayan.

The committee oversaw a mission in which agents of the Israeli foreign intelligence service, the Mossad, systematically hunted down and killed the Black September members responsible for the Olympic massacre. Beginning in October 1972, the killings continued over the next year resulting in thirteen deaths.[6] Israel's war with the Palestine Liberation Organisation (PLO) escalated in April 1973 when three of its leaders were killed in separate apartments in Beirut. Ehud Barak, the future Prime Minister, led the successful operation.

The 1980s saw Israel attempt to kill two Palestinian leaders, one of which was successful. The failed effort occurred following the Israeli intervention into Lebanon in the spring of 1982, when Israel tried several times to kill PLO leader Yasser Arafat. Despite the use of booby trapped cars and air attacks, Arafat emerged unscathed. Israeli efforts proved more successful when an Israeli hit squad killed Arafat's second-in-command, Abu Jihad (Khalil el-Wazir) in Tunisia in the spring of 1988. The decision to kill Jihad stemmed from his role in planning several terrorist actions against Israel, including the bloody hijacking of an Israeli bus in March 1988. More important, Israel saw Abu Jihad as an irreplaceable leader who held the PLO together and was central to the success of the first Arab intifada that began in 1987. Ehud Barak reportedly drew on his 1973 Beirut experience in planning the joint IDF/Mossad raid that killed Jihad.[7]

Three major targeted killing operations took place in the 1990s. One was successful, one a failure, and one achieved mixed results. The successful operation killed Palestinian Islamic Jihad head, Fathi Shikaki, in Malta in October 1995. No competent successor emerged to replace Shikaki, leaving Islamic Jihad in disarray.[8] The mixed outcome stemmed from the January 1996 killing of Yahya Ayyash, known as 'the engineer', in Gaza. Ayyash was killed while speaking on a mobile telephone that had been booby trapped by the Israeli domestic intelligence agency, Shin Bet. Ayyash had been one of Hamas' most skilled and prolific bomb-makers whose handiwork proved critical to many terror attacks against Israel. Although Jerusalem succeeded in removing a key figure from Hamas, Ayyash's death also unleashed four suicide bus bombings in the next two months, killing more than fifty Israelis.

Finally, in an embarrassing, almost comic episode, Israel failed to kill Khaled Meshal, the chief of Hamas' political bureau in Amman, Jordan, in September 1997. Two Mossad agents succeeded in poisoning Meshal, but were captured by Jordanian authorities before they could leave the country. In order to secure the return of the two operatives, Israeli Prime Minister Benjamin Netanyahu agreed to provide the antidote for the poison (thus bringing about Meshal's recovery) and released Hamas' founder, Sheik Ahmed Yassin, from an Israeli prison. As a result of this episode, Israel damaged its relationship with Jordan, a friendly Arab country, and infuriated Canada when it was revealed that the Mossad agents had used Canadian passports.[9] Meshal, now operating from Syria, has emerged as the principal leader of Hamas and is believed to have been behind the 2006 kidnapping of an Israeli soldier that sparked the ensuing Israeli–Hezbollah war.

TARGETED KILLINGS DURING THE SECOND INTIFADA

A wave of targeted killing began in November 2000, as a consequence of the beginning of the second Palestinian intifada. Following the failure of the Camp David accords in the summer of 2000 and Ariel Sharon's visit to the Temple Mount in late September, the Palestinians unleashed a violent revolt against Israel. Unlike the first intifada, in which the ratio of Palestinians to Jews killed was roughly 25 to 1, in the second intifada, a well-armed Palestinian force making free use of suicide bombers reduced that proportion to three to one.[10] Israel responded to these increasingly lethal attacks with military incursions into Palestinian-controlled areas; an increase in the use of checkpoints to control Palestinian movements; the building of a security barrier; and a dramatic rise in the slaying of Palestinian militants.

In one sense, there was nothing new about Israel's policy of targeted killing during the second intifada. As indicated above, Israel has pursued targeted killings throughout its history. What was new was the scale of the effort – never have so many militants been killed in such a short span of time. Also new were some of the tactics, particularly the use of helicopter gunships and fighter aircraft to execute individuals. Because of the extent of the campaign and the obvious use of Israeli military assets, the Israeli government has been forced to acknowledge its role in targeted killings to a much greater extent than previously, although it still refuses routinely to claim responsibility for its operations.[11]

Several high ranking Palestinians have been killed during the second intifada. They include the head of the Popular Front for the Liberation of Palestine (PFLP), Abu Ali Mustafa, the secretary-general of the PFLP, Mustafa Zibri, one of the leaders of the Tanzim movement, Raed al-Karmi, and a senior official of Hamas, Sheik Salah Shehada. Most of those killed, however, were mid-level fighters, important enough to disrupt a terrorist cell but not so important as to provoke murderous retaliation. The targets of the attack usually knew they were being sought. Israel identified them through its intelligence apparatus and through collaborators. Israel claims that she only targets those who are on their way to a terrorist attack or are actively planning one. During the early months of the second intifada, when the Israelis had ongoing talks with the Palestinian Authority (PA), they would hand over a list to the PA of the suspected terrorists. If the PA did not arrest the individuals, Israel killed them.[12] Once talks broke down with the PA in the spring of 2002, and especially with the emergence of a Hamas government in 2006, efforts to enlist the help of the PA to arrest the militants presumably ended.

HOW EFFECTIVE IS THE POLICY OF TARGETED KILLING?

There is no question that Israel's policy of targeted killing has hurt the capability of its Arab adversaries to prosecute attacks against Israel. Terrorism is essentially an offensive action, making counter-offensive actions such as targeted killing an especially effective response. It is exceedingly difficult for Israel to defend or deter terror attacks from Palestinians. In terms of defence, there are literally tens of thousands of targets in Israel for Palestinian terrorists. Power stations, government officials, bus depots, airports, skyscrapers, open air markets, sport stadiums – the list is endless. It is impossible to defend them all, especially against a determined adversary that can choose the time and place of attack. Although, as discussed below, some level of deterrence of terrorism is achievable, dissuading potential terrorists is not easy when they are eager to die for their cause. In such situations, the best response to terrorism is to go on the counter-offensive, that is, to eliminate the terrorist threat before it can be launched, hence the policy of targeted killing.[13]

In fact, Israel's policy of targeted killing has done much to reduce the threat of suicide bombings during the second intifada. As Daniel Byman notes, Hamas, the principal antagonist of Israel, killed 185 Israelis in 2002, but only twenty-one in 2005. The sharp decline in Israeli deaths did not come about because of a decline in attacks by Hamas, which actually skyrocketed from thirty-four in 2002 to 179 in 2005. Instead, each Hamas attack proved much less destructive.[14] The reasons for this dramatic decline have much to do with the success of targeted killing in eliminating, discouraging and disrupting terrorist operations.

Targeted killings have impeded the effectiveness of Palestinian terrorist organisations because leadership, planning, and tactical skills are confined to a few key individuals. There are a limited number of people who have the technical ability to make bombs and plan attacks. If these people are eliminated, the ability to mount attacks is degraded. There is some evidence that targeted killings have reduced the performance of Palestinian operations. The large number of intercepted suicide bombers (Israelis estimate they stop over 80 per cent of attempts) and poorly planned attacks (e.g. suicide bombers who appear with wires sticking out of their bag or detonations that occur with little loss of life) indicates that there are problems either with the organisation of operations or those available to carry them out.[15] There are individual leaders whose charisma and organisational skills keep a group together. If they are eliminated, they are not easily replaced.[16] Shikaki of the Islamic Jihad falls into this category.

Another clear benefit of targeting killing is keeping would-be bombers and bomb-makers on the run. When the Israelis informed the PA who they were after, this information was often passed on to the targeted individuals so that they knew they were being hunted. Some voluntarily chose to place themselves in Palestinian custody to avoid being slain. The threat they posed to Israel was consequently diminished. There are numerous accounts of others on the 'hit' list taking precautions against being killed such as sleeping in a different location every night and not letting others know of their whereabouts.[17] Even for those Palestinians who have not been told they are being hunted, the very possibility they might be targeted is likely to cause a change in behaviour. Time and effort undertaken to avoid Israeli dragnets are time and effort not used to plan or carry out operations against Israel.

Targeted killing also acts as a deterrent. In one sense, it appears virtually impossible to deter people willing, and even eager, to lose their life. However, behind every suicide bomber are others who might not be as ready for martyrdom. The large numbers of Palestinian commanders who surrendered meekly to Israeli forces during the large-scale military incursions in the spring of 2002 lends support to the notion that many senior officials do not wish to die for their cause. It is also reasonable to assume that there are skilled, capable Palestinians who do not engage in terrorist operations for fear of Israeli reprisals.

Most important, there is strong evidence that the policy of targeted killing hurts Palestinian organisations to the extent that they are willing to alter their behaviour. Former Israeli Prime Minister Ariel Sharon met with three Palestinian leaders (though not Yasser Arafat) on 30 January 2002. When Sharon asked the Palestinians what they wanted from him, first on their list was an end to targeted killings.[18] Islamic Jihad and Hamas agreed to refrain from launching attacks in pre-1967 Israel in December 2001 so long as Israel refrained from killing its leaders. The ceasefire adopted by Hamas and other Palestinian groups in 2005 was, at least in part, due to the harm inflicted on the group by Israel's policy of targeted killing.

Targeted killing is popular with the Israeli public. A poll conducted by *Ma'ariv* and the Mutagim Institute in July 2001 found that 90 per cent of the Israeli public supported the policy. There appears to be a near universal belief that targeted killing represents an appropriate response to terror attacks. No other Israeli policy including incursions into Palestinian territory, the arrest of militants, the erection of a barrier, or the forced transfer of Palestinians from the territories to neighbouring Arab countries, enjoys the same level of support as the targeted killing policy. Since the approval spans the Israeli body politic, it is well received by all political parties representing diverse Israeli views. Democracies follow public opinion and targeted killing is a policy that has never lost favour with the Israeli electorate.

Targeted killing has also proven effective in the battle for public relations throughout the world. Although Israel has been criticised in the media for slaying Palestinian militants, the criticism has been far less than that levelled at other policies. When, for example, Israel attacks Palestinian cities, there is no lack of coverage of the innocent deaths that result or the widespread suffering imposed on a mostly non-combatant society. Targeted killings, at least, focus on specific adversaries who mean Israel harm. That there is rarely television coverage of the actual operation is another benefit. Israel's image was greatly tarnished in the summer of 2006 due to air strikes that killed hundreds of innocent Lebanese civilians. The Israeli effort to hunt down and eliminate Hezbollah's leaders received far less criticism.

To be sure, targeted killing has drawbacks. Despite its effectiveness in limiting Israeli casualties over time more than 1000 Israelis were killed during the second intifada at a time when targeted killing was at its peak. Why has targeted killing not worked better?

Organisations promoting terror against Israel such as Hamas, Islamic Jihad and the PA are very decentralised. They are made up of many cells, the destruction of some having little or no impact on others. There is also no doubt that targeted killing, at least in some instances, increases the terrorist threat against Israel by producing murderous retaliation. The killings of 'the engineer' (Yahiya Ayyash), Tanzim chief Raed al-Karmi and Hamas head Sheik Salah Shehada all resulted in dramatic escalations in attacks against Israelis with revenge explicitly cited as the motivation for the actions. Targeted killing hurts Israeli interests by removing current adversaries who may prove to be useful negotiating partners in the future. When Israel killed Arafat's second in command, Abu Jihad, in 1988, it eliminated not only an individual behind several bloody operations, but also someone on the right wing of the PLO who many saw as a pragmatist capable of making peaceful compromises.

Locating and killing key Palestinian terrorists requires timely intelligence, much of which can only be supplied by informers. Given that a limited number of people will know the whereabouts of the targets, it will not be difficult to isolate those who have collaborated with Israel. Increasing reports of informers being killed during the second intifada, with their bodies publicly displayed, may partly be a result of their identities becoming known as a result of the targeting killing policy.[19] Targeted killing has also helped weaken Palestinian society as the search for real and suspected collaborators undermines the trust necessary to build a sense of community.[20] Finally, Israel's policy of targeted killing has been condemned by the Arab world, Europe, the United Nations and even the United States. Clearly, targeted killing is a policy with serious shortcomings.

Nevertheless, despite its drawbacks, it is hard to argue with the success of targeted killing in stemming the tide of terrorism that Israel experienced during the second intifada. Largely because of this policy Israel has reduced the terror threat to pre-intifada levels. Targeted killing has prevented count-less attacks against Israel, weakened the effectiveness of terrorist organisations, kept potential bomb-makers on the run, deterred terrorist operations, gained the support of an overwhelming per centage of the Israeli population, and done so while largely avoiding the sharp glare of publicity. It has not prevented all acts of terrorism, nor can it. But as part of a larger array of policies, including the security barrier, checkpoints, and incursions, it is seen to be a successful response to an intolerable threat.

IN SUPPORT OF THE ISRAELI POLICY OF TARGETED KILLING

Despite some shortcomings, the policy of targeted killing makes sense for Israel. It does so first on moral grounds. Yes, there is widespread agreement that targeted killing raises disturbing moral issues. After all, Israel is killing individuals without any trial or due process. Innocent people are sometimes killed in these operations. It offends our sense of moral sensibility when government officials are reduced to the role of hit squads, as if they were part of some Mafia-like organisation. The bedrock of Western democracy established by philosophers such as Thomas Hobbes and John Locke is limited government. How can that principle reconcile itself with a government that deprives people of their life without proper judicial proceedings? The moral squeamishness that the policy entails is demonstrated by the reluctance that Israel manifests when it refuses to comment on various killings for which it is clearly responsible. Israel may defend its right in the abstract to pursue a policy of targeted killing, but clearly the specifics of doing so is not something with which it is comfortable.

All this notwithstanding, the Israeli policy of targeted killing rests on an unassailable moral foundation. Just War tradition from the time of Saint Augustine to the present has emphasized the need for armed conflict to be discriminate and proportionate in the pursuit of legitimate ends for the use of force to be moral.[21] There is no question that the policy of targeted killing meets these criteria. Targeted killing is discriminatory in that it focuses exclusively on one's adversaries. Civilian casualties and collateral damage are minimised. It is proportionate in that only enough force is used to accomplish the task. Targeted killings does not employ large numbers of troops, bombers, artillery and other means that can leave in their wake far more destruction than they prevent; and targeted killing serves a legitimate end by striking at those who threaten the lives of innocents. Since the policy is applied against those on their way to terrorist attacks or those who make such attacks possible, targeted killing enables Israel to protect its civilians by eliminating those who would murder them. Far from being morally questionable, it would be difficult to come up with an approach in warfare that rests on stronger moral ground.

Retribution is an even more powerful justification for the Israeli policy of targeted killing. Retribution, in its purest sense, has no utilitarian component. It is not motivated by vengeance. Even if the victims do not care about the offence committed or are opposed to punishing the aggressors, punishment nevertheless must be carried out. Nor is retribution motivated by deterrence or a need to satisfy the demands of an aggrieved population. If it can be shown that deterrence will not be enhanced by retaliation or that the community has no wish to strike back, retribution still demands the punishment of the guilty. Retribution is driven by the belief that offenders need to be punished because such punishment is warranted. This concept of 'just deserts' is compellingly put forward by the theorist Michael Moore who writes, 'Retributivism is the view that punishment is justified by the moral culpability of those who receive it. A retributivist punishes because, and only because, the offender deserves it.'[22]

Israel's policy of targeted killing, stripped of its utilitarian aspects, is retribution, plain and simple. Palestinian suicide bombers seek out the most innocent of Israeli civilians – old men, women, children and infants – and attempt to kill as many of them as they can. Stopping these operations before they can inflict their horrific harm is of obvious importance and provides some of the justification for targeted killings. But what of those who plan the attacks, arm the bombers and send them on their way? How are they to be punished? The Palestinian Authority is unwilling or unable to arrest the perpetrators, many of whom are PA officials. Who, then, aside from Israel will provide the just desserts to these terrorists? Even if the policy of targeted killing does not reduce Israeli causalities, even if it increases them, such a policy is justified because it is only through this approach that the terrorists get what they inflict on others – a violent death.

There is a danger that retribution, like revenge, can get out of hand. In order to prevent this from happening, two limits on retribution need to be imposed, both of which are consistent with Israel's policy of targeted killing. First, the punishment must fit the crime. Retributivists emphasise that the response to an action must be proportionate to that action. Since Palestinian terrorists are bent on killing Israeli civilians, killing them in return (or those who send them on their missions) is a fitting reaction. Second, the punishment must be focused on those who are actually committing the offence, with innocents spared. As the moral philosopher Judith Lichtenberg writes,

> while the principle of retribution says that the guilty must be punished, equally important is its demand that only the guilty may be punished. Punishment must be tailored to reach those who have done wrong and leave untouched those who have not.[23]

Targeted killing, when done properly, achieves this goal by focusing retaliation on the actual perpetrators of terrorism. It is true that targeted killing that also results in innocent casualties weakens the retributive rationale. But given the greater risks of innocent Palestinians being killed by other forms of retaliation such as military strikes against urban areas, targeted killing best fits the retributive model of appropriate punishment for the guilty.

Targeted killing supports Israel's interests because among the possible responses Israel can mount against terrorism, it is the least bad option. As discussed, Israel has responded to terror in several ways, all of which have major drawbacks. Checkpoints humiliate and inconvenience a large portion of the Palestinian population, producing resentment and seething hatred. Israeli raids to arrest militants result in civilian casualties. Air strikes kill hundreds of innocents. Not only are these actions morally repugnant, they also plant seeds of hatred, fomenting further terrorism in the future.

Aside from anti-Israeli extremists and pacifists, few counsel Israel to simply endure suicide bombing attacks and do nothing. The question then becomes what, for Israel, is the correct response to terrorism. From hawks, military strikes along with continued occupation are attractive options, though not so much to replace targeted killings as to supplement them. From Israel's international critics, there are few suggestions for how Israel should combat terrorism, only condemnation of whatever armed response Israel undertakes along with demands for Israeli political concessions. Targeted killing may achieve international approval not so much for what the policy has achieved, but rather because it is less objectionable than the alternatives. Although not a ringing endorsement, targeted killing may survive because it is indeed the least bad choice for a state confronted with the threat of terrorism.

CONCLUSIONS

The policy of targeted killing is very much in Israel's interest. Terrorists on their way to operations against Israeli civilians are intercepted before they unleash their carnage. Bomb-makers and commanders are eliminated, with skilled replacements not always available. Enemies spend time trying to survive rather than planning attacks and potential recruits are discouraged from offering their support. Targeted killing signals to the Israeli people, adversaries of Israel, and the world at large that those who seek to kill the innocent in an effort to spread fear for political purposes will pay the ultimate penalty. Targeted killing provides retribution. Given the Palestinian Authority's inability, or unwillingness, to punish terrorists, the task of rendering justice to those who attack innocent civilians falls into the hands of the Israelis. It is true that targeted killing sometimes provokes murderous retaliation, but given the range of options open to the Israeli government to respond to terror, it remains the most effective and least morally problematic policy for Israel to follow.

There is little doubt that Israel will continue to pursue targeted killing, raising the question of how this policy can be improved. I suggest four improvements, all designed to make certain that the benefits of targeted killing are not overwhelmed by the very real dangers that such a policy can bring about. First, Israel should be open and unapologetic about its pursuit of targeted killings. Targeted killing is a legitimate and moral response to terrorist attacks. There is no need for Israel to evade responsibility for carrying out this policy, especially when Israeli involvement is obvious. Denial or refusal to comment leaves Jerusalem open to the charge that it is behaving improperly or has something to hide. Neither is the case and Israel should not behave like it is.

Second, Israel needs to make sure that its pursuit of targeted killing does not degenerate into lawlessness and savagery that makes it undistinguishable from the threat it seeks to counter. The guidelines that Israel has already instituted for targeted killing need to be strengthened and become the subject of open debate. Along with the directive that targeted killing should be carried out only against combatants on their way to committing terrorist acts or against those who are known to be behind them, Israel must also do more to ensure that decisions on actual killings are overseen by elected officials. As a democracy, Israel needs to entrust the monumental decisions on who to kill to those who are responsible to the Israeli people.

Third, Israel must refrain from killing political leaders when they are not engaged in waging war against the Jewish state. Granted, the distinction between political leaders and those who plan terrorist attacks is at best ambiguous and at times non-existent. Nevertheless, for the norm against assassination to survive – a norm that Israel needs as much as any state – a distinction must be drawn between political leaders and combatants. Just as the Israeli government tolerated Yasser Arafat, despite his active backing of terrorist operations, so too must it avoid the targeting of lesser leaders provided their main activities are political. If, however, it is determined that a leader's principal role is launching attacks against Israel, than he becomes a legitimate target.

Finally, Israel needs to announce publicly that the policy of targeted killing is a temporary expedient while it is engaged in armed conflict with its enemies. Israel must unambiguously declare that if a leadership emerges that makes peace with Israel, and proves itself capable and willing to curb terrorism, targeted killing will stop. Targeted killing makes sense and is justifiable only as a weapon of war. Once that war is over, the policy must end.

Targeted killing is an unsavoury practice for an unsavoury time. It can never take the place of a political settlement, which is the only solution to the terror that confronts Israel. Until such a settlement is achieved, however, targeted killing stands out as a measured response to a horrific threat. It is distinctly attractive because it focuses on the actual perpetrators of terror, while largely sparing the innocent. For a dangerous region in an imperfect world, targeted killing is the worst possible policy – except for all the others.

NOTES

1 Samantha M. Shapiro, 'Announced Assassinations', *New York Times Magazine*, 9 December 2001.
2 Nachman Ben-Yehuda, *Political Assassinations by Jews: A Rhetorical Device for Justice*, Albany, NY, 1993, pp. 99–104.
3 Ibid., p. 304; Dan Raviv and Yossi Melman, *Every Spy a Prince: The Complete History of Israel's Intelligence Community*, Boston, MA, 1990, p. 122.
4 Raviv and Melman, *Every Spy a Prince*, p. 122.
5 Ibid., p. 247.
6 Ian Black and Benny Morris, *Israel's Secret Wars: A History of Israel's Intelligence Services*, New York, 1991, pp. 272–7; Ali Hassan Salameh, the Black September operations officer who planned the Munich massacre and was the target of the Lillihammer attack, was eventually killed by a car bomb in Beirut in 1979.
7 Ibid., p. 392.
8 Michael Eisenstadt, 'Pre-Emptive Targeted Killings as a Counter-Terror Tool: An Assessment of Israel's Approach', *Peacewatch*, No. 342, 28 August 2001, Washington D.C., p. 1.
9 Barton Gellman, 'For Many Israelis, Assassination is only as Bad as its Execution', *Washington Post*, 12 October 1997.
10 James Bennet, *New York Times*, 12 March 2002.
11 Shapiro, 'Announced Assassinations', p. 54.
12 Aaron Harel and Gideon Alon, 'IDF Lawyers Set 'Conditions' for Assassination Policy', *Ha'aretz*, 4 February 2002; Shapiro, 'Announced Assassinations', p. 54.
13 For a similar view regarding dealing with terrorism in general see Richard K. Betts, 'The

Soft Underbelly of American Primacy: Tactical Advantages of Terror', *Political Science Quarterly* (Spring 2002) p. 33.

14 Daniel Byman, 'Do Targeted Killings Work?', *Foreign Affairs*, March–April 2006, p. 103.
15 Eisenstadt, 'Pre-Emptive Targeted Killings as a Counter-Terror Tool', p. 2 .
16 Brian Michael Jenkins, 'Should our Arsenal Against Terrorism Include Assassination?', The Rand Corporation, Santa Monica, p. 4.
17 See, for example, the account of a victim in Yael Stein, 'Israel's Assassination Policy: Extra Judicial Executions' (Translated By Maya Johnson), www.btselem.org, p. 6.
18 William Safire, 'Sharon enters Armistice Talks', *New York Times*, 4 February 2002.
19 On the killing of informers see, for example, Joel Brinkley, 'Israel Promises a Pullback as Death Toll Keeps Rising', *New York Times*, 15 March 2002.
20 This is a principal argument of Michael L. Gross in 'Fighting by Other Means in the Mideast: A Critical Analysis of Israel's Assassination Policy', *Political Studies*, 51 (2003), pp. 358–9.
21 For one of the best accounts of Just War Theory see Michael Walzer, *Just and Unjust Wars*, New York, 1992.
22 Michael S. Moore, 'The Moral Worth of Retribution', in Jeffrie G. Murphy (ed.), *Punishment and Rehabilitation*, 3rd edn, Belmont, CA, pp. 94, 97.
23 Judith Lichtenberg, 'The Ethics of Retaliation', *Philosophy and Public Policy Quarterly*, 21, 4 (Autumn 2001), p. 5.

Dirty War? Targeting terrorists in Northern Ireland

Simon Kingston

It is now more than nine years since the declaration of a second ceasefire by the Provisional IRA. Recently, after prolonged circumlocution, the group has declared that its 'war' is over and, based on the hope that this really is the case, a faltering and tortuous progress towards the re-establishment of normal political life in Northern Ireland is underway. While considerable scepticism about the Provisional movement's present *modus vivendi* and commitment to exclusively democratic methods in the future is understandable, there is no doubt that the IRA campaign has, for now at least, ended. The question of how this situation was brought about has been widely discussed. Northern Irish Republicans have certainly not relinquished their desire to create a united Ireland, regardless of the wishes of the majority population in the province and the tepid response that the prospect provokes in the Irish Republic. Some argue that this is the latest in a series of Republican ruses and that a violent campaign could begin again, with arms currently held or with new material which it could readily acquire. Others feel that the IRA's capacity to undertake terrorist operations has been eroded to the point that, although a reduced campaign could still be waged in the province, augmented by 'spectaculars' in Britain, there is no prospect of a return to major violence.

Certainly, by the early 1990s, British counter-terrorist measures had become highly sophisticated and the state's capacity to limit the IRA's room for manoeuvre was significant. Much of this effort relied on the commitment of considerable numbers of troops, in support of an armed police force, The Royal Ulster Constabulary (RUC). The routine apparatus of security, roadblocks; body searches in public places; control zones in city centres, and so on, were an inconvenient fact of life for anyone who lived in Northern Ireland. Combined with increasingly sophisticated military techniques, ranging from the use of advanced surveillance technology to the honing of counter-sniper procedures in places like South Armagh, these were a major means of inhibiting terrorist activity. The importance of this campaign of attrition cannot be underestimated and, to come to a somewhat brutal point, many of the IRA terrorists killed died in encounters with policemen and soldiers on regular duty. In what follows, however, I propose to offer a survey of the direct action taken by the security forces that falls outside the 'regular'.

Over the twenty years from the mid-1970s, a variety of organisations were created by the RUC, British Army and intelligence organisations to 'take the fight to the terrorists'. They did not always collaborate effectively and some were short-lived, but the evidence suggests that ultimately they made a considerable difference. Intelligence gathering and the running of informers ('touts' in Northern Irish slang) was a major focus of activities. By the mid-1980s, this intelligence was capable of being used to apprehend or engage IRA active service units in the preparation and prosecution of their operations. Most frequently, this direct engagement fell to the Special Air Service (SAS) to carry out.

At the outset, it is worth being clear about some of the numerical facts. The vast majority of those who lost their lives in Northern Ireland's 'Troubles' were killed by Republican or Loyalist paramilitaries, not by the state. This was a militarily low-intensity campaign, frequently characterised by inter-community conflict rather than a sustained insurgency aimed chiefly at the forces of the state. To be precise, between 1969 and 1999, the British army was responsible for the deaths of 239 people in Northern Ireland, in addition, in the period 1976–92, the SAS accounted for a further sixty-two deaths. The RUC was responsible for some fifty-two deaths in the same period and the, locally raised, Ulster Defence Regiment eight. In total, of the 3636 people who lost their lives in the period, the combined security forces of the British state were directly responsible for the deaths of 362 (one IRA man was killed by police in Britain).[1]

It is not within the scope of this chapter to discuss the possible influence that elements of the security forces may, or may not, have had on other deaths in the course of the 'Troubles'. Whatever the truth of some of the claims that are still made on this score, the fact remains that the security forces were directly responsible for a small proportion of those killed in the conflict – somewhere around 10 per cent. This point is important in our thinking about Northern Ireland in relation to other conflicts around the world. The killings we are concerned with here are a minority even of that small per centage and are to be understood as part of a counter-terrorist strategy, distinct from the counter-insurgency methods deployed in other situations.

This approach, the very careful intelligence-led targeting of terrorist suspects, took time to develop. To digress briefly, the distinction between the counter-terrorist and counter-insurgency approach continues to be very important for the British army in its engagements elsewhere in the world, particularly when either is confused with 'peace keeping' as it would seem to have been by government ministers recently in Afghanistan. A muddled approach to 'the lessons learned in Northern Ireland' was also evident in early, somewhat hubristic, remarks about winning hearts and minds on the streets of Basra. Tyrone was not Helmand or southern Iraq, anymore than South Armagh was the West Bank. It is not the intention here to suggest any such analogy.

Rather, the purpose here is to consider specifically the impact of the use of lethal force by the security forces in tackling the threat of Irish Republican terrorism. This should facilitate a comparison, and show a contrast, with Israel's approach to dealing with its own conflict with the Palestinians, as addressed in the previous chapter by Professor David. Loyalist terrorism was viewed for much of the period as a lower level threat; significantly less well-organised than its Republican counterpart; and susceptible to more traditional law and order responses, given the different level of co-operation the police and army received from its 'host' community.

The number of fatal interventions by the security forces reflects the difference in how the threats were perceived. The army was responsible for the deaths of seven Ulster Defence Association (UDA)/Ulster Freedom Fighters (UFF) members and three Ulster Volunteer Force (UVF) members; the RUC for three and two respectively. By contrast, in the thirty-three years of the 'Troubles', the army (including the SAS and other Special Forces units) killed 104 Provisional IRA volunteers; eleven Official IRA members; five members of the Irish National Liberation Army (INLA); and one member of the Irish Peoples Liberation Organisation (IPLO). The RUC killed eleven IRA members and four INLA members.[2] It is the impact of these killings and the strategies that lay behind them with which we are concerned here.

What part did the use of lethal force by the security forces play in the pattern of events in Northern Ireland? What role, if any, did this factor play in the Provisional movement's decision to pursue political, as well as military means in achieving its ends? While some claim the IRA bombed its way to the table, is it also true that paradoxically it may have been forced there by the activities of the British military?

TERROR AND COUNTER-TERROR IN NORTHERN IRELAND

In August 1969, the British Prime Minister, Harold Wilson, approved the dispatch of troops to Northern Ireland to help restore order. This followed the outbreak of inter-community violence in the province that proved too intense and widespread to be contained by the RUC. The conflict between the Protestant and Roman Catholic communities radicalised elements in both, and paramilitary groups were created to 'defend' their respective territories.

The revival of armed Republican groups in the Catholic community saw the emergence in late 1969 of the Provisional IRA (hereafter, the IRA). This terrorist organisation mounted a sustained and intelligent campaign in the ensuing years aimed at the removal of the British presence in Northern Ireland and the creation of a new all-Ireland republic. In the course of the early 1970s, the IRA's campaign grew in scale, drawing initially on the resentment felt within the Roman Catholic community against the temporary use of internment without trial in 1971 and civilian deaths caused by army ineptitude. The most notorious of these incidents was the killing of thirteen demonstrators in Londonderry in January 1972 by members of the Parachute Regiment. The year of 1972 was the bloodiest year of the 'Troubles' with nearly 500 people losing their lives. While this level of fatality was not reached again, the killing continued at a high level for the rest of the decade and was not finally brought under control until the mid-1990s. As the IRA evolved, so did the British military response to it.

Responsibility for intelligence gathering and combating the IRA was shared between a number of organisations. Within the RUC, the Criminal Investigations Department (CID) had a reactive role in dealing with terrorist crimes, while the Special Branch ran a network of informers. In the mid-1970s, these organisations were supplemented by the creation of the mobile anti-terrorist Special Patrol Group. These efforts were not always well co-ordinated with those of the army. For its part, the army had specialist intelligence and surveillance units, notably fourteen Intelligence Company and, from 1976, the SAS. As one commentator on this complex mix of organisations has summarised:

> By mid 1978 an IRA suspect might have been under observation from men and women from one of Fourteen Company's three detachments, one of the four SAS troops in Northern Ireland, or the seven Army Close Observation Platoons, the Special Patrol Section's Bronze Section, or one of several squads from [RUC surveillance unit] E4A[3]

The somewhat amateurish early attempts to counter the IRA are widely known. This applied to all aspects of the army's campaign and went beyond surveillance techniques, verging on the comical on occasion.[4] An early attempt to apply lessons learned elsewhere was the creation of the Mobile Reconnaissance Force (MRF). This was established in 1970 by Brigadier Frank Kitson, a veteran of colonial conflicts in Kenya and Malaya. Perhaps its best known operation was the establishment of the Four Square Laundry as a cover for surveillance operations in Belfast. The 'Laundry' offered its services in predominantly nationalist areas of Belfast aiming to use the access it gained to gather intelligence. It also developed a somewhat haphazard network of 'Freds' (Republican sympathisers whom the group believed it had turned sufficiently to feed it information). Tactics appropriate to tropical insurgencies proved ineffective in Ulster and MRF operations were compromised. By 1973, a new surveillance unit, 14 Intelligence Company, had been established. It was '14 Int', along with the SAS, that was to score the most notable successes in the army's war with the IRA.

The situation remained confused, however, as the famous case of Captain Robert Nairac illustrates. Nairac, who was killed in May 1977, was abducted from a bar in South Armagh by Republican sympathisers who were not even members of the IRA. Often described as an SAS officer, Nairac was a former member of '14 Int' and at the time of his abduction was in fact a liaison officer between his Brigade Headquarters, the SAS and the RUC. He frequently seems to have acted in a virtually freelance capacity and though his bravado was impressive in a Buchanesque sort of way, at the time of his death his way of doing things was being replaced by a more systematised approach.

Between its first deployment in 1976 and November 1978, the SAS was responsible for the deaths of seven IRA men. However, it also had operational teething troubles, in one incident worthy of Flann O'Brien, a single member of *An Garda Síochana* (the Irish police force) succeeded in arresting eight members of the SAS, as in three separate cars they successively lost their way and found themselves south of the border. This embarrassing evanescence on the part of the Irish border was a persistent problem for security forces in the early days of the Troubles, something that itself provides a useful reminder of the diffuse nature of the conflict. More controversial, in these years, were the circumstances of the deaths of some IRA men killed by the SAS and the mistaken shooting of a Protestant farmer on whose land the IRA had cached some arms.

From late 1978, the SAS seemed to change tactics and did not use lethal force again until 1983. The feasibility, on occasion, of detaining rather than shooting IRA members seemed to be proven by the arrest of two by the SAS in Tyrone in 1980 and the capture of four IRA men in Fermanagh in 1981.

In this period, in which the SAS role was relatively muted, some of the most controversial killings of the Troubles occurred. In three incidents in late 1982, RUC undercover units (the Headquarters Mobile Support Unit, a part of Bronze Section) killed three IRA men and two members of the smaller Republican Irish National Liberation Army (INLA). While these operations need to be seen in the context of an ongoing assertion of the principle of 'Police Primacy', the controversy that they caused was intense: all of those killed were unarmed at the time of their deaths and a civilian with no proven connection to any paramilitary group was also killed. The Stalker Inquiry, launched in 1984, raised serious questions about the conduct of these operations. The apparent obstruction by the RUC Special Branch of its own

CID investigations into the killings cast the force in a poor light and the revelation that in one case the scene of the incident had been bugged by MI5, unbeknown to the RUC, highlighted inter-service operational difficulties.⁵ The impression was one of a clumsy and poorly co-ordinated local settling of scores by elements of the police force. The result appears to have been a renewed focus on the army as both a source of training for RUC specialist units and as the leading participant in actively engaging the IRA.

In 1983, the SAS returned to more aggressive tactics with the killing of two IRA men retrieving arms from a cache in Tyrone. The next year saw mixed fortunes with the SAS accidentally killing a bystander in an exchange of fire with an IRA unit it was seeking to apprehend. In subsequent incidents in 1984, 1985 and 1986, SAS and '14 Int' operatives killed seven IRA men, for the loss of one SAS soldier. These operations were episodic in nature and it is hard to argue that they significantly affected IRA strategy in the period. Indeed, during these years, the IRA was not prevented from perfecting new technologies, such as its mortar capabilities. However, this was to change from 1987, when a sustained intelligence-led campaign by the SAS broke the back of two big pushes planned by the IRA.

By the mid-1980s, the IRA's ruling Army Council recognised that its campaign was effectively being contained by the British. The military strategy it chose to adopt in the face of this was a massive escalation in levels of violence in an attempt to take and hold significant areas of the border region. This was designed to 'force the British either to use maximum force or to hold off'.⁶ The plan was modelled on the Tet Offensive in Vietnam in 1968 and the intention was the same: to shock the 'occupying' force and, more importantly, its political class, into thinking the war was unsustainable.

To achieve this, the IRA acquired a significant quantity of weaponry, including RPG-7 rocket launchers; Sam-7 missiles; and semtex from Libya. In four trips in 1985 and 1986, the IRA succeeded in landing almost 150 tonnes of material. A fifth, even larger, consignment on board a ship called the *Eksund* was intercepted off the coast of France as a result of the work of an informer at a senior level within the IRA whose identity remains disputed. Although 'Tet' was scaled down as a result, the IRA nevertheless had a formidable arsenal with which to mount a fresh campaign.

The East Tyrone brigade, which included the charismatic Jim Lynagh, was chosen to lead 'Tet 2'. On 8 May 1987, eight IRA volunteers attempted to carry out an attack against the RUC station at Loughgall. Some of its most experienced volunteers were involved and they deployed a well-tried technique, rushing the RUC base with a mechanical digger carrying an explosive charge. Some twenty-four SAS soldiers, accompanied by Army and RUC surveillance teams and RUC HMSU personnel, were lying in wait. When the IRA teams attacked and the bomb exploded the SAS opened fire. In the ensuing, decidedly one-sided, firefight all eight IRA men were killed. The source of the intelligence which led to this interception remains disputed. A listening device or an informer may have been involved. What is clear is that this, and a series of subsequent engagements, effectively neutralised the IRA's East Tyrone Brigade.

In the five years following Loughgall, the SAS was responsible for killing some twenty-eight IRA volunteers in Tyrone. This stands in stark comparison to the twenty-five members of the brigade killed in the previous seventeen years. The brigade's capacity to wage 'war' was effectively broken and its contribution to the IRA's total activities dipped from 21 per cent in 1986 to 9 per cent in 1993.[7] The intelligence that the British were receiving was clearly excellent, but the 'hard nuts' in the Brigade also contributed to their own downfall with some reckless attacks. These included a somewhat cinematographic gun attack, with a heavy machine gun mounted on the back of a lorry flying the Irish tricolour, on a police station in Coalisland in February 1992. The SAS was clearly prepared for this attack and the IRA unit was caught in gunfire as it attempted to transfer into getaway vehicles at a nearby church. Four young volunteers, the post-Loughgall generation, were killed and two others wounded in this incident.

Whatever the source of the intelligence that enabled Special Forces to intervene in this way, there is little doubt that it forced the IRA's activities in the area, intended to be the frontline of the Tet campaign, to a halt. It has been suggested that it was only with the connivance of members of the IRA's Executive or Army Council that this volume of intelligence could have been leaked. This theory, advanced by Ed Moloney, effectively argues that a faction, led by Gerry Adams and Martin McGuinness, had recognised in the mid-1980s that the IRA's violent campaign was not going to drive the British from Northern Ireland and that some form of political accommodation was necessary.

In order to bring the IRA (and Sinn Féin, its political arm) to a point where negotiation was possible two things needed to be achieved: the British government's attitude needed to change from the tough stance adopted by Margaret Thatcher and the IRA hardliners such as Lynagh had to be removed. The implication from Moloney is that to achieve the latter goal the IRA leadership not only ensured the emasculation of the Tet offensive through facilitating the capture of the *Eksund*, but also that it allowed, or even worked to ensure, that 'Tet 2' floundered in East Tyrone.

That the IRA was penetrated at a senior level by different elements of British intelligence has come to light very publicly in the years since the ceasefire. In May 2003, it was revealed that Freddie Scappaticci, the head of the IRA's counter-informer Internal Security Unit (known as 'the Nutting Squad'), had been a paid agent of the Force Research Unit. This unit had been formed in 1980 to co-ordinate the gathering of intelligence across the Army's operations. At the time, it was said that Scappaticci had been permitted to take part in or facilitate the 'execution' of other informers to disguise his own role and that of other, even more senior, spies within the Provisional movement.

The identity of one of these other senior informers emerged in December 2005, when Dennis Donaldson, who had been Sinn Féin's head of administration at Stormont, was publicly expelled from the movement after having admitted to working for Special Branch. In April 2006, he was murdered at the cottage in Donegal to which he had fled in the wake of this revelation. In the reporting of both cases, it was alleged that a still more senior member of the IRA, by implication Martin McGuinness, had also been in the pay of the British (it is usually alleged that he was an MI6 agent). The grounds on which this claim is made are flimsy at present. In any event, it is surely not necessary to the Moloney case that McGuinness (or Adams) was actually in the pay of the British, merely that they saw a strategic advantage in allowing them to have information at certain points.[8]

Indeed, a direct relationship between the IRA's leadership and the British need not have existed at all for the Tyrone 'Tet' to have been doomed from the outset. A modification of the Moloney conspiracy theory is offered by others, including the informer turned political commentator Sean O'Callaghan.[9] They argue that in fact there was no need for a major conspiracy at the top of the Provisional movement to achieve the goal of getting rid of the 'hard nuts'. Rather, given that the East Tyrone Brigade was riddled with informers and that the British had become so effective at eliminating its Active Service Units, the Adams leadership merely had to decide not actively to prevent Lynagh and others from mounting operations. The Belfast leadership took the view that 'on your own heads be it' and the outcome suited them.

Of course, it was not just the East Tyrone Brigade which was met with this force, and a much contested use of the SAS occurred when three IRA volunteers were killed as they prepared a bomb attack on Gibraltar on 6 March 1988. The intelligence that enabled this operation has been read by some as further evidence of how completely the upper echelons of the IRA had been infiltrated by the British. Protracted litigation ensued and there was an intense outbreak of violence in Northern Ireland when a loyalist gunman attacked mourners at the funeral of the three IRA personnel. This in turn gave rise to the murder of two soldiers at the funeral of one of those killed.

After 1992, there were no more killings of IRA personnel by the SAS. This did not mean that the celebrated unit ceased to operate, but in the 1990s the SAS was deployed in the arrest rather than ambush of IRA operatives. A good example of this was the 1997 arrest of members of an IRA sniper team which had operated around the Republican stronghold of Crossmaglen in South Armagh.[10] This doubtless reflects a change in the political environment, as well as in the nature of the IRA campaign the security forces were working to inhibit.

THE EFFICACY OF LETHAL FORCE

The SAS was deployed aggressively between 1976 and 1978; it is clear that in this period its techniques and the intelligence on which it acted were very far from perfect, and it is difficult to assert any tangible military advantage that the unit's presence created. As a clear statement of British resolve there was, nevertheless, an intangible benefit to their deployment. By contrast, in any reading of the events of the late 1980s, it is clear that the intervention of the SAS and other specialist units of the security forces did have a significant impact in degrading the IRA's capacity to wage a seriously destabilising campaign. They broke the 'Tet' offensive. This view is held by a variety of those within the Republican movement at the time, as well as by, it would seem, British and Irish officials. One member of the Irish Department of Foreign Affairs volunteered to this author the view that this campaign had been critical in bringing the IRA to the negotiating table.

Militarily the actions were, however, a qualified success as there was minimal penetration of the Republican stronghold of South Armagh. There, the greatest success in the fight against the Provisionals came between the ceasefires of 1994 and 1998, that is, *after* the aggressive tactics of the late 1980s.

THE MORAL ISSUE

The morality of the sort of actions described above is of course open to question. The fatal shooting in London in July 2005 of Jean Charles de Menezes, erroneously suspected of being a terrorist, brought concerns about the use of lethal force by the security services to the fore again in Britain. At the time, parallels between campaigns against the IRA and the new Islamist terrorist threat were drawn by some commentators.[11] However problematic such comparisons may be, in episodes such as those at Loughgall and on Gibraltar, British Special Forces did use lethal force as a first resort. In many of these incidents, and in those relating to RUC activities in 1982, it is clear that the normal 'yellow card' procedure of repeatedly challenging suspects before opening fire was not followed. A special vocabulary was coined to describe increasingly robust tactics.

In his book *Big Boys Rules*, Mark Urban makes much of expressions such as 'covert patrol' and 'Observation Post/Reactive' used as euphemisms for ambushes staged against IRA units. The 'fudge factor' principle, with comforting echoes of Church of England theology, was elaborated to describe the granting of some discretionary latitude to Special Forces soldiers who believed they had caught IRA volunteers 'red-handed'. In certain instances, they opened fire even when they did not feel their own lives were at immediate risk. Even allowing for the stress and uncertainty to which these soldiers would have been subject and the impossibility of reconstructing events perfectly, it seems clear that some of the actions of the SAS crept closer to the *modus operandi* of war than it was advisable for their military superiors and political leaders to concede publicly. One might add that this coincided with periods when the IRA's own campaign was increasing in intensity.

A number of important caveats are worth entering alongside this apparent criticism of British actions. This is especially the case when the argument is made that the health of Britain as a liberal democracy was somehow risked in this period. The first is that there were relatively few incidents where lethal force was actually used. It was clearly not the norm for the security forces to 'shoot-to-kill' as Republican apologists are wont to claim.[12] In a limited set of cases, a small group of specialist troops were given the opportunity to engage known terrorists aggressively. Second, after each incident there was considerable public and judicial scrutiny, which the state facilitated. While not everyone may have been satisfied with the answers provided by Special Forces troops (who were obliged to give evidence before civilian judges in many cases), it is unreasonable to suggest that elements of the military acted with impunity. Again, the relatively small total number of incidents supports this view.

Third, in the vast majority of cases, the people shot by Special Forces were indeed members of terrorist organisations engaged in, or intent on, violent acts. Mistakes were made and as at Loughgall, innocent bystanders were sometimes killed in error. In the Gibraltar case, it is certainly arguable that a non-lethal intervention would not have given rise to the cycle of violence and loss of life that the shooting of the IRA personnel caused in Northern Ireland. Nevertheless, crude though it sounds, in general the SAS and other special units shot the 'right' people in these engagements. Given the clear contribution their efforts made to the shortening of the IRA's campaign, a strong case can be made in defence of their actions.

A more serious allegation is that intelligence gathered for use by the army found its way to the Loyalist Ulster Volunteer Force (UVF) and was used by it in a 'complementary' campaign in Tyrone. As with other claims of collusion this falls outside the scope of this chapter. None of the cases described here involved any participation from Loyalist elements. Even if one were to accept, as this author does not, all of the claims of collusion made, the UVF campaign would not have been a pivotal part in the dismantling of the IRA's capability in Tyrone.

'DOCTRINAL' MUDDLE?

How to define the sort of campaign in which the British were engaged in Northern Ireland remains a questions which still dogs military operations. Frank Kitson in his classic work, *Low Intensity Operations*, describes a kind of sliding scale of progressively more intense conflict between the forces of the state and terrorists, moving from subversion to insurgency and finally to insurrection. The MRF, which Kitson established, was a product of an approach which saw the Northern Ireland situation as one of insurgency following a pattern he had observed in rural campaigns in under-developed countries. Vague and reactive in its tactical goals and relying on the network of 'Freds', in practice the MRF, was easily detected by a determined and well-organised opponent in an urban, Western, context. In a relatively stable society, much more sophisticated and long-term approaches to developing human intelligence were required. These took time to develop and, it would seem, the efforts of the different arms of the security forces were never entirely co-ordinated. A degree of muddle would appear to persist in the doctrine followed by British agencies tasked with counter-terrorism to this day.

CONCLUSIONS

The contribution of the SAS and other Special Forces units to the military defeat of the IRA was of great significance. However, it evolved in a wider security and political context than is usually considered. *Inter alia*, the technology of 'jarking' (placing tracing devices on terrorist weapons) and bugging improved steadily during the thirty years of the 'Troubles'. Alongside this, a network of informers, the scale of which is only now coming to light, was also developed. All of this supported the increasingly acutely targeted use of specialist military units. Other factors and a clear desire by those at the heart of the Republican movement to arrive at some sort of accommodation with the British were also at work over the same period. Nevertheless, this, and the more agitated speculation about conspiracies to protect an informer 'right at the top' of the IRA, is a distraction from the strategic point here. Intelligence-led use of lethal force by SAS and '14 Int' was certainly effective, most strikingly in Tyrone in the late 1980s. By the early 1990s, the SAS had proved itself to be a sharp instrument in the pursuit of a sophisticated, if still imperfect, counter-terrorism strategy, often as important for the fear which it instilled in its opponent as the actual damage done. In response, the IRA resorted to techniques which even its own 'base' disliked, the proxy bomb campaign being perhaps the most notorious.[13]

It would be a mistake to claim that what its critics describe as 'the dirty war' was solely responsible for achieving the measure of peace that now exists. However, it would seem fair to suggest that it contributed, after considerable error (and a number of trials) to significantly reducing the IRA's military options. In the end, the IRA's loss of freedom of manoeuvre helped the Adams/McGuinness leadership to sell a political approach to the Republican movement. Having lost the 'War', the Provisional movement has set out to win the peace, whether it succeeds will fall to political not military specialists to determine.

NOTES

1   David McKittrick, Seamus Kelters, Brian Feeney and Chris Thornton, *Lost Lives*, Edinburgh and London, 1999, pp. 1473–93.
2   Ibid. p.1483.
3   Mark Urban, *Big Boys' Rules, the SAS and the Secret Struggle against the IRA*, London, 1992, pp. 47–8.
4   This author, for example, has heard from one former officer of how, as a young man, he observed with incredulity his superiors testing new rubber bullet designs by firing them against squash court walls. Author conversation with anonymous British officer
5   See McKittrick *et al.*, *Lost Lives*, p. 926. John Stalker was removed from the inquiry into this episode before he published his final report. The report of Colin Sampson, who took over from him, was not made public. He published his version of events in a subsequent autobiography, John Stalker, *Stalker*, London, 1988.
6   See view of anonymous IRA volunteer quoted in Ed Moloney, *A Secret History of the IRA*, London, 2002, p. 21.
7   As calculated by Moloney, *A Secret History of the IRA*, p. 319.
8   Ed Moloney, 'The Killing of a Spy', *Irish Times*, 8 April 2006, http://www.ireland.com/ newspaper/weekend/2006/0408/3433760127WK08DONALDSON.html The dissident Republican view was provided in characteristically trenchant style by Anthony McIntyre, 'We Believe Freddie McGuinness', *The Blanket*, 30 May 2006 http://www. phoblacht. net/phprint.php.
9   Sean O'Callaghan in discussion with the author.
10 A good account of this operation is provided by Toby Harnden, although one might question whether, as his account suggests, the success was achieved without informer intelligence. Toby Harnden, *'Bandit Country': The IRA and South Armagh*, London, 1999, pp.303–7.
11 Liam Clarke and Tony Geraghty, 'Shoot to Kill Error Echoes Irish Dirty War', *Sunday Times*, 24 July 2005.
12 It is worth noting that even in the case of the 1982 'Shoot-to-kill' cases no evidence of a general policy was found by the European Court of Human Rights. It ruled in 2001, in the case of Gervaise McKerr, one of those killed in this period, that while there had been a violation of Article 2 of the Convention for the Protection of Human Rights and Fundamental Freedoms in respect of failings in investigative procedures, there was no evidence, in its view, of a policy unwarrantably targeting members of the Catholic or nationalist community. Case of McKerr v. The United Kingdom (Application no. 28883/95).
13 The first proxy bomb attacks were in October 1990, when three civilians whose families were being held hostage were forced to drive bombs at military installations on the border, in Newry and in Omagh. Such attacks continued in the latter part of that year, but were highly unpopular. There is debate about the motivation, Moloney argues that they were a deliberate ploy by the Adams' leadership of the IRA to discredit the 'armed struggle'.

Approaches to power-sharing in Northern Ireland and Lebanon

Michael Kerr

On 12 July 2006 the likelihood of power-sharing agreements stabilising ethnic conflict in Northern Ireland and Lebanon appeared equally remote.[1] The Israeli response to Hezbollah's capture of two of its soldiers was an intense bombing campaign – mainly targeted at Lebanon's Shi'a dominated areas – and a land invasion which aimed to loosen the Islamic militia's control over the border area. On the day that tensions boiled over in the Middle East, veteran unionist hardliner Ian Paisley told a crowd of independent Orangemen in Northern Ireland that only over their 'dead bodies' would Sinn Féin be readmitted into any devolved government at Stormont.[2] His rhetoric hid the fact that all Northern Ireland's main parties were prepared to work within the power-sharing institutions established under the 1998 Belfast Agreement.[3] Some, however, sought a more opportune moment to do so than the 24 November 2006 deadline set by the British and Irish governments. In contrast, Lebanon's Christian–Muslim power-sharing administration desperately sought international support for its newfound independence from Syria.

In Northern Ireland, the Democratic Unionist Party (DUP) leader's festive rabble rousing held no relation to his party's official policy on power-sharing with Sinn Féin. With the governments' deadline fast approaching Paisley, however, remained characteristically unwilling to articulate that policy publicly. Within days, DUP sources suggested that he would retire to the House of Lords following any resumption of power-sharing at Stormont, in remarks that directly contradicted his 12 July views.[4]

It had been clear for some time that the DUP was in fact willing to enter a power-sharing executive with Sinn Féin. But having defeated David

Trimble's Ulster Unionist Party (UUP) the previous year on an electoral platform ruling out power-sharing with republicans for 'a generation', Paisley's party was, understandably, in no hurry to make such a dramatic u-turn.[5] On the surface, Northern Ireland's political process appeared as intractable as the conflict in Lebanon, its two main protagonists stubbornly divided over the intergovernmental devolution programme. Yet this deadlock masked the progress the British and Irish governments had made since the Belfast Agreement was negotiated.

Both had learnt political lessons from the failure of Northern Ireland's first power-sharing executive under the 1973 Sunningdale Agreement.[6] It became apparent that power-sharing could only regulate Northern Ireland's conflict if the two governments were able to force the main local parties to negotiate an inclusive agreement and establish a stable environment for its implementation. Neither of the two British administrations tasked with Sunningdale's implementation, nor their Irish counterparts, had been politically equipped to do this in 1973–74.

Having ended unionism's political dominance by imposing power-sharing, British Prime Minister Edward Heath's approach had been to stem Northern Ireland's escalating violence through tough security measures against the Provisional Irish Republican Army (IRA).[7] For its part, the Irish government sought to influence British policy on Northern Ireland, represent its nationalist minority and prevent violence spreading across the border.[8] The domestic weakness of both governments then seriously hampered efforts to implement the Sunningdale Agreement.

Northern Ireland's political isolation from London and Dublin meant that neither administration was prepared for the outbreak of political violence. Prior to Sunningdale, Anglo-Irish relations had been lukewarm and it was only due to the unfolding security crisis that Britain accepted Irish intervention.[9] Sunningdale's Council of Ireland symbolised this influence, fuelling an anti-agreement unionist campaign to break the Northern Ireland executive under the slogan: 'Dublin is just a Sunningdale away'.[10] The Council of Ireland dilemma may have been alleviated had the Irish government removed its irredentist claim to Northern Ireland through amendments to Articles 2 and 3 of its constitution. Ulster Unionist leader Brian Faulkner had, however, accepted an all-Ireland body, with a large remit and the potential to expand, prior to the Sunningdale negotiations.[11] This split his party and prompted fierce resistance from opposition leader William Craig, his Vanguard movement and the DUP. The Republic of Ireland's Fine Gael-Labour coalition, led by Liam Cosgrave, was not best placed to make fundamental amendments to the Irish constitution. As the traditional republican party, Fianna Fáil would have been more authoritative in putting this question to the Irish people in a referendum. Furthermore, had Cosgrave attempted to do so and lost such a referendum, it would most likely have cost him his government.

In Britain, Heath's domestic weakness was exposed at the February 1974 General Election when Harold Wilson's Labour Party defeated the Conservatives and Northern Ireland's pro-agreement parties held only one seat. The threat of violence prompted Wilson to abandon what Heath had hastily created, leaving Faulkner and his coalition partners to the fate of the Ulster Workers' Council Strike in May 1974.[12] Loyalist paramilitaries, backed by the majority of Northern Ireland's unionist politicians, brought the country to a standstill and undermined the Sunningdale executive's authority.[13] Lacking security powers, the Sunningdale executive was completely reliant on a tough military response to the strike from Wilson. Fearful of the potential for a confrontation between British troops and striking 'workers', Wilson did nothing to prevent its collapse.

A quarter of a century later, British Prime Minister Tony Blair and Irish Taoiseach Bertie Ahern brought a unity of purpose to a political process in Northern Ireland that had developed incrementally at different levels since the politicisation of Sinn Féin in the 1980s. The two premiers took ownership of the process, pushing the Northern Ireland parties towards a constitutional settlement with political incentives and coercion. For nationalists, the Belfast Agreement provided extensive reform at all levels of society with a fully inclusive government premised on the concept of political equality.[14] For unionists, it offered the opportunity to constitutionally underpin Northern Ireland's position within the United Kingdom in a British-Irish agreement; gain nationalist acceptance for the principle of consent regarding any future change to this constitutional position; and control its all-Ireland bodies through a power-sharing assembly.[15]

Not all parties accepted or supported this settlement in 1998 and Trimble required the support of Northern Ireland's two small loyalist parties to achieve a majority of the divided unionist electorate in the negotiations.[16] On the nationalist side, Sinn Féin was very uncomfortable accepting publicly an agreement based on the principle of consent, which recognised Northern Ireland's constitutional position within the United Kingdom. Consequently, republicans left the negotiation of the accord's constitutional aspects and the formulation of its devolved institutions to the Social Democratic and Labour Party (SDLP).[17]

Initial attempts to implement the Belfast Agreement stalled over the symbolic issue of decommissioning and trust between unionists and republicans. The unionist community, which only backed the accord by a slender majority in 1998, lost confidence in Trimble's ability to lead them in the political process. The rise of Sinn Féin as a potent electoral force during this period strengthened unionist opposition to the direction the British Government had taken in its implementation of the Belfast Agreement. Conversely, the security aspects of the agreement and the symbolic victories they brought Sinn Féin assuaged republican fears that they had compromised on key ideological principles.

By 2006, the gulf between unionism and Sinn Féin seemed unbridgeable. When Tony Blair took office in 1997, Trimble readily engaged with a prime minister who made clear his intention to achieve a comprehensive political settlement in Northern Ireland. After the 2005 General Election, his close relationship with Trimble at the heart of UK politics was replaced by the distance of Paisley's intransigence at the heart of Northern Ireland's divide.

Having defeated Trimble's Ulster Unionists on an anti-agreement platform, the DUP needed time to prepare its constituency for power-sharing with Sinn Féin. The more Blair pushed Paisley towards agreement, the more rooted to his 12 July stance the DUP leader appeared. The prime minister desperately wanted to conclude a deal between Northern Ireland's two largest parties, which might allow him to leave office on a domestic high note and divert attention from his crumbling Middle East diplomacy in Afghanistan, Iraq and Lebanon.

Paisley, on the other hand, wanted to delay the historic moment when his party would enter an executive with the IRA's political representatives and gain confidence-building concessions from the government for any such move. Sinn Féin had begun preparing the ground for critical political u-turns on republican ideology before 1986 when its leaders Gerry Adams and Martin McGuinness shifted republican strategy towards a duality of violence and electoral politics. The unionist dilemma in 2006 was that no parallel political trajectory existed between Sinn Féin and the DUP. Having risen to dominance on the back of anti-agreement policies, the DUP had not begun to gather grassroots support for a return to the Belfast Agreement.

Blair's main objective under that accord was to end the IRA's paramilitary campaign against the state. To achieve this, Sinn Féin was brought fully into the political process with a series of political and military incentives. The government needed the UUP's support for this strategy and, in return, Blair backed Trimble on the constitutional issues that Sunningdale had been weak on.[18] Blair's inclusive approach tied republicans into accepting Northern Ireland as a political entity, as well as Britain's jurisdiction over it and the necessity of securing the unionist community's consent for any future change to its constitutional position.[19] It also tied unionists into accepting a fully inclusive power-sharing framework for Northern Ireland's governance, political equality at every level of society and the Republic of Ireland's right to represent the nationalist community within it.[20]

During the 1970s, Heath's primary objective had been the reduction of republican violence and he sought support from the Irish government and the SDLP for robust security measures against the IRA. In 1998, Blair understood that bringing Sinn Féin into the political process would considerably reduce the likelihood of any future resumption of republican violence. The justification for the IRA's armed campaign diminished when Britain demonstrated that it had no strategic selfish interest in Northern Ireland through its efforts to implement the Belfast Agreement.[21]

Furthermore, in the United States, following the 11 September 2001 al Qaeda attacks on Washington and New York, political and financial support for the IRA decreased. Closer to home, Sinn Féin could no longer point to the Republic of Ireland's constitutional claim over Northern Ireland in its justification of political violence. On the unionist side, most of those who stood in opposition to Faulkner supported and negotiated the Belfast Agreement. Their position was reinforced by the fact that many of the paramilitaries who led the Ulster Workers' Council Strike subsequently came out in favour of the new power-sharing arrangements.

The success of this conflict regulation approach in Northern Ireland marked an end to both anti-agreement unionism and the IRA's modern campaign of violence. The British and Irish governments then acted in unison to implement the Belfast Agreement as Anglo-Irish relations entered a new phase of political cordiality. Blair and Ahern's joint management of Northern Ireland's political process provided the stability that had been absent during the early 1970s. Within this framework the two governments indicated to the Northern Ireland parties that they would proceed with the Belfast Agreement agenda regardless of the difficulties its implementation entailed, and punish those that forced any departure from that template.

While this may not have been apparent to Unionists in the agreement's first implementation phase, which lasted up until the UUP lost the 2005 General Election, the British government tied Sinn Féin further into the straitjacket of democratic politics, after the devolved institutions collapsed in 2002, by continuing to implement the security aspect of the accord. By 2007, republican support for Northern Ireland's new police and judicial institutions resolved the only major aspect of the agreement outstanding between the British government and Sinn Féin.

Of the two main political parties, Sinn Féin appeared the more comfortable with the Anglo-Irish plans to restore Northern Ireland's power-sharing institutions. Following the 2005 General Election, it came under no great pressure to do so, as the DUP was ideologically and politically unprepared for the power-sharing agenda it inherited from the defeated UUP. In the short term, the British government needed to refocus its approach in Northern Ireland to address the deep alienation from the political process now felt by unionists. Support for those in the DUP willing to create the conditions for a return to devolution was a prerequisite for progress. It was logical that the British Government should have initially concentrated on the republican side of the agreement, even if it was at the expense of unionism. After all, permanently ending IRA violence was necessarily its first priority in Northern Ireland. When the institutions failed due to unionist division and republican intransigence over the decommissioning issue, it did not distract the British Government from pursuing that goal. The challenge in the Belfast Agreement's second implementation phase is for the two governments to allay unionist concerns over the settlement, maintain the conditions for the restoration of the devolved institutions at Stormont and consolidate power-sharing.

FROM BELFAST TO BEIRUT

In the Middle East, regional and international tensions conspired to put the clock back in Beirut. Lebanon's Christian–Muslim power-sharing system buckled under inter-confessional divisions that deepened in the vacuum that followed Syria's 2005 military withdrawal from the country. Shi'a militant Islamic group Hezbollah (Party of God) – Lebanon's largest political party in 2006 with two government ministers and fourteen members of parliament – was at the heart of these tensions. Through its increased attacks on Israel, Hezbollah sought to support Hamas, the Palestinian Islamic Resistance Movement in Gaza; consolidate its politico-military position in Lebanon; and enhance its regional status as the only non-Palestinian Arab force willing to challenge Israel.

In the war that followed, Israel sought to remove Hezbollah's forces from its Lebanon border, weaken its political support base and reduce Iran's influence in the Israeli–Palestinian conflict. The Israeli–Hezbollah war continued for over a month until the two sides agreed a ceasefire on 14 August, with Lebanese and UN troops slowly occupying the south.

The Lebanese imbroglio reflected the deadlock that existed between the United States and Iran over the Islamic Republic's nuclear development programme and its regional challenge to Israeli hegemony. In the United States, the Bush administration sought to weaken Hezbollah, further isolate Syria and limit Iran's role in Arab politics through its support for Islamist groups.

When Syria withdrew from Lebanon following the assassination of Lebanese Prime Minister Rafik Hariri in 2005, the Lebanese Government unsuccessfully attempted to resolve the political anomaly of Hezbollah's position within the state. Following the 1989 Ta'if Accords, which marked an internationally agreed end to Lebanon's civil war through Syrian inter- vention, all Lebanese militias were disarmed with the exception of Hezbollah.[22] Syria and Iran subsequently used the Islamist group to pressure Israel in its occupation of southern Lebanon and as a bargaining chip in any future negotiations towards a regional settlement.

When Israel withdrew in May 2000, low-level conflict continued between Syria, Iran and Israel through Hezbollah over the contested Shebaa Farms. The farms were captured by Israel from Syria during the Six Day War of 1967, but Lebanon claimed them as part of its sovereign territory. This granted Hezbollah a thin pretext for its continued military presence in the Shi'a dominated south.

The purpose of Israel's 1982 invasion was to eliminate the Palestinian Liberation Organisation's (PLO) capacity to launch cross-border attacks from

Lebanese soil and weaken Syrian influence in Lebanon. The PLO previously enjoyed the freedom to strike against Israel through the Arab-sponsored 1969 Cairo Agreement. Lebanon's unstable power-sharing formula imploded in 1975, as the PLO's activity divided a power-sharing government that exercised little control over its foreign policy. Christian ministers were fearful that the PLO would provoke an Israeli invasion, whereas most Sunni ministers felt compelled to support the Palestinians and many viewed 'their cause as our cause'.[23]

Conflict over the distribution of power in Lebanon's Christian–Muslim power-sharing government also contributed to the outbreak of civil war in 1975. This system, known as the National Pact, had been Lebanon's governmental formula since Britain pressed Charles de Gaulle's Free French administration to grant Lebanon independence in 1943.[24] The country's two most influential communities – the Maronites and the Sunnis – agreed power-sharing arrangements during the Second World War. Under this pact they occupied Lebanon's two most powerful political positions; the presidency and the office of prime minister respectively. This political system remained largely static between 1943 and 1975, as it contained no mechanism for significantly amending Lebanon's power balance.

By the 1970s, having matured politically, Lebanon's large Shi'a community used the PLO issue to press for radical constitutional reforms that would reflect its enhanced demographic weight. The Shi'a were one of Lebanon's three largest communities but their political influence remained subordinate to Maronite–Sunni dominance enshrined in the 1943 agreement. It was Christian-Muslim tension over the PLO–Israeli issue, however, which was the catalyst for civil war and fighting broke out between Maronite militiamen and Palestinian guerrillas in April 1975. Syria intervened in the conflict at the behest of the Christians in 1976, preventing a Maronite defeat by the PLO and ensuring no faction became powerful enough to achieve a comprehensive military victory.[25]

In 1983, the US government sought to impose a new order in the region under the auspices of an Israeli–Lebanese agreement, which aimed to reduce both Syrian and Soviet influence.[26] On 17 May, Lebanese President Amin Gemayel, hoping to regain some authority over his country, accepted a deal, granting political normalisation to Israel in return for a troop withdrawal in the south. This was not acceptable to Syria or the Soviet Union, whose ambassador Alexander Soldatov commented, 'we won't let the US get out safely from this Lebanese swamp'.[27]

A heavy military defeat by the advancing Israeli army had weakened Syria's position the previous year. Israel subsequently besieged Beirut and accomplished its military objective of removing the Palestinian leadership from Lebanon. The United States, however, had underestimated Syrian President Hafiz al-Asad's resolve to block any settlement that reduced his influence in the Arab–Israeli conflict.

Reinforced by Soviet military aid, Asad escalated a Christian–Druze war in Lebanon's mountainous Chouf region where the Israeli's were stationed,[28] testing their resolve to implement the 17 May Agreement. Israeli forces quickly withdrew to southern Lebanon before Iranian-inspired Shi'a suicide bombers blew up the US and French military headquarters in Beirut, killing hundreds. The United States immediately withdrew, leaving Lebanon's government at the mercy of the militias and a rejuvenated Asad. This conflict marked the period in the Lebanese civil war when Syria began to consolidate its control over the country. President Reagan's attempt to reshape the Middle East at Syria's expense by installing a pro-Western government in Beirut had dramatically backfired. It was also a significant victory for Iran through its support for militant Shi'a Islamists in Lebanon.

For the Lebanese there was a sense of *déjà vu* about the events of July 2006. The anti-Syrian members of the Lebanese Government sought to strengthen the state by resolving Hezbollah's Janus-faced political-military duality, something that was not on Iran's agenda. There had been no diplomatic solution to the Lebanese civil war, as the US–Saudi sponsored negotiations at Ta'if masked the reality of Syria's military control over the shattered state. Through its political and military support for the United States during the first Gulf War, Syria consolidated its hegemonic grip over its western neighbour, setting aside the reformulation of Lebanon's National Pact that had been negotiated at Ta'if. The old Lebanese elite went to Ta'if in the hope that the Arab states, with US support, would limit Syrian influence in Lebanon by supporting a new power-sharing democracy.

Plans for the country's political rehabilitation lay unimplemented, however, as the regional interests of its neighbours took precedence. Lebanon's new President, René Moawad, was assassinated on 22 November 1989 in the first of a series of events that enabled Syria to replace the old elite with a Christian–Muslim coalition, that was not preoccupied with implementing the Ta'if Accords.

Syria's unrivalled hegemony in Lebanon lasted until 2005, when it came under enormous international pressure to withdraw its forces. Suspicion that its intelligence services were responsible for the assassination of Hariri – who had grown beyond Syrian political control – led to the Asad regime's international isolation. Following Syria's withdrawal, Lebanon's different communities sought to reconstruct their divided state and avoid civil war over the issue of Hezbollah's armed status.

These efforts were only successful in preventing the outbreak of internal conflict and the authority of Prime Minister Fouad Siniora's technocratic government dwindled in the months leading up to the Israeli invasion. An extra-governmental National Dialogue Committee, consisting of representatives from the different Lebanese factions and militia leaders, met regularly in 2006. This committee mirrored the division between the two Lebanese camps – the pro-Syrian alliance of Hezbollah and Christian leader

General Michel Aoun and the pro-Hariri/anti-Syrian coalition of Sunnis, Christians and Druze.

The anti-Syrian coalition sought strong western support to enable Lebanon's democratically elected government to survive the crisis and fill the political void created by Syria's departure. The US attempted to redress the regional power balance by further isolating Syria and weakening Iran's position in Lebanon. Those who had not learnt the lessons of the civil war hoped that US–Israeli pressure would successfully stunt Hezbollah's growth. The outcome of the Israeli invasion had the opposite effect and diminished what little authority Siniora's government enjoyed, further exacerbating tensions between the country's pro- and anti-Syrian camps.

The problem was that the civil war had ended in 1989 without actually resolving many of the internal conflicts that broke the National Pact in 1975. Syrian hegemonic control brought a false sense of stability to Lebanon's deep divisions. While Syria prevented Ta'if's implementation, by 2005 the accord no longer accurately reflected the power balance between Lebanon's different communities and their external sponsors.

Hezbollah subsequently became the strongest political and military force in Lebanon and the failure of US-Israeli policy the following summer enabled it to consolidate its domestic position. Consequently, the war significantly shifted the centre of gravity in Lebanon's inter-confessional system towards Tehran. The consolidation of Hezbollah's position in Lebanon's government was apparent before the war ended. Siniora was forced to publicly back its leader Hassan Nasrallah after the 'Qana massacre', branding the victims 'martyrs' and denouncing the Israeli Government as 'war criminals'.[29] As the dust settled in its aftermath and the rebuilding process began, he promised, in a statement that could have been penned by Nasrallah himself, that Lebanon would be the 'last Arab country' to make peace with Israel.[30]

Without positive external support, division between the Lebanese factions was self-perpetuating. Each community was fearful of being dominated by others or having their political influence reduced in any reformulation of the old National Pact. All the major communities looked to foreign sponsors to protect their position within Lebanon and following the departure of Syria, Hezbollah's double life as an armed militia and a governing coalition partner provided Iran with an opportunity to extend its influence. How, then, could Lebanon's government have built on its newfound independence after 2005, with an unaccountable armed militia acting at the behest of external powers from within the state? Free from the yolk of Syrian authoritarian control, Lebanon's government was limited in its capacity to control its own borders. Those outside the pro-Damascus camp viewed Hezbollah's actions as damaging to the interests of the Lebanese collectively, but while they held a majority of seats in Lebanon's parliament, they lacked the military strength of the Islamic group.

This deadlock indicated that, even after the long years of civil war, the question of what it meant to be 'a Lebanese' remained unresolved. The polarisation between the two camps reflected two different visions of Lebanon's future place in the Middle East and what sort of independence it should have. The anti-Syrian camp wanted to build on the progress Hariri had made in reconstructing Lebanon as a modern capitalist country. However, they needed western diplomatic support, as well as Saudi financial investment, to succeed in those endeavours. In contrast, the pro-Syrian Hezbollah-led faction wanted Lebanon to take a leading role in supporting the Iranian challenge to US/Israeli hegemony in the region.

The irony of gaining independence from Syria and accepting Hezbollah's presence along the southern border was that this left the state open to attack from Israel in retaliation for the Islamist group's actions. In accordance with UN Resolution 1559, Christian and Sunni leaders called for the Lebanese army to replace a disarmed Hezbollah on the border.[31] The choice Siniora's government faced was whether to accept the status quo, with Hezbollah in control of the south, or risk another Lebanese civil war. They initially opted for an inclusive process, which finally saw the Islamists take ministerial seats in a power-sharing coalition. Most anti-Syrian ministers in that government hoped that the United States would support its efforts to help solve their problems diplomatically. But given Hezbollah's internal strength and external backing any change to its domestic position was unlikely outside the rubric of regional and international relations.

Ultimately, this left the fate of power-sharing in Lebanon at the mercy of intervening states and their propensity to use Lebanon as a battlefield for the pursuit of conflicting foreign policy agendas. The Lebanese government's attempts to avoid civil war by including Hezbollah invited Iran, Syria, Israel and the United States to manipulate the weakness of its pluralist position. Events in July/August 2006 illustrate Lebanon's perpetual weakness as a divided state at the centre of a regional power struggle. Some might be tempted to conclude that in the absence of robust Western support for its power-sharing government, Lebanon may have been better off under the stability of Syrian authoritarian rule.

The main beneficiaries of the 2006 war was Iran and its sponsor, Hezbollah, who strengthened their political position in Lebanon. Regionally the Islamic group made Egypt, Jordan and Saudi Arabia look inept as it took credit among their populations for withstanding the region's most potent army. The Sunni populations of these states looked increasingly to Hezbollah as a role model for militant Islamic resistance. They appeared to be the only Arab force willing to both support the Palestinians in their struggle against Israel and oppose US policy in the region. In contrast, the United States failed in its attempts to weaken Iran's political and financial support for Sunni and Shi'a Islamists. This considerably strengthened Tehran's position vis-à-vis Israel and its influence on the security situation in Iraq and Afghanistan.

In both Northern Ireland and Lebanon, democratically-elected political parties with military wings obstructed the stabilisation of agreed power-sharing systems of government. In contrast to the IRA, Hezbollah maintained its external struggle on the basis of Israel's clearly expressed selfish, strategic interest in Lebanon. It also increased its relevance to Iran and Syria in their regional power struggle with Israel and the US. Domestically, Hezbollah did not share the level of political authority Sinn Féin enjoyed in Northern Ireland. Neither the Ta'if Accords, nor the power-sharing arrangements that followed Syria's departure, constitutionally enhanced the Shi'a community's political role in proportion to its demographic weight or Hezbollah's military standing.

On the other side of the border, Israel enjoyed the cover of the US-led War on Terror and a pre-emptive self-defence doctrine, which fitted neatly with the Bush administration's regional agenda. Therefore the decommissioning obstacle had a completely different magnitude in Lebanon compared to Northern Ireland, due to the conflicting interests of intervening governments.

CONCLUSIONS

Northern Ireland and Lebanon clearly share a history of power-sharing, brought about by internationally sponsored constitutional agreements between rival ethno-national or religious communities. Consociational arrangements have repeatedly been used to regulate ethnic conflict in these divided societies by intervening powers.[32] Many lessons can be learnt from the varied approaches intervening states have taken towards implementing or hampering power-sharing arrangements in these two cases. For inter-nationally brokered consociational agreements to stabilise, long-term support is essential. If external powers are to negotiate and implement power-sharing accords, they must act as stanchions between the rival communities in order to create and maintain a political environment where inter-communal antagonisms may be regulated through political co-operation.

In 2007, Northern Ireland and Lebanon reached critical junctures in their approaches to power-sharing. What can be learnt from these two cases and from US-led attempts to impose a confederal system on Iraq, is that for consociation to be successful in managing a divided society, regional and international powers must have an interest in constructing and supporting its institutions.

This has been the case in Northern Ireland, where intervening governments have worked in tandem to restore devolution. The Middle East state system, as it stands in the post-Cold War era, offers precious little protec-tion for weak pluralist states. What this means for decentralised governments such as Lebanon and Iraq is that in the absence of long-term Western support, balanced with regional legitimacy, the prospects of regulating ethnic conflict through power-sharing administrations are at best remote.

In contrast, the fate of the Belfast Agreement in 2007 hinged on the ability of the British and Irish governments to garner republican support for Northern Ireland's new policing and judicial system, while illustrating to the unionist community that the IRA had truly become redundant. The DUP needed positive political developments to create an environment where it could comfortably enter into government with Sinn Féin. In Lebanon, Siniora's administration sought external support to avoid civil war and consolidate its independence from Syria. Lacking this variable and the authority to prevent Hezbollah promoting Iran's regional agenda, the resuscitation of Lebanon's democratic power-sharing institutions once again took second place to the international struggle for the Middle East. This dilemma illustrates the inconsistency in Western approaches to implementing power-sharing agreements and promoting democratisation.

Different approaches are certainly required in different regions. The problems incurred by the British in Northern Ireland – a democratic part of the United Kingdom – are very different from those experienced in Iraq, where US policy objectives are both economic and strategic. The unwillingness of the US and British governments to prevent the outbreak of war in Lebanon seriously undermined the credibility of their efforts to impose power-sharing in Iraq and end the civil war that had broken out in certain parts of the country.

While the British government had little choice but to support US policy during the Israeli-Hezbollah war, many of its foreign office officials were acutely aware of the potential consequences military action in Lebanon might entail. Having firmly supported US president George Bush in toppling Saddam Hussein in Iraq three years earlier, it was of little surprise that Tony Blair did not attempt to influence his administration's black and white view of how it should deal with the democratically elected Islamic parties that surround Israel. In the Middle East the Bush–Blair approach was to back Israeli might, in what the British prime minister deemed an 'elemental struggle' over 'the values that will shape our future'.[33] At the end of his premiership Blair's Middle Eastern diplomacy showed no trace of the subtlety and even-handedness he had brought to Northern Ireland's political process when he first took office and exposed the inherent contradictions in Western approaches to conflict regulation in the post 9/11 international system.

NOTES

1   Michael Kerr *Imposing Power-Sharing: Conflict and Coexistence in Northern Ireland and Lebanon*, Dublin, 2005.
2   BBC News, http://news.bbc.co.uk/1/hi/northern_ireland/5174000.stm, 12 July 2006.
3   *Agreement between the Government of the United Kingdom of Great Britain and Northern Ireland and the Government of Ireland*, London, Her Majesty's Stationary Office, 1998.
4   *Sunday Times*, 16 July 2006.

5   Michal Kerr, *Transforming Unionism: David Trimble and the 2005 General Election*, Dublin, 2005 p. 88.
6   *The Sunningdale Communiqué*, London, Her Majesty's Stationary Office, 1973.
7   Author interview with Sir Edward Heath, 7 February 2001.
8   Author interview with Garret FitzGerald, 12 September 2001.
9   Author interview with David Blatherwick, 21 July 2001.
10 Kerr, *Imposing Power-Sharing*, pp. 47–53.
11 Author interview with Sir Ken Bloomfield, 23 August 2001.
12 Kerr, *Imposing Power-Sharing*, pp. 41–72.
13 Robert Fisk, *The Point of no Return: The Strike that Broke the British in Ulster*, London, 1975.
14 Author interview with Jim Gibney, 17 September 2004.
15 B. O'Leary, 'The British–Irish Agreement', in J. McGarry (ed.), *Northern Ireland and the Divided World: Post-Agreement Northern Ireland in Comparative Perspective*, London & New York, 2001, pp. 53–88.
16 Author interview with David Kerr, 5 September 2001.
17 Author interview with Mark Durkan, 14 September 2001.
18 Author interview with David Kerr, 5 September 2001.
19 Kerr, *Imposing Power-Sharing* pp. 87–111.
20 O'Leary, 'The British–Irish Agreement', pp. 69–81.
21 Author interview with Lord Brooke, London, 6 July 2001.
22 Theodor Hanf, *Coexistence in Wartime Lebanon: The Decline of a State and the Rise of a Nation*, London, 1993, pp. 621–4.
23 Author interview with Muhieddin Chehab (Former *Mourabitoun* combatant), 28 November 2001.
24 F. el-Khazen, *The Communal Pact of National Identities: The Making and Politics of the 1943 National Pact*, Oxford, 1991.
25 Hanf, *Coexistence in Wartime Lebanon*, pp. 216–28.
26 Kerr, *Imposing Power-Sharing*, pp. 148–9.
27 Author interview with Amin Gemayel, 2 December 2001.
28 Author interview with Walid Jumblat, 9 April 2002.
29 Prime Minister Fouad Siniora's statement at the Islamic Summit held in Kuala Lumpur, 3 August 2006.
30 *Ha'aretz*, 30 August 2006.
31 UN Security Council Resolution 1559, 2 September 2004.
32 J. McGarry and B. O'Leary, *The Northern Ireland Conflict: Consociational Arrangements*, Oxford, 2004; and 'Consociational theory, Northern Ireland's Conflict, and its Agreement. Part 1: What Consociationalists can Learn from Northern Ireland', *Government and Opposition*, 41, 1 (2006), pp. 43–63; Arend Lijphart, *Democracy in Plural Societies*, New Haven, CT, 1977.
33 Speech by Tony Blair to the Los Angeles World Affairs Council, 1 August 2006, Downing Street Press Office: http://www.number-10.gov.uk/output/Page9948.asp

Conflict Resolution and Civil Society in Northern Ireland and Iraq

Gary Kent

We didn't ask you to come in but we'd like a say on when you go
Abdullah Muhsin, Iraqi Federation of Trade Unions, 2004

> Things fall apart; the centre cannot hold;
> Mere anarchy is loosed upon the world,
> The blood-dimmed tide is loosed, and everywhere
> The ceremony of innocence is drowned;
> The best lack all conviction, while the worst
> Are full of passionate intensity.
> William Butler Yeats, 'The Second Coming', 1921

The Provisional IRA was once the most sophisticated terrorist organisation in Europe and a key threat to the well-being and stability of the United Kingdom and the Republic of Ireland. Anglo-Irish relations were poisonous and a British ambassador to Dublin was murdered. Over four decades hundreds of thousands of British soldiers served in the province. Britain's human rights record was in the international dock and civil liberties were curtailed, not least with mass internment in 1971. Terror disfigured Belfast and regularly hit London. The 'Provos' murdered the Queen's cousin, very nearly assassinated Prime Minister Margaret Thatcher and came close to murdering her successor John Major.

In his valedictory speech to the 2006 Labour Party Conference, the British Prime Minister Tony Blair looked at the changes of the previous decade, saying almost ruefully 'Terrorism meant the IRA.' The long Northern Ireland war led to long ceasefires and then 9/11 changed the meaning and scope of terror.

After all, nearly as many people were murdered that morning as in the whole course of the Troubles. This chapter aims to establish key parallels between the Northern Ireland conflict and that in contemporary Iraq. The Iraqi conflict continues, but hope and history appear to have rhymed in Northern Ireland where an increasingly astute mixture of soft and hard power, international political co-operation and independent peace and labour movement activities helped end the 'Troubles' and bring about the decommissioning of paramilitary weapons.

Northern Ireland and Iraq are poles apart. They may have been constructions of British imperialism and 'artificial entities' but are part of entirely different political and cultural contexts. At least all the actors in the Northern Ireland conflict shared the English language, if markedly divergent views of history! Nonetheless, there are several key parallels. Both are societies deeply divided by sectarian identities largely masked and repressed during a long period of one-party rule although it would be monstrous to equate exactly the 'Protestant Parliament for a Protestant People' with the Ba'athist dictatorship.

Both experienced the use of the military to police civil conflict and curb terrorism. Both saw the credibility and viability of counter-insurgency operations undermined by counter-productive actions. Both saw vociferous and sometimes popular demands for 'troops out now'. Both saw complex conditions distorted by a media always keen on the moving image which led many to believe that conflict was intractable. Both contained consciously non-sectarian forces which sought to overcome division and terror and required external support. Both required possible resolution through power-sharing or federalism.

As someone who has been involved for twenty years in Northern Irish peace movement activities, this author has been a vocal critic of terrorism. In recent years, as Director of Labour Friends of Iraq, I have been helping to provide solidarity to those forces in Iraq which seek to defeat terror and build a democratic, federal and pluralist society. As such, this chapter breaks new ground in being one of the first to examine the crossover between the two conflicts.

'TROOPS OUT NOW'

Northern Ireland is a part of the United Kingdom and the presence of troops required no international legal sanction while Saddam's Iraq was a sovereign country and the presence of foreign forces required such sanction, which was later provided by UN Security Council Resolution 1546. However, it is striking that large parts of the left, often the same people and groups, used the same slogans in both cases: 'Troops Out Now' and 'Time to Go'. Troops are not best suited to enforce civil peace and almost always take on the appearance and reality of an occupying force. They are trained to use violence and were responsible for events that inflamed people and thereby acted as the recruiting sergeants to insurgents. Think of Bloody Sunday in Derry in 1972 or the Abu Ghraib scandal in Iraq in more recent times.

The British army was sent to Northern Ireland in 1969. The British State had precious little experience or understanding of Northern Ireland. Only one Cabinet Minister visited Belfast before the 'Troubles' and then only for an afternoon. Just one Home Office official was responsible for Northern Ireland along with nationalised pubs and dog licensing. The army had much to learn about its new patch. Many squaddies had just been stationed in Aden. Once, during a riot in Belfast, they took up a protective 'brick' formation and unfurled a flag to read out the riot act – it was in Arabic. They may have learned the wrong lessons from Aden but the lessons painfully learned in Belfast were to be applied on the streets of Basra where by common consent the troops were initially more capable of reducing tensions than US forces in the areas that they controlled.

Yet the argument for 'Troops Out Now' in both cases is that the mere presence of external forces aggravates conditions and their removal would allow, and force, local political players to come to a settlement. This seemed extremely unlikely in Northern Ireland. The withdrawal of troops would have allowed republican and loyalist paramilitary groups to operate with far less impediment and the security vacuum would have resulted in a bloodbath. The rationale of the far-left argument was precisely to give such support to its adopted side – the Provisional IRA – so that it could take physical control of nationalist areas, force ethnic cleansing and encourage Protestants to leave mixed areas or leave Northern Ireland altogether.

The withdrawal of troops was more than a way of finding more congenial policing methods, it was also a shorthand for the disengagement of the British state from Northern Ireland. The fanciful theory was that this would force the Protestant majority to make its peace with a united Ireland. Unfortunately thousands died for this illusion. The Provisionals now look like a somewhat less bloody war machine than their equivalents in Iraq, although they are credited, if that is the right word, with pioneering the use of car bombs. The field of battle and the casualties were much smaller. The Provisionals were no saints. They were relatively unrestrained in the early 1970s when war crimes were carried out against civilians. Take Bloody Friday in Belfast on the afternoon of Friday 21 July 1972: twenty-two bombs exploded, nine people were killed and 130 seriously injured. Warnings were either withheld or were useless.

The point of such attacks was to weaken the will of the British state to remain in Northern Ireland. They were aimed at sickening the British public and building momentum for disengagement. The 'Provos' may have known what this meant but some supporters were more naive. A senior unionist once told me that when Tony Benn introduced a House of Commons Bill to set a date for disengagement, he (the unionist) asked for six months' notice. When asked why, he replied 'so we can buy some weapons' to which an astounded Benn said, 'you can't do that' to which the reply was obvious – 'we'll do what we like if you disengage'. I am not sure to this day if the unionist was joking.

The 'Troops Out' movement was always ready to exploit right-wing instincts that we should let the Irish fight it out amongst themselves. Former military personnel who had deserted or despaired and their families were also exploited to make the same point. The demand for troops out often found support in opinion polls but was always resisted by successive British governments who refused to concede to this pressure. The ultimate settlement was based on recognising that majority consent was required for a united Ireland.

SUICIDE AND MARTYRDOM

The 'Provos' may have been relatively unrestrained in large parts of their armed campaign but they were aware that widespread civilian casualties would count against their cause domestically and internationally. This became a more pressing issue as the political wing became more dominant than the military wing in the republican movement. The scope of paramilitary operations was also circumscribed by the need to ensure that their volunteers always had an exit strategy: that is, they survived to carry out further operations. By the mid-1980s, increased infiltration of the 'Provos' and the scale of both human and signals intelligence meant that 80 per cent of their operations in Belfast were either intercepted or aborted because they had been compromised.

The contrast with al-Qaeda in Iraq is striking. The London *Times* reporter Sean O'Neill quotes Deputy Assistant Commissioner Peter Clarke, head of the new Counter-Terrorism Command (replacing Special Branch) on the differences between the IRA and Al Qaeda – the report states:

The new type of terrorism, pursued by Islamist groups under the al-Qaeda banner, was entirely different in character. Mr Clarke said: 'If you take all those characteristics [of the IRA campaign] and reverse them . . . you are not too far from describing the nature of the threat we now face. Far from being domestic, it is global in origin, global in ambition and global in reach. There is clearly no determination to avoid capture because we have seen that the use of suicide attacks is a frequent terrorist method. Far from there being any attempt, for political or other reasons, to restrict casualties, what we see time and again is an ambition to kill as many people as possible. There are no warnings and we have seen efforts here, and overseas, around unconventional weapons.[1]

However, al-Qaeda is only a minority component of the armed resistance in Iraq and has been both allied to and attacked by Sunnis. It is also detested by the majority Shia population who are viewed as sub-human apostates by al-Qaeda. Apart from a criminal element composed of thousands of prisoners released by Saddam before his fall, the main elements are aggrieved former members of the armed forces and those who want to reinstate Sunni minority rule. There have been negotiations between these more nationalist-minded, former Ba'athist forces and the US authorities, the details of which are not fully in the open. I am reminded of the secret talks in 1972 between the then Secretary of State for Northern Ireland, William Whitelaw and Gerry Adams, who had been released from internment, Martin McGuinness and other IRA leaders. Negotiating with the IRA proved impossible unless it meant simply conceding demands for disengagement. In time, it became possible to have more than a dialogue of the deaf with the 'Provos'. One hopes that this stage is being reached more quickly in Iraq.

Another key similarity was the initial welcome given in both jurisdictions to the troops, even if their presence also came to be resented by significant parts of society. However, the elected Iraqi government does not wish the multinational forces to be withdrawn until they can rely on their own security forces. Unlike Northern Ireland, anti-occupation feeling is high in Sunni and Shia areas, although this co-exists with a more positive view that the overthrow of Saddam was good and that Iraq will improve in a relatively short period of time. And voters plump for parties which do not demand an immediate end to the occupation.

If 'Troops Out Now' has come to be a cardinal principle of the anti-imperialist left then 'Troops in Now' is not an eternal principle of the anti-fascist or liberal interventionist left. There is always a balance to be struck between the ability of troops to prevent or provoke violence. Yet in both cases significant parts of the left and wider public opinion argue for troops out – some on the grounds that they wish to see the defeat of the occupying powers and others because they wish to wash their hands of a difficult struggle.

The left-wing former Labour MP Harry Barnes makes a very astute point about the demand for 'Troops Out' of Iraq:

> In fact, merely to concentrate on the invasion and on the current position of the armed forces is a rather Western-centred approach. These matters are, of course, also of key importance to the Iraqi people. But their daily struggles show that we need to go beyond our own two big issues if we are to link in with their needs. After all, whose side will we be on when the troops leave? If the answer includes the trade unions, then shouldn't we be active at their side already?[2]

It is a fair estimate that if British troops had been withdrawn from Northern Ireland there would have been a downward spiral of violence. Iraq is more complex with more ethnic identities and disparate terrorist forces and sectarian militias in play. It seems true that some of the violence is sparked by the very presence of foreign troops and their actions, but it would be wrong to suggest that all political violence would end with the withdrawal of US and UK forces. It is highly probable that it would lead to 'Troops In' – that is, troops from neighbouring countries such as Iran, Syria and Turkey. It is also likely that it would embolden al-Qaeda, and possibly provide them with the opportunity to further organise and also to spark full-scale civil war.

RISK-FREE RADICALISM

This raises the wider question of the political irresponsibility of parts of the Left and the ease with which a minority is prepared to fight to the last drop of someone else's blood. I recall one particular argument in 1979 over troops out of Northern Ireland with a then far left activist whose answer to my suggestion that there would be a bloodbath in Northern Ireland was to ask if I had read Lenin; he then went on to suggest that it would be best to get the bloodletting over and done with quickly. We were many miles from the conflict and would have been immune from the lethal consequences of such a policy.

Michael Walzer, co-editor of the US left-wing magazine *Dissent* wrote a very influential essay in the spring of 2002 on the US 'Leftist Opposition to the War in Afghanistan', in which he made a number of highly pertinent points that can be applied retrospectively to Northern Ireland and to the current situation in Iraq. Walzer argued that

> The radical failure of the left's response to the events of [9/11] raises a disturbing question: can there be a decent left in a superpower? Or, more accurately, in the only superpower? Maybe the guilt produced by living in such a country and enjoying its privileges makes it impossible to sustain a decent (intelligent, responsible, morally nuanced) politics. Maybe festering resentment, ingrown anger, and self-hate are the inevitable result of the long years spent in fruitless opposition to the global reach of American power. Certainly, all those emotions were plain to see in the left's reaction to September 11, in the failure to register the horror of the attack or to acknowledge the human pain it caused, in the *schadenfreude* of so many of the first responses, the barely concealed glee that the imperial state had finally gotten what it deserved.[3]

The Observer's Ireland Correspondent Henry McDonald examined a major sectarian slaughter in Karbala in 2004 and drew parallels with Northern Ireland, when faced with similar atrocities:

The cheerleaders from the Irish and British ultra-left who for so long lent republican violence some spurious radical edge would have left the field instantly once their 'heroes' started fomenting total sectarian conflict. The fact that by and large the paramilitaries avoided an inevitable all-out 'war' via a series of Karbala-style atrocities shows that there were limits, both moral and political, even to the cold-hearted calculations of republicans and loyalists.[4]

He then asked just

why does the left in Ireland have no problem siding objectively with those determined to strangle democracy at birth in Iraq? And why in turn did they not support those Iraqis including the party, which holds membership of the Socialist International, attempting to build up their country after the nightmare years of Saddam's rule?

The answer to what he calls 'the moral vacuum at the heart of the Irish left's stance on Iraq' is that 'the Irish left, blinded by unthinking anti-Americanism, took the easy option'. The same applies to much of the British Left.

Andrew Murray, a key leader of the British anti-war movement argues that 'Empire, and resistance to it, is the central issue of our time.'[5] His comrade George Galloway argues that there is no third way between resistance and imperialism. Galloway described the international representative of the Iraqi trade union movement as a 'Quisling' – an odd description for someone who spent his life opposing Ba'athist fascism and whose comrade, Hadi Saleh, paid the ultimate price for being a member of the Iraqi Communist Party and a leading member of the new Iraqi labour movement which he had rushed back from exile to help rebuild. Hadi was brutally murdered in January 2005 by former members of Saddam's secret police, who tortured him before strangling him and riddling his body with bullets and then stealing union records. The murder of Hadi Saleh was a *cause célèbre* for the international labour movement including Irish Labour leader Pat Rabbitte.

The British anti-war coalition issued a controversial statement in October 2004 which 'reaffirms its call for an end to the occupation, the return of all British troops in Iraq to this country and recognises once more the legitimacy of the struggle of Iraqis, by whatever means they find necessary, to secure such ends'. The statement also expressed doubts that 'genuinely independent trade unionism in Iraq can develop under a regime of military occupation'[6] – a triumph of arcane theory over actual practice.

One of the main victims of Saddam was the trade union movement. It was once one of the biggest and most powerful in the Middle East. Back in 1959 the May Day rally in Baghdad attracted half a million people out of a population of about 7 million. The Iraqi Communist Party was one of the largest in the region. Saddam virtually extinguished independent trade unionism, banning all public sector unions, a major blow, as about 80 per cent of the economy was in state hands and because it rendered the rest of the movement vulnerable to Saddam's apparatus of state terror.

By the time of his fall in 2003 the labour movement had been reduced to a few hundred clandestine cadres or exiles. In the period since then, the movement has grown to a million members throughout Iraq. My then employer, Harry Barnes, MP, and I had initiated solidarity efforts with the then emerging Iraqi labour movement in the months following the fall of Saddam Hussein. In April 2006, I organised a labour movement delegation to Iraqi Kurdistan. We held a five-hour summit meeting in Erbil with Iraqi trade union leaders from Basra, Babel and Baghdad who described how, in the face of major obstacles, they had built-up a devastated movement from nowhere to a million people throughout Iraq.

They argued that the trade unions are a key bedrock of non-sectarianism, and are determined to help rebuild Iraq as a democratic and federal society. One issue that was not mentioned by them, though we raised it, was the demand for the immediate withdrawal of troops. I am still struck by the wise dialectical words of Abdullah Muhsin, the international representative of the Iraqi trade union movement, who told us 'we didn't ask you to come in but we'd like a say on when you go'. In conversation with Iraqi labour leaders, the general view was that even if they had opposed the original invasion, preferring Saddam to be toppled through an internal process, they were fearful that the early withdrawal of foreign forces would worsen the security vacuum and that non-sectarian networks like their own would suffer most.[7]

One parallel between the two situations is that some people take a pre-existing position in favour of 'troops out' on the grounds that its implementation would remove the apparent aggravation of occupation and invasion. This is a fallacy. Because the troops are being shot at – sometimes by both sides – removing them would add to the problem of civil conflict. No government would be right to take out the troops before a successful peace process, as this would presumably turn over security to highly organised and armed paramilitary groups – in Iraq even more so than in Northern Ireland. Withdrawing troops would prolong conflict as it would be seen as denying victory to one side or another and this would mean that both sides would have an interest in continuing their violence.

THE ROLE OF THE MEDIA

Bloodshed makes news. It takes precedence in coverage over more mundane and less photogenic realities. The media should seek to report on the widest range of events and allow the widest range of opinions to be heard. Roger Darlington identifies another key difference between the two cases:

The British and the Americans know Northern Ireland or think they do because, although they have never been there, they know people who were born in Ireland or are descended from people born in Ireland. For most in the UK and the USA, very little is known about Iraq which – to paraphrase – is 'a far away country... of which we known nothing'. This illustrates the need for a decent liberal press that does much more to convey the complexity of Iraq and to cover those groups which are trying, in the most desperate circumstances, to hold the country together.[8]

It would be equally foolish to look at post-war Iraq through rose-tinted spectacles. Nonetheless, there are some important advances to mention. Iraqi Kurdistan is safe and has been able to restart building a pluralist society and reconstruct its economy thanks to US/UK no-fly zones imposed and policed since 1991 and the 'liberation', as everyone I met during my visit to Iraq termed the 2003 invasion.

Christopher Hitchens lists other positive changes:

I am glad that all previous demands for withdrawal or disengagement from Iraq were unheeded, because otherwise we would not be able to celebrate the arrest and trial of Saddam Hussein; the removal from the planet of his two sadistic kids and putative successors; the certified disarmament of a former WMD – and gangster – sponsoring rogue state; the recuperation of the marshes and their ecology and society; the introduction of a convertible currency... the killing of al-Qaida's most dangerous and wicked leader, Abu Musab al-Zarqawi, and many of his associates; the opening of dozens of newspapers and radio and TV stations; the holding of elections for an assembly and to approve a constitution; and the introduction of the idea of federal democracy as the only solution for Iraq short of outright partition and/or civil war.[9]

In the *Guardian*, however, there has been a relentless emphasis, with a trickle of dissenting views, on withdrawing troops and very little on the positive strides made by trade unions and others. The uninvolved liberal is generally unaware of their very existence. A journalist joined the Labour Friends of Iraq delegation in Erbil for that unique five-hour meeting with leaders of trade unions across Iraq but his subsequent article on this meeting was not deemed newsworthy by a leading liberal newspaper. This is not academic. The widespread ignorance of the trade union movement makes it harder for them to secure solidarity and material assistance. Democratic governments with military forces in conflict zones also answer to electorates who often assume the worst based on those images. No modern democracy can, or should, be cavalier with the lives of its military forces; and while the use of military force should not be lightly entered into it may sometimes be required.

It is often said that the reason the United States was defeated in Vietnam was that its public came to believe that the intervention was illegitimate, futile and costly in terms of blood and treasure. This in turn gives rise, especially in America, to a strong aversion to putting 'boots on the ground' and to extreme sensitivity to military casualties. Ronald Reagan quickly withdrew American forces from Lebanon when 241 marines were blown up. The eighteen soldiers who died in Somalia – captured in the film *Blackhawk Down* – led to a swift and humiliating US retreat from that country. Aversion to casualties led to an emphasis on high-level bombing rather than ground operations in the former Yugoslavia.

Remote operations are more ineffective and cause more collateral damage than ground forces. The US failure to deal effectively, and fairly, with post-invasion Iraq results from this, especially when combined with the emphasis placed by former US Defence Secretary Donald Rumsfeld on a military strategy minimising the number of troops on the ground. This allowed Iraq's porous borders to be penetrated by interfering neighbours and for the massive Iraqi arsenals and state infrastructure to be plundered, not least by thousands of men whose incomes had been swiftly halted by a radical policy of disbandment of the army and dramatic de-ba'athification. US troops may have played a positive role in some places but have also been extremely heavy-handed to the point of brutality in shooting first and asking questions later. The casual atrocities that flow from such actions by 19-year-old recruits then cause and ventilate popular grievances.

It led to inexplicable decisions such as the US invasion of the new free trade union's head offices in Baghdad in December 2003 and the overnight arrest of its key leaders, despite their being a force wholly opposed to sectarian terror. In fact, the marauding US troops tore up anti-terror posters as they rampaged through the building, which was eventually retrieved from US control.

However, the conflict exists independently of US actions. In both cases, the drivers of change and reconciliation are to be found inside the borders of the conflict zone. External support for such forces is vital but made much more difficult if airbrushed out of the equation by media coverage that exaggerates the bad and ignores the good.

THE ROLE OF NON-SECTARIAN MOVEMENTS AND PEACE GROUPS

The early 1970s in Northern Ireland saw the Provisionals at their most bloody. Five hundred people died in 1972. Each of these years was claimed to be 'the year of victory'. One response was the formation in 1976 of the Peace People following an horrific incident in which the British army shot dead a member of the Provisional IRA whose out of control car then careered into children on the pavement. The movement attracted thousands of people across the religious divide. The Northern Ireland writer John O'Farrell says that 'everyone knows that the Peace People fell apart and scattered but what isn't appreciated is that they were successful in putting a cap on the murderous ambitions of both sets of paramilitary groups'.[10]

The later British–Irish peace movement included organisations such as Families Against Intimidation and Terror, the Peace Train and New Consensus. Its members sought to learn the lessons of the Peace People and to construct a more sustainable and cross-community movement. Slowly, the peace movement was able to rally Irish and British people behind the view that the IRA's activities were 'not in my name', a slogan later adopted by the movement against the invasion of Iraq. Arguably, this helped deprive the Provisionals of legitimacy and may have played a role in encouraging them to embrace a more political approach and so helped create the right conditions for the peace process, along with other actors and factors.

Parts of the organised labour movement in Ireland and Britain were keen supporters of the peace movement. The Northern Ireland trade unions had been unable to resist working-class loyalist opposition to power-sharing in 1974 but came to play a positive role in fighting workplace sectarianism – most notably in its 'Hands off my mate' campaign. The peace movement and the labour movement in Northern Ireland did come to have a significant influence but not when the conflict was at its height. It was too dangerous, though few activists or journalists were murdered. In today's conditions, the Iraqi and al-Qaeda death squads are making it extremely difficult to mobilise such a movement in Iraq. The assassination of Hadi Saleh was part of a concerted campaign to eliminate the leadership of the nascent and non-sectarian labour movement. As the leaders of that movement told us when we saw them in Erbil, they just want external support so 'we can stand on our own two feet'. They have the ability to unite Iraq but can do so better with concerted assistance, rather than being abandoned to extremist forces or despair borne out of crude historical determinism.

History is plentiful in Ireland and in Iraq and it is always possible to find an event that paints the British in a bad light: from Drogheda to the RAF gassing of Iraqi Kurds in the 1920s. One of the most prolific exponents of this is Robert Fisk, whose reaction to the death sentence passed on Saddam in late 2006 was to list previous Western collaboration with Saddam against his own people and his neighbours. For instance, he mentions these UK exports: 'the £200,000 worth of thiodiglycol, one of two components of mustard gas *we* [my emphasis] exported to Baghdad in 1988, and another £50,000 worth of the same vile substances the following year'.[11]

It is right to criticise the actions of past UK and US governments and the cynical way in which they applied Realpolitik, during the Cold War, to backing Iraq against the newly fundamentalist Iran. It is vital to have a sense of history, but it is also vital not to be transfixed by past crimes which lead those such as Fisk to reject any claim that 'we' (even those who opposed such crimes) in the UK or the US can ever play a progressive role in the present or in the future.

DIVIDED SOCIETIES AND POWER-SHARING

Both societies are deeply divided. It is arguable that Northern Ireland has become more segregated since the peace process with 90 per cent of Protestants and Catholics living in largely homogenous areas. Only 5 per cent of pupils attend integrated schools. Iraq is a construct of British colonial rulers and brings together three main ethnic identities: the majority Shia community accounts for 60 per cent, while Kurds and Sunnis number about 20 per cent each, with a far smaller number of Christians, Jews, Assyrians and Turkomen. The violence of post-war Iraq is driving people into more homogenous areas, especially in Baghdad.

Roger Darlington says 'both involve a long history and are not problems simply created in the last few decades. Both involve religion – one a division in Christianity; the other a division in Islam'.[12] The divide was largely concealed and suppressed in Northern Ireland for about 50 years until the Troubles erupted and the Shias were largely repressed for the period of minority Sunni and Ba'athist rule.

The conflict in Northern Ireland was on 'narrow ground' and therefore affected many more people's lives, especially in large cities such as Belfast and Derry. The current eruption of sectarian strife is also more acute in mixed cities such as Baghdad and in Kirkuk which suffered forced 'Arabisation' and is now a key to the long-term resolution of conflict as ways and means are found to restore its Kurdish character. As was also the case in the former Yugoslavia and in the former Soviet Union, once such 'ancestral quarrels' – to use Conor Cruise O'Brien's memorable phrase – are unleashed they can take a long-time to resolve and this emphasises the crucial role of institutions and bodies that seek to overcome such differences. In Northern Ireland this has been, and is being done, within the boundaries of a once heavily disputed jurisdiction.

SDLP leader John Hume told the *Jerusalem Post* in 2000 that the Good Friday Agreement could be applied to the Israel–Palestine conflict but Robert Fisk concludes that 'other people's peace treaties don't travel well'.[13] The Iraqi Foreign Minister Hoshyar Zebari who visited Northern Ireland as an exile before the 1998 Belfast Agreement told the *Irish Times* that Iraqi ministers were studying the North 'very closely'. Zebari noted one key difference:

> We are not dealing with Sinn Féin and the IRA; what we have in Iraq is all IRA. The motto of those who are fighting us is very simple: 'Either we rule Iraq or we burn Iraq'. Sinn Féin had a political agenda. Okay, it used a

military wing to pursue this through a variety of violent means – terror attacks sometimes. But there was some care for civilians, and when there was a bomb there was a warning to the police. There is no warning in Iraq.[14]

He concluded that: 'When people realise that violence is futile, when there is hope in the political process that they will be treated equally, and when there is participatory, consensual democracy, people will start to change their views.'[15]

The ideal solution for Iraq is based on the need for power-sharing and federalism, as outlined in the Iraqi constitution, but this remains an unresolved issue. During the Troubles, Northern Ireland was seen as an insoluble problem. Few writers on the subject fail to remind readers of Churchill's pessimistic assessment of 1922 that 'The whole map of Europe has been changed...but as the deluge subsides and the waters fall short we see the dreary steeples of Fermanagh and Tyrone emerging once again'. Yet the intractable conflict has been resolved on the basis of an astute mixture of soft and hard power, economic investment and international co-operation.

This was far from inevitable. In fact, it looked impossible three decades ago. Roger Darlington worked for Shadow Home Secretary Jim Callaghan and then Merlyn Rees, the first Labour Direct Ruler after the suspension of Stormont. He has noted that:

Expectations are so important in politics and in war. I was astonished when I went into the Northern Ireland Office in 1974 as part of a newly-elected Labour Administration to appreciate that sections of the Provisional IRA genuinely thought that a Labour Government would pull out the troops. There was no objective reason to believe this. How terrorists/ insurgents expect politicians to behave is important to their campaign. Equally astonishing to me was that many in the 'Troops Out Now' movement expected the result of the withdrawal of troops to be a united Ireland at peace with itself. In fact, the reality would have been a civil war resulting in an independent, smaller, largely Protestant, neo-fascist statelet with a more unstable state on its southern border. Those arguing for troops out of Iraq have to think very hard about what the consequences would be and how that squares with their sometimes socialist principles of peace and prosperity for Iraqis and a more stable world order.[16]

Likewise, Alison Gordon, a diplomat at the British embassy in Baghdad accompanied a senior delegation of Shia and Sunni leaders from Iraq in November 2006 to Northern Ireland to examine the decommissioning of paramilitary weapons, combating sectarianism and preventing the infiltration of the police by paramilitary gangs. She said 'The road to disarmament and peace in Northern Ireland was slow and painful. But with strong political and religious leadership, reconciliation is possible, even in Iraq.'[17]

CONCLUSIONS

Parts of the Irish and British left have embraced the 'anti-imperialist' terror of a minority in both Northern Ireland and Iraq. In the former this meant accepting that the primary cause of terror was partition and in the case of Iraq it means accepting that the primary cause of violence is the 'occupation' and the presence of foreign troops. In both cases, a vociferous minority wanted the immediate withdrawal of troops and tended to franchise its thinking to extremist forces, rather than the majority in the two polities who wanted the troops withdrawn or scaled down but only when it was safe to do so. We can now see Northern Ireland as a testing ground for a reactionary left with a world view based on the principle that any enemy of the imperialist metropolis is a friend of ours. It seems fanciful now but parts of this constituency entertained the idea that the 'Provos' could bring about a socialist state – a sort of Cuba without the sunshine.

The former SDLP Deputy leader Seamus Mallon described the 1998 Belfast Agreement as 'Sunningdale for slow learners'. The lesson for Iraq is that conflicts acquire a deadly momentum of their own. It has been said that a general rule of thumb is that peace-making takes as long as the initial war or conflict. By that reckoning Northern Ireland is about a third of the way to full resolution. However, Northern Ireland's conflict was relatively small fry compared to Iraq's misery. An almost fascist-type and totalitarian dictatorship ruled for 35 years casting a long shadow over the new Iraq, whose people can justly claim to be amongst the most oppressed ever. Combined with four years of increasingly intense violence aimed at fomenting sectarian strife, the process of establishing liberal values, institutions and a representative and federal government is a long-term process. At the time of writing it is an open question as to whether the elected coalition government can establish a monopoly of force, maintain the territorial integrity of the country, replace foreign troops and rebuild a shattered infrastructure while diversifying its oil-based economy.

The last thing they need is partial solidarity based on redundant stereotypes. My own epiphany on the Irish Question came from the realisation that some on the British left were more preoccupied with achieving a united Ireland, whatever the cost, than the Irish left, not to mention Irish public opinion. It seemed that this group divided the world into 'good' and 'bad' peoples. The Catholics of Northern Ireland had suffered terribly at the hands of the 'Prods' and deserved solidarity. This drew from the poisonous and primitive 'Provo' analysis that Protestants were a stooge, comprador class whose existence was due to British gerrymandering that had established an artificial statelet against the wishes of the majority. It would be a great tragedy if some parts of the left start to view, and present, the Iraqi Kurds in similarly unfavourable terms, for having been sheltered by Western forces since they ejected Ba'athism after the first Gulf War of 1991.

However, in both Northern Ireland and Iraq there were, and are, people of all religions and forces in civil society that can do much to stabilise society, assist government, eradicate and reverse extremism. Victory for the Sunni and Shia extremists and al-Qaeda would help condemn Iraq, and the wider Middle East, to languish in its own oil wealth without having to nurture a civil society or create the jobs for a restless youth who may then become more susceptible to the millenarian claims of Islamic totalitarianism.

I note for future exploration other parallels: the role of diasporas in the conflict (pressurising the American government in both cases) and the impact on the economy and society of exiles and the brain drain; the growing role of the Internet in allowing otherwise external observers to play a larger role – the contribution of www.nuzhound.com over ten years in relation to Northern Ireland should be praised; the discussion of how the Irish in Britain were once termed a 'suspect community' and how this is often applied to Muslims in Britain, and more widely.

Harry Barnes lists five key lessons based on his long Northern Ireland experience that are relevant to Iraq:

(a) we need to support the people and forces of good will, (b) there needs to be strong restraints to prevent illegal and counter-productive acts by whoever is acting as a force of law and order (c) the authorities need to protect the innocent and advance their quality of life, (d) certain extremists can sometimes be drawn into political discussions (which will often come to alter their game plan) and (e) efforts need to take place to create an artificial centre in politics, which will help shape its future parameters.[18]

Professor Fred Halliday, a keen observer of Middle East politics has seen the failure of the Left in addressing both Northern Ireland and Iraq. He has recalled that

I was ten years old when the 1956 IRA bombing campaign, organised from my town [Dundalk] began. I had heard tell of 'progressive atrocities'. I well recall the nationalist who in Belfast in 1969, told me that the Protestants had the right to self-determination, 'provided they went and did it somewhere else'.[19]

In these terms, Halliday has praised the work of Isaac Deutscher and Hannah Arendt which:

contains truths that the contemporary Middle East, and the world, sorely need. Their relevance is to much more than the Arab–Israeli question; it applies in principle to any of the numerous other national or inter-ethnic conflicts across the world where local rhetoric and partisan solidarity from outsiders have reinforced each other in a dance of death, as if one side were angels and the other devils – Cyprus, ex-Yugoslavia, Nagorno-Karabakh, Sri Lanka, Northern Ireland.[20]

Recently, Dr Ali Al Saleh, Imam at the Ahlulalbait Islamic Centre in Milltown, Dublin, penned a powerful piece in the *Irish Times* in which he concluded that

> The issue now is not being for or against the United States, for or against the invasion, or whether or not anyone lied about weapons of mass destruction. The only thing that matters now is supporting Iraq's democratic development and helping the Iraqi government to develop a strong and professional police and military. Then we can tell foreign military forces that their services are no longer needed, thank them for their help and ask them to leave – a goal that Iraqis, Americans, British, Irish and all free people of the world should share.[21]

An optimistic view is that Iraq is at the equivalent – though far more bloody – stage that Northern Ireland was at in the early 1970s. The hope is that sustained international involvement and support for the government and non-sectarian forces, using a combination of soft and hard power, can stop Iraq falling apart with the 'blood-dimmed tide' conquering all in its path. The solution is in Iraqi hands – as it was in the gift of Northern Irish actors and factors – but this requires that the best of the left, and others, acquire conviction and passionate intensity for solidarity, not least with people like Hadi Saleh and the Iraqi labour movement. It would be ideal if they could then also be able to state with confidence 'our day will come'.

ACKNOWLEDGEMENT

I am very grateful for sound advice and comments from Harry Barnes, Professor Thomas Cushman, Roger Darlington, John Lloyd, David Mapstone, Austen Morgan, John O'Farrell, Eamonn Rafferty, Dave Spector, Jonathan Tanner, Bert Ward, Professor Paul Bew, Mick Fealty and Ruth Dudley Edwards. All errors are mine. I hope that the essay begins a conversation about how to encourage practical solidarity with progressive forces in Iraq and I dedicate the essay to a fallen comrade, Hadi Saleh.

NOTES

1   Sean O'Neill, 'Special Branch absorbed into counter-terror unit' *London Times*, http://www.timesonline.co.uk/article/0,,29389-2385406.html.
2   http://www.labourfriendsofiraq.org.uk/archives/001006.html.

3 Michael Walzer, 'Can there be a Decent Left?', *Dissent Magazine* (Spring 2002), http://www.dissentmagazine.org/article/?article=598.
4 Henry McDonald, 'This Moral Vacuum on Iraq', *The Observer*, 7 March 2004, http://observer.guardian.co.uk/comment/story/0,6903,1163750,00.html
5 Andrew Murray, 'Empire and its Resistance is the Central Issue of Our Time', *The Guardian*, 26 August 2006.
6 http://www.labourfriendsofiraq.org.uk/archives/000176.html.
7 On this Labour Friends of Iraq visit to Iraq see 'The Other Iraq-report of LFIQ Delegation to Iraq', http://www.labourfriendsofiraq.org.uk/archives/2006_04.html.
8 Author conversation with Roger Darlington.
9 Christopher Hitchens, 'The Indecent Haste to Exit Iraq', *Slate*, 30 October 2006, http://www.slate.com/id/2152548.
10 Author conversation with John O'Farrell.
11 Robert Fisk, 'This was a guilty verdict on America as well', *The Independent*, 10 November 2006.
12 Author conversation with Roger Darlington.
13 Robert Fisk, 'Why Peace Treaties Don't Travel Very Well', *The Independent*, 10 July 2006.
14 Deaglán de Bréadún, 'Iraqi Politician Studying North Peace "Very Closely"', *Irish Times*, 14 November 2005, http://www.ireland.com/newspaper/front/2005/1114/785203311HM1IRAQIPOL.html.
15 Ibid.
16 Author conversation with Roger Darlington.
17 *The Sunday Times*, 5 November 2006.
18 Conversation with author.
19 Halliday, 'In Time of War: Reason Amid Rockets'; *openDemocracy*, 11 August 2006, http://www.opendemocracy.net/globalizationmiddle_east_politics/arendt_deutscher_3813.jsp
20 Ibid.
21 Ali Al Saleh, 'What Future do Iraqis Want?', *Irish Times*, 18 March 2006, http://www.ireland.com/newspaper/opinion/2006/0318/350186149OP18IRAQI.html

Irish Aid to the Palestinian Authority in the Bilateral and EU Context

Constantin Gurdgiev

In the mid-1990s, at the height of the Oslo peace process, Ireland significantly increased its bilateral financial aid to the Palestinian Authority (PA). In January 1996, Ireland committed some US$2.9 million to the PA as a part of the Oslo Agreement.[1] In October 1998, on the back of the Israeli–Palestinian Wye River Agreement, Ireland promised to continue its aid to the PA for the period between 1999 and 2003 in the amount of US$2 million per annum.[2] Following the outbreak of the Al-Aqsa intifada in September 2000, Irish aid to the PA continued to rise as Israeli-Irish political relations became increasingly strained. Indeed, diplomatic and political tensions between Ireland and Israel have had an impact on the nature and volume of bilateral aid flows from Ireland to the PA.

The majority of Irish aid to the PA since the mid-1990s falls into the category of direct state-to-state aid and emergency/humanitarian assistance. The former has been primarily allocated directly to the PA in the form of support for education and health services. The latter has been largely administered through the Irish Non-Governmental Organisation (NGO) sector and has taken the form of payments for medical and food assistance. In the process the whole issue of efficiency of such aid, along with the issues of aid conditionality, monitoring and preventative measures to ensure that Irish aid does not provide either direct or indirect support for anti-Israeli, and even terrorist, groups have become secondary to the objective of engaging in providing direct support for the PA.

In May 1999 during Palestinian leader Yasser Arafat's visit to Dublin, the Irish authorities announced their intent to establish a development aid office in Ramallah that would administer Irish aid to the PA. At the time this development was billed as part of the Irish government's desire to give 'increased status' to Palestine. In September 1999 during another visit to Ireland, Arafat thanked the Irish government and people for their support for the Palestinians. He especially praised Irish educational aid to Palestine.[3]

In mid-October 2001, during another visit to Dublin, Arafat stated that Ireland was a 'good friend' of the Palestinians and that the Palestinians and the Irish had a 'historical and very important relationship together, more than friends'.[4] A similar statement was made by Arafat in his March 2002 interview with the *Irish Times*, in which he noted that ties between 'our two peoples are very strong and very old and we are proud of it'.[5]

According to Rory Miller, the Irish representative office in Ramallah co-ordinated the significant increase in Irish bilateral aid to the PA, which in 2002 alone reached €5 million (€780,703 more than the previous year)[6].

Ireland's aid to PA follows three major pathways:

1) Direct bilateral aid;
2) NGO-administered aid;
3) Aid flows through EU programmes: These programmes, run by the European Commission and individual member states, provide the largest financial contribution to the PA to the extent of €500 million per annum since 2003.

This chapter will first examine direct Irish aid to the PA. It will then place the Irish contribution in the context of EU-wide aid programmes. The chapter will conclude with an analysis of the effectiveness of Irish aid, both bilateral and through the EU, to the PA.

IRISH AID SUPPORT TO THE PA

Following the 1998 Wye River Agreement, Ireland pledged to maintain its annual contribution to the Palestinians at €1.5 million during the period 1999–2003. In reality, while the majority of other donors failed to meet their planned aid budgets, Ireland's contribution to Palestine over this time has exceeded its pledges. In 2000, Ireland deepened its commitment to Palestine by opening a Representative Office in Ramallah. Following two programming missions to Palestine in 2004, a three-year (2005–07) Country Strategy Programme (CSP) was adopted in October 2004. The CSP commenced in 2005 with a proposed budget of €3.35m for 2005; €3.5m for 2006 and €3.5m for 2007; thus providing for over €10m during the three-year period. The principal components of the CSP for the period 2005–07 are intended to provide support for:

Basic Education
This is the main focus of the strategy. Funding in 2005 was provided to the

Palestinian Ministry of Education and Higher Education to support the development of the new Palestinian curriculum for the printing of textbooks for use in government and United Nations Relief and Works Agency (hereafter, UNRWA) schools in Gaza and the West Bank.

Health
Funding is provided to Bethlehem University for community outreach programmes in physiotherapy, occupational therapy, water quality, neonatal nursing, midwifery and education development.

Local government
Funding is provided to the United Nations Development Programme (UNDP) for local rural development programmes in the Jenin region.

Human rights and democratisation
Funding is provided to Palestinian and Israeli NGOs who focus on the rights of Palestinian prisoners, women and children and also on reconciliation, civil society and the building of democratic institutions.

Palestinian Development Assistance Programmes
Support to local civil society groups for economic and social regeneration.

UNOCHA
Funding is provided to the UN Office for the Coordination of Humanitarian Affairs (UNOCHA) to assist it in its on-going monitoring and advocacy work in Palestine.

Support to UNRWA
This is the key UN agency with responsibility to deliver humanitarian assistance to approximately 4 million Palestinian refugees. UNRWA's relief efforts are focused on education, health, basic services and the provision of micro-finance facilities. Irish Aid's assistance to UNRWA is delivered through core funding and in specific response to UNRWA emergency appeals.

In 2005, over €4.4 million was provided in assistance to the PA as follows: €2.35 million under the Bilateral Aid Programme; €1.50 million to UNRWA; and over €400,000 under Irish Aid's Civil Society Funds (in support of the NGO Christian Aid, agricultural development and personnel co-financing); €200,000 in support of the EU Border Assistance Mission (EU BAM); and €50,000 in support of the Office of the Delegate General of Palestine.

In the wake of the Hamas victory in the January 2006 Palestinian legislative elections, Ireland was the first EU country to pledge increased funding for the PA. According to the Department of Foreign Affairs, 'Ireland is committed to continuing our development and humanitarian support to

Palestine. It is envisaged that Ireland's support in 2006 will exceed that of 2005.'' So far, Ireland pledged US$4.9 million in aid, of which US$923,400 was in direct aid to the PA. The rest was channelled through aid groups and the UN agencies, making Ireland the tenth largest donor among OECD nations.

At 18.8 per cent of Irish aid being direct aid to the PA, Ireland's contribution is slightly above that of The Netherlands and Denmark (both at 15 per cent). Interestingly, Sweden, Greece, Luxembourg and Spain provide virtually no direct aid to the PA. The EU Commission gives 14.6 per cent (US$148 million) of its aid in the form of direct aid – a 57.1 per cent reduction of aid on 2005.

THE EU AID FRAMEWORK

Ireland is a party to the EU-wide agreements aimed at financing development activities and social policy spending by the PA. These agreements include the MEDA (Mediterranean Development Assistance) partnership and subsequent development programmes outlined below.

According to the European Parliament, the MEDA programme is 'the main financial instrument of the EU for the implementation of the Euro-Mediterranean Partnership. This partnership, also known as the Barcelona process, involves the fifteen Member States and twelve Mediterranean Partners situated in the Southern and Eastern Mediterranean'.[8]

The partnership is based on three pillars:

- A political and security pillar establishing a common Euro-Mediterranean area of peace and stability based on fundamental principles, including respect for human rights and democracy;
- An economic pillar, involving the creation of a free-trade area between the EU and its twelve Mediterranean Partners and among the Mediterranean Partners themselves. According to the European Parliament 'this partnership is accompanied by a substantial EU financial support for economic transition in the Partner countries and for the social and economic consequences of this reform process';[9]
- A social, cultural and human pillar, with a view to developing human resources, promoting understanding between cultures and rapprochement of the peoples in the Euro-Mediterranean region, as well as to developing free and flourishing civil societies.

The MEDA programme for the period 1995–99 was adopted in July 1996 and amended by the Council in November 2000, providing the legal basis for MEDA II covering the period 2000–06.

Co-operation under MEDA operates at both bilateral and regional levels, the former involving some financing programmes carried out by the member states, including Ireland. Bilateral programmes aim at increasing the competitiveness of the private sector with a view to achieving sustainable economic growth, paving the way for the implementation of free trade, while providing for a smoother economic transition through social policy measures.

MEDA I amounted to €3,474 million, or on average €694.8 million per annum. MEDA II funding was €5,350 million – averaging €764.3 million per annum. However, during MEDA I, only 26 per cent of pledged funds were actually disbursed, as shown in Table 1 below. The EU identified several reasons for this low disbursement to commitment ratio, including the fact that 'bilateral co-operation was hampered by domestic/political problems...or by the slow implementation...of the necessary structural reforms' and due to 'poor co-ordination of implementation and management of projects by Commission services'.[10] Under MEDA II, the ratio of payments/commitments averages 63.3 per cent despite the fact that there was little noticeable improvement in the recipient countries record on reforms implementation or in the Commission's ability to monitor conditional reforms. Thus, 'this improvement derives from a better organisation of Commission services: the restructuring of external aid services of the Commission and the creation of Europe Aid'.[11]

Table 1. MEDA I–II: Payments versus commitments for the period
1995–2003, € million

	1995	1996	1997	1998	1999	2000	2001	2002	2003
Commitments	173	403	981	941	937	879·1	757·4	632·6	640·4
Payments	50	155	211	231	243	330·5	403·7	588·7	520
Commitment Ratio %	28.9	38.5	21.5	24.5	25.9	37.6	53.3	93.1	81.2

European Parliament (2003), Tables 1 and 2.

The European Union aid to Palestine was a considerable part of the appropriations provided by the EU budget under heading 4 (external actions) and extends beyond the MEDA partnership arrangements. According to the EU programmes, aid to Palestine can be roughly divided in three different forms of assistance:

Direct Budgetary Assistance
Following the outbreak of the second intifada in September 2000 the Israeli Government suspended the monthly transfer of tax revenues (VAT and customs duties) to the PA and closed off the Palestinian Territories. In response, the EU released €27.7 million of Special Cash Facility (SCF I) in November

2000 and in December 2000 established a second Special Cash Facility (SCF II) with an amount of €90 million to support the PA's administrative functions. In January 2001, the Commission released €30 million of the SCF II.

EU Direct Budgetary Assistance (DBA), was established as a long-term strategy at the end of May 2001, when the EU converted the remaining €60 million of the SCF II into DBA, which was disbursed to the PA between June and November 2002. This aid was conditional on a fiscal austerity spending plan to be prepared and implemented by the PA; the increased authority of the various ministries of finance for the administration and supervision of spending programmes, and the preparation of future reforms.

Since SCF II, the EU has made six more rounds of funding: DBA II–VI in the amount of €150 million (between December 2001 and February 2003), all subject to the submission of the budget law and monthly global breakdown of expenditures; further evolution on the consolidation of the investment budget; the establishment of a modern system of internal audit and financial control; and the reform of the General Control Institute in order to transform it into a supreme audit institution.

DBA transfers represent about 9 per cent of the monthly expenditure of the PA. Although the Israeli government recommenced transfers of VAT and duties proceeds to the PA in late 2002, the European Commission continues its budgetary assistance (albeit on a scaled-down level) to the PA. Furthermore, the direct assistance to the budget of the PA was financed from the MEDA and other programmes (B7-410) in 2000–01. Despite the European Parliament conclusion in 2003 that 'this procedure is not very transparent and coherent', and the recommendation that 'the Commission should envisage future financing of direct budgetary assistance only through one budget item',[12] DBA to the PA continues along several lines of financing.

UN Relief and Works Agency
The renewed convention on the EU budget support for the UN Relief and Works Agency for Palestinian Refugees in the Near East (UNWRA) was agreed in 2002 for a total of €237.1 million through 2006. Previously, €97.5 million was disbursed in 2000–01 through budget line B7-421. The EU also supports UNRWA Food Aid programmes: €43.8 million in 2000–02 (chapter B7-20). According to an EU Parliamentary assessment, 'the management by UNRWA can be considered as reasonable and has not been questioned'.[13] All of the UNWRA programmes take form of zero-conditionality aid.

Other projects
These miscellaneous programmes are funded by the EU budget with €238.3 million in 2000–02 covering a range of financing for humanitarian and development aid, such as 'emergency aid for victims of the escalation of the ongoing conflict in certain parts of the Palestine territories and in neighbouring countries, shelter rehabilitation, water and electricity

reconstruction, health projects, education, risk capital, interest subsidies for EIB operations, training of local administration, etc'.[14]

As with UNWRA, these programmes bear no policy or institutional reform conditions. However, these projects require a call for tender and control from the Commission. According to the EU Parliamentary assessment:

> the projects in the Palestine territories suffer from particular problems. The most important problem is that NGOs and independent organisations encounter difficulties for their work in the field and are rather regularly hindered by Israeli authorities in implementing projects. This makes the implementation of projects through NGOs increasingly difficult.[15]

Surprisingly, the EU Parliamentary reports do not identify the problems of non-transparent operations of the PA and partnering NGOs, or the accounting and verification deficiencies of EU aid donors.

Overall, between 1994 and 2002, the contributions to UNRWA have increased by 50 per cent; humanitarian aid has increased five-fold in volume between 1994 and 2002. Aid for other projects has more than doubled (from €84 million to €202 million). In total, the appropriations provided for Palestine have been increased by 119 per cent in this 9-year period (from €135.8 million to €297.5 million).

THE EFFECTIVENESS OF IRISH AND EU AID TO THE PA

Problems of accountability

Direct budgetary aid to the PA is fraught with difficulties in ensuring an adequate control and follow-up mechanism. Other aid programmes to Palestine are either managed from other budget lines under external actions or by the United Nations.

However, direct budgetary assistance together with other direct aid outflows to the treasury accounts of the recipient countries, such as macro-financial aid, constitute a special case of EU support. According to the European Parliament, over time, 'some Members have expressed the fear that the direct budgetary assistance entered into the accounts of the PA could be re-directed to destinations where it could be used for terrorist acts'.[16]

For these reasons, DBA to the PA was the focus of discussions between the European Parliament and the Commission on aid to Palestine, in particular when the Commission presented transfer request no. 14/2002. The Committee on Budgets approved the transfer concerning budget article B7-420 only on the condition that budgetary assistance to the PA is accompanied by complete and permanent information to the European Parliament and by reinforced monitoring measures, aimed in particular at:

- improving the PA's audit system;
- conducting an external audit;
- changing the Palestinian law related to budget and audit;
- ensuring that social policy is included in the PA budget.

Apart from the internal PA control mechanisms, disbursements of DBA is subject to information collected by the International Monetary Fund (IMF). This information is a crucial input for the analysis and evaluation of conditionalities of the macro-economic situation conducted by the Commission. The IMF information includes revenue developments; employment; the wage bill and non-wage current outlays (with emergency expenditure broken down into health, social assistance and others); estimates by the PA of unpaid outlays; capital expenditure financed by the PA; disbursements of external budgetary support; the evolution of domestic bank financing; and economic policy decisions by the PA pertaining to fiscal matters.

Payments are made upon compliance with conditionalities agreed with the PA. These relate to transparency in the PA's public finances, the strengthening of budgetary management (containment of expenditure and the cost of the public sector payroll) and progress regarding overall financial and administrative reform. In particular:

- Proper implementation of the austerity budget with a ceiling of US$90 million for current expenditure;
- Budgetary revenue, including donors' contributions, should not exceed the austerity budget's expenditures;
- Containment of arrears and expenditure (in particular of the cost of the public sector payroll);
- Pursuance of the financial and administrative reform platform;
- Integration of the investment budget into the overall budget of the PA in order to reinforce transparency in the PA's public finances;
- Strengthening the transparency of public finances;
- Legal reform through the promulgation of the Judiciary Independence Law.

According to the European Parliament, 'EU direct budgetary assistance has led to positive developments in the PA and the Palestinian territories'. In particular, the following were highlighted:

- Improved co-operation by the PA, including discussion on possible improvements, such as a more detailed breakdown of the budget, etc.;
- Reinforced transparency in the PA's public finances following the monitored consolidation of accounts;
- Viable management of the PA's public finances through the containment of expenditure and particularly of payroll in the context of the implementation of the austerity budget;

- A renewed discussion process with the Israeli government leading to a re-start of payments from Israel to the PA.[17]

However, given the scope of the original requirements and the fact that these requirements were in place for nearly 4 years, it is clear that DBA from the EU is far from being compliant with the EU-imposed standards. The same criticism applies to the direct aid to the PA budget by EU member states, including Ireland.

More importantly, since the January 2006 elections, the issue of conditionality of EU aid has come under increased criticism from the PA. As was reported in the Russian daily *Vremya Novostei*, during his visit to Moscow in early 2006 senior Hamas official Khaled Meshal stated that

> The Palestinian people cannot sell their legitimate claims...There can be no trading on that, with money on one side and on the other side our homeland and our rights...Humanitarian aid should not be given with conditions. It's inadmissible.[18]

This strongly suggests that there remain significant difficulties in assuring that 'humanitarian aid' money disbursed by the international donors, including the EU, is not being used by the current leadership of the PA to finance illegal and terrorist activities both inside and outside Palestinian-controlled areas.

The Problem of targeting

Along with the issue of insufficient conditionality and enforcement, Irish aid to the PA suffers from the problem of proper targeting of objectives. In other words, Irish aid to the PA, although directed to worthwhile causes, contributes little to the improvement of the institutional, social and human capital deficit suffered by Palestinian society. As mentioned above, the main objectives of Irish aid to the PA are in the following areas:

- Education;
- Institutional assistance;
- Relief programmes.

On the other hand the major challenges facing the PA administered areas include

- A lack of private sector development and excessive dependency on state funding for economic activity and employment;
- Shortages of entrepreneurship, marketable skills and employable labour force;
- A non-marketable system of religious education.

In the case of PA-administered territories, over 70 per cent of GDP is accounted for by central government expenditures – well above the average for the region which stands at around 35–50 per cent. An even higher share of personal income and wages depend on direct disbursements by the PA. As a result, the public sector dominates virtually all economic activities from the retail distribution of food to the provision of health services.

Such state activities are associated with significant inefficiencies, a lack of transparency and moral hazard. However, perhaps the most detrimental impact of the disproportionate role of the state structures in the Palestinian economy is the effect that public spending has on crowding out competitive markets in the provision of goods and services.

Closely linked to the PA's high spending share in the economy is the problem of the extremely high dependency of the Palestinian economy on low-skilled labour and extremely high labour intensity of all economic activities. Over 45 per cent of the workforce in the region is employed in agriculture or agriculture-related rural economic activities. Another 40 per cent are employed in pre-industrial manufacturing, characterised by an extremely low value-added per unit of labour. These activities tend to generate up to 80 per cent discount on average wages earned in the region.

Thus, while the average wages in the Middle East are approximately 70 per cent below those in industrial countries, in the PA-administered territories, average wages are around 90 per cent lower than those in developed countries. This pattern also extends to Palestinians employed in Israel and to the Palestinian entrepreneurs engaged in individual economic activity in the Israeli territories.

The dire state of Palestinian entrepreneurship is also evident outside the PA-administered territories. In Syria and Lebanon, native Palestinian businesses account for a negligible effect on these countries Gross Domestic Product. Blanchflower has provided some indirect evidence of the low level human capital investment in entrepreneurship amongst the Palestinian Diaspora residing in the United States. When considering the rate of self-employment among the various groups of immigrants residing in the US, Blanchflower finds that Palestinian natives tend to exhibit a below average propensity for self-employment relative to other groups. This suggests that Palestinians residing in the United States are less likely to engage in entrepreneurial activities than an average immigrant into the United States. This stands in stark contrast to their next door neighbours. Israelis residing in the US tend to be at least 2.7 times more entrepreneurial, Syrians 4.4 times, while Lebanese are 2.4 times more entrepreneurial than Palestinians.[19]

These factors help to explain both the lack of jobs and the lack of economic activity, as well as the fact that within the PA-administered territories, there is virtually no capital and wealth accumulation, with the majority of Palestinian native entrepreneurs preferring to invest their savings outside the jurisdiction of the PA.

Table 2. Macroeconomic parameters of the PA-administered territories

	2000	2001	2002	2003	2004
Agriculture, value added (% of GDP)	7.56	7.31	6.31	6.18	
Exports of goods and services (% of GDP)	14.79	14.57	12.3	9.99	
Fixed line and mobile phone subscribers (per 1,000 people)	151.1	191.22	192.38	236.38	379.59
GDP (current billion US$)	4.64	4.03	3.40	3.45	
GDP growth (annual %)	−1.17	−16.01	−19.12	−1.67	
GNI per capita, Atlas method (current US$)	1750	1370	1110	1120	
GNI, Atlas method (current billion US$)	5.18	4.23	3.58	3.77	
Gross capital formation (% of GDP)	21.52	5.65	3.53	2.5	
Imports of goods and services (% of GDP)	60.37	48.25	46.57	49.01	
Industry, value added (% of GDP)	22.58	16.38	13.25	12	
Inflation, GDP deflator (annual %)	9.98	6.86	17.23 7		
Internet users (per 1,000 people)	11.8	19.38	32.5	43.07	45.61
Market capitalization of listed companies (% of GDP)	16.51	17.92	16.97	18.83	
Official development assistance and official aid (current US$, billion)	0.637	0.870	1.62	0.972 1.14	
Population growth (annual %)	4.27	4.29	4.27	4.11	4.11
Population, total	29,66,000	3,096,000	3,231,000	3,366,702	3,508,104
Services, etc., value added (% of GDP)	69.86	76.3	80.43	81.81	
Workers' remittances and compensation of employees, received (billion US$)	1.12	0.799	0.679	0.692	0.692

According to World Bank, the West Bank and Gaza had GNI per capita of US$1220, ranking the two territories the 139th economy in the world. Using PPP (Purchasing Power Parity) comparisons, the territories' GNI (Gross National Income) stood around US$3,035 ranking them in 148th place just above Vietnam. This income per capita was over 55.6 per cent above that of India and just 18 per cent below that in Syria. Both the direct GNI and the PPP-adjusted GNI for the two PA-administered territories suggest that the Palestinian areas do not present a case for urgent humanitarian aid relief.[20]

These problems are further amplified by the rapidly growing population, with fertility rates ranging between 5.14 new born per woman in 1999 to 4.93 in 2002, the latest year for which data is available. 97.4 per cent of all births in 2000 were attended by skilled health staff. In 2002, 78 per cent of the urban population in the PA-administered territories had access to sanitation facilities, while 94 per cent of the population had access to improved water sources. Subsequently, life expectancy at birth has increased between 2000 and 2004 from 72.12 years to 72.99 years in line with the developed nations and above the regional average.

In 2004, the literacy rate for the adult population was recorded at 92.39 per cent – higher than the OECD average. At the same time, over the last 5 years, despite increasing funding for educational programmes by foreign donors, the primary education completion rate has fallen from 103.46 per cent of the relevant age group population to 98.11 per cent, indicative of two factors: increased enrolment in religious schools and decreasing enrolment in adult education programmes. Primary schools enrolment declined from 109.31 per cent in 2000 to 92.94 per cent in 2004.

Both secondary and third-level school enrolment rates increased, with the latter rising from 25.65 per cent in 2000 to 37.9 per cent in 2004. Despite the questionable validity of some of these figures, the data presents PA-administered territories as being at, or above, the average performance for the region of the Middle East and North Africa, again raising the question of the urgency of external funding increases.[21]

Indeed, the daunting task of increasing economic growth in the face of extremely rapid population growth and other adverse factors is not being served by continued aid inflows for emergency assistance and health subsidies. Under the conditions of the second intifada, real growth in PA-administered areas all but collapsed. The real GNI growth averaged 9.28 per cent per annum between 1994 and 1999. This fell to a 13.3 per cent per annum contraction for the period 2000–03. In per capita terms, the figures are even more bleak – between 1994 and 1999 per capita GNI expanded by 3.7 per cent per annum, while in the period 2000–03 there was a 17.3 per cent per annum contraction in the PA economy. The unemployment rate increased from 11.8 per cent in 1999 to 31.3 per cent in 2002.

These figures suggest that the second intifada had an effect of reversing all gains made by the PA-administration, despite the fact that aid inflows remained robust. As shown in Figures 1 and 2 below, there is zero relationship between the growth rate in aid to the PA and the per capita real GNI growth rate. In fact, according to the IMF, virtually all loss of economic performance in income growth terms during the period of the second intifada can be attributed to the loss of trade and workers' mobility with Israel.[22]

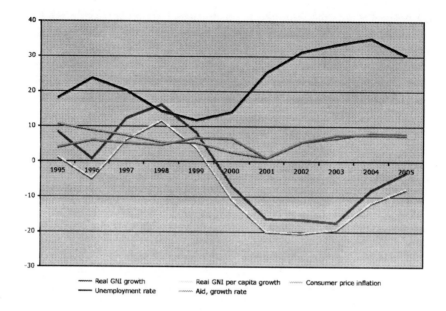

Figure 1. Real GDP and GNI growth and aid flows, 1995–2005

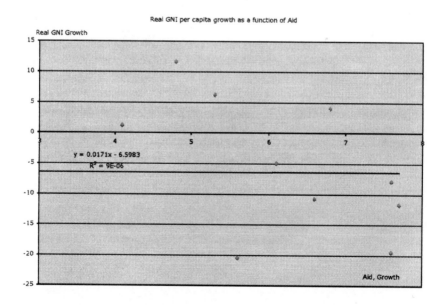

Figure 2. Per capita real GNI growth rate and aid flows

Confirming the above, aid has a positive, but relatively weak, correlation with unemployment when measured year on year. This relationship is present both during the period preceding the second intifada and since 2000, suggesting that international aid is not successful in reducing unemployment in the territories. Changes in aid flows account for zero change in the real growth rate for the period 1995–2005. However, the relationship strengthens when we consider a one-year lag in aid inflows, implying that past aid inflows are associated with higher unemployment in the future. This refutes any potential argument that aid flows follow higher unemployment, as would be anticipated in the case of humanitarian aid. Instead, it appears that in the case of the PA, higher unemployment is a response to the previously higher aid contributions.

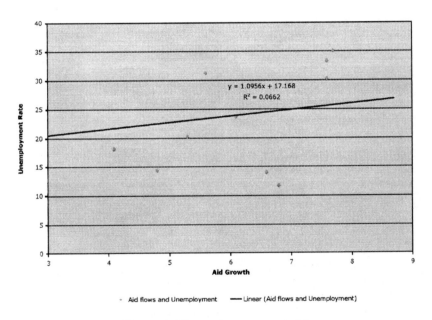

Figure 3. Unemployment and aid

Perhaps the most worrisome aspect of aid to the PA is that over time, the strongest effect of aid on macroeconomic performance in the PA-administered territories has been the effect of increasing inflation. Once again, when one considers aid lags, higher aid clearly triggers higher inflation.

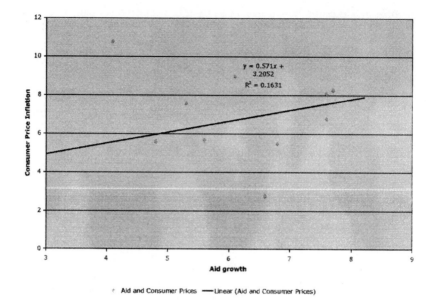

Figure 4. Inflation and aid

    This latter conclusion is not surprising given the state of national accounts for the PA. As net current transfers have increased from 15.1 per cent of GDP in 1994 to 59 per cent in 2002, private consumption increased by only 29 per cent over the same period, while public consumption increased by 85.4 per cent. Similarly, private gross fixed investment contracted by more than 37 per cent while gross public investment fell 47 per cent between 1994 and 2002. These figures suggest that aid flows were not used to build either private consumption or private and public investment.

    Instead, the majority of aid flows appear to have been used for the purposes of public consumption. It is worth noting that the PA's own work-force has increased from 52,000 in 1995 to 125,000 in 2003 (a 140 per cent increase); while non-agricultural private sector employment grew from 245,000 to 272,000 (only an 11 per cent increase) over the same period. For overall employment (inclusive of Palestinians working in Israel), public sector employment grew by 8.08 per cent between 1994 and 2003. Over the same period of time, private sector employment grew by just 3.71 per cent.

CONCLUSIONS

According to the World Bank:

Creating a good business environment is key to creating jobs, fighting poverty, and improving growth. Developing economies in Eastern Europe are streamlining business regulations and taxes, but there's still a lot of red tape in Middle East and North African countries.[23]

For example, it takes 47 days in Iran to complete the required procedures for legally operating business, and 36 days in Egypt, 11 days in Morocco and 24 days in the high-income economies, on average. In the PA-administered territories, this figure is around 110 days.[24]

A lack of proper governance reforms, not a shortage of aid, explains the difficult development situation faced by the Palestinians. In contrast with the rest of the region, in PA-administered territories even the first trench of reforms, primarily comprising of regulatory reforms that are easy to adopt, such as streamlining court and collections procedures; taxation rates and collection; exchange rate and central banking regulations; and zoning and development regulations are all lagging behind regional norms. Similarly, even the first round of trade tariffs and barriers reforms were not implemented in the PA-administered areas.

With respect to the more substantive reforms, which may have direct adverse effects on the entrenched interest groups – in the financial and education sectors, for example – deeper reforms are still decades away. Thus, the declining resources, rents, and the building of pressures in the labour markets – high labour force growth, high unemployment, almost stagnant or declining real wages – suggest that the labour market pressures are untenable at present levels. These factors also suggest that the existing system of education, while yielding impressively high rates of secondary and tertiary education completion, is not capable of delivering the requisite entrepreneurial and professional skills. Aid inflows, including those targeted for education programmes appear to have no direct positive effect on unemployment, despite the fact that the earlier cohorts of aid recipients (1994–2002) have already completed their education.

Furthermore, aid conditionalities have so far failed to deliver any significant improvement in the legal and regulatory environment. Piecemeal reforms and a lack of top-down reforms imply that any deeper changes in policies, especially those related to improving the business climate, are being delayed. The PA-administered territories remain largely closed to the prospect of integration into the global economy through trade and Foreign Direct Investment (FDI).

In terms of FDI and capital formation, PA-administered territories remain far behind their regional neighbours. Overall, since the mid-1990s less than

5 per cent of the global capital flows were directed to the Middle East and North Africa region. Of these, less than 0.25 per cent landed in the Palestinian territories, or roughly US$180 million. This figure includes both the FDI and the capital acquisitions through remittances.

The growth rate in foreign capital inflows has slowed down since 2002. At the same time, the PA's own public investment programmes have remained extremely low, having only commenced in 2000. Instead, virtually all public investment programmes are financed by external donors. This, perhaps, represents one of the examples of the positive contribution of foreign aid to Palestinian development.

The Oslo period (1994–2000) saw the establishment of a number of modern enterprises in telecommunications, beverages, and tourism. In part, this was spurred by the investment promotion law, which granted investments an income tax exemption for 10 years. However, this positive development was undermined by the nature of some of the enterprises that were created. Most of the PA tax revenue diverted away from the budgets was used for investment in PA commercial operations. Monopolies on cement and petroleum acquired early on generated substantial profits, which were also hidden from the budget.

Due to a lack of transparency and accountability in the PA's commercial activities, the IMF estimates that between 1995 and 2000, approximately US$300 million in commercial profits were channelled outside the budget. All in all, excise tax revenue and profits from commercial activities diverted away from the budget may have exceeded US$898 million. This figure represents 19.1 per cent of overall PA revenues.

In general, as pointed out by the IMF in 2003, income tax revenues and proceeds collected from various fees and charges are characterized by the overall lack of control and accountability.

> Fees and charges are levied by about fifteen PA ministries and constitute 12-15 per cent of all PA revenues. In addition to education and health fees, there are transportation fees (automobile licensing and fines) as well as agricultural and judicial fees. These fees were remitted to the ministries' bank accounts and remained under the ministries control and discretion until very recently.[25]

Once again, soft budget constraints arising from aid inflows helped to remedy the situation without the need for significant reforms. Only the revenue crises at the beginning of the second intifada prompted the PA to initiate the reform of tax revenue collection and to strengthen the audit powers of the ministry of finance.

Aid inflows propped up an increase in PA employment that is unprecedented for the region. In 2003, the PA's civil service employment stood at 73,933, up from 32,600 in 1995, while security personnel amounted to

56,128, up from 24,400 in 1995. These figures exclude health and education services employment. Excluding the refugee population (serviced directly by UNRWA programmes), the proportion of the PA's civil service to employment on a per capita basis is 4 per cent. This, in the words of the IMF, 'exceeds that of most countries in the region as well as comparator countries'.[26]

Increases in civil service employment up to 2002 'greatly exceeded what would have been warranted'[27] by the demographics and private sector growth. Overall, public sector employment grew at more than twice the rate of what was fundamentally warranted in the years between the two intifadas. The PA's wage bill quickly exceeded all comparator countries, undercutting the PA's ability to provide effective investment in infrastructure, health and education services. According to the IMF, in 1999 the wage bill accounted for 15 per cent of GDP and 55 per cent of current expenditures. By 2002 the PA's wages absorbed 70 per cent of current expenditures, 'leaving inadequate resource for non-wage expenditures and resulting in accumulation of unpaid bills and arrears to the private sector'.[28]

Overall, the central government wage bill in 2001 stood at 15.2 per cent of GDP – the highest ratio in the region (the regional average was 8.95 per cent). As a ratio of total expenditure, including capital expenditure, the PA's wage bill was 49.3 per cent in 2001 – the highest in the region and 89.4 per cent above the regional average.

The budgetary crisis of 2002–03 was not resolved by the appointment of the so-called 'reform cabinet' in June 2002. Instead, civil service employment continued to expand. The cabinet was able to begin the implementation of the Presidential Decree of 10 January 2000, which established the Palestinian Investment Fund (PIF), charged with 'managing all of the PA's assets and commercial activities in the WBG (World Bank Group) as well as abroad and also with executing the PA's privatization strategy once it has been finalized'.[29]

The Fund was formally established in October 2002, some 34 months after the decree. The decree establishing the PIF (Palestinian Investment Fund) made it illegal for the PA to conduct any commercial activity or hold assets outside of the PIF. Upon its first valuation, the Fund had US$633 million in sixty-seven commercial entities and liquid assets, including several major foreign investments in high-risk venture capital. According to the IMF, 'since there was neither transparency nor accountability surrounding these investments, one may surmise that the only strategy was to build up equity with little regard to risk'.[30]

Some of the commercial activities such as the Cement Company failed the transparency test because of 'anti competitive behaviour, unfair or preferential relationship with the Palestinian Authority and corruption'.[31] Once again, an argument can be made that the reforms aimed at deregulating monopolies and privatising PA-owned enterprises, commonly seen as potential triggers for the greater opening of the PA-administered territories to world capital markets are being unnecessarily delayed by the soft budget constraints represented by the aid inflows.

In their groundbreaking 1997 article Burnside and Dollar argued that aid accelerates growth and poverty reduction only in developing countries that pursue sound economic policies. Aid has had no measurable effect in countries with poor policies.

> By 'sound policies' we mean measures that have been shown in a wide range of studies to promote growth: open trade regimes, fiscal discipline, and avoidance of high inflation. These results imply that aid would be more effective overall if it were well targeted to poor countries with sound policies.[32]

Given the fact that Irish aid to the PA does not present a departure from the practices of other donors, it is hard to conclude that the conditions of Irish aid are sufficiently different to present a case of effective support for economic development in the PA-administered territories.

The central problems with Irish aid to the PA are very much in line with those presented by the aid inflows from other countries. Lack of transparency and accountability in revenues utilisation and allocation by the PA imply that a potentially large share of Irish aid is being used for public consumption maintenance instead of development and investment.

The lack of specific conditionalities aimed at reducing monopoly power of the PA-owned companies implies that Irish aid is simply being used to soften the budget constraints of an inefficient, corrupt and anti-competitive economic system run by the PA. The inability, or unwillingness, of the Irish donors, in-line with other donors, to impose controls over the education curriculum and education-spending imply that educational grants are being directed towards areas of education that are largely irrelevant to skills acquisition and entrepreneurship promotion. All of these points suggest that there is little difference between bilateral aid from Ireland and bilateral aid from any other donor to the PA.

NOTES

1   'Irish Aid: Ireland's Official Development Assistance 1996', Department of Foreign Affairs (hereafter, DFA), 1996, p. 23 and Annex 2, p. 2.
2   'Palestinian-Administered Areas (PAA)', *Ireland Aid, Annual Report*, 1999.
3   A. Quinlan, 'Ahern, Arafat talk during Shannon Stop', *Irish Times*, 22 September 1999.
4   Deaglán De Bréadún 'Ahern Tells of Irish 'special' Role', *Irish Times*, 16 October 2001.
5   See Arafat's interview with Deaglán De Bréadún in the *Irish Times*, 18 March 2002: Deaglán De Bréadún, 'Arafat says he is Willing to meet Sharon if Troops Leave', *Irish Times*, 18 March 2002.
6   Rory Miller, *Ireland and the Palestine Question, 1948-2004*, Dublin, 2005, p. 184.
7   From statement provided to the author by the Department of Foreign Affairs, 4 August 2006.

8 'Working document on MEDA and Financial Assistance to Palestine', European Parliament, Committee on Budget Rapporteur Salvador Garriga Polledo, 20 January 2003, p. 1.
9 Ibid., p. 1.
10 Ibid., p. 2.
11 Ibid., p.3.
12 Ibid., p. 6.
13 Ibid., p. 6.
14 Ibid., p. 7.
15 Ibid., p. 7.
16 Ibid., p. 8.
17 Ibid., p. 10.
18 See 'Russia Faces Tough Task to Soften Hamas Stance on Israel', *Agence France-Presse*, 3 March 2006.
19 David G. Blanchflower, 'Self-employment: More May not be Better', NBER (National Bureau of Economic Research) working paper 10286, February 2004.
20 See World Development Indicators database, World Bank, 1 July 2006.
21 Ibid.
22 See A. Bennett, K. Nashashibi, S. Beidas, S. Reichold, and J. Toujas-Bernaté, 'Economic Performance and Reform under Conflict Conditions', Middle Eastern Department, IMF, 15 September 2003.
23 See World Development Indicators database, World Bank, 1 July 2006.
24 Ibid.
25 See Bennett, Nashashibi *et al.*, 'Economic Performance and Reform under Conflict Conditions'.
26 Ibid.
27 Ibid.
28 Ibid.
29 Ibid.
30 Ibid.
31 Ibid.
32 Craig Burnside and David Dollar, 'Aid Spurs Growth – in a Sound Policy Environment', *Finance & Development* (December 1997).

'The Luck of the Irish': Perceptions of the 'Celtic Tiger' in Egypt, Lebanon and Israel

Rory Miller

Ireland's meteoric transformation from one of Europe's poorest and least developed economies into the 'Celtic Tiger' over the last decade has left politicians, economists and businessmen from California to Bulgaria and from China to the Baltic States desperately trying to work out the best way to emulate the Irish model. This concluding chapter will examine the newest developments in Ireland's Middle Eastern involvement by focusing on the extent that three of the region's nations – Egypt, Lebanon and Israel – have come to perceive the Irish economic 'miracle' as an important model for their own economic development. It also assesses whether the Irish achievement in harnessing an educated, English-speaking workforce to a number of progressive economic policies – most notably low tax rates, flexible business practices, and a strategic goal of promoting a competitive enterprise environment – is relevant to the development of these three nations.

Ireland's highly developed beef industry and its traditional expertise in the areas of electricity generation, healthcare, construction and education have meant that from the 1970s, long before the rise of the 'Celtic Tiger', there had been Irish economic involvement in the Middle East – for example, in 1987 an Arab–Irish Chamber of Commerce was established in Dublin by the Arab League Union of Chambers of Commerce.[1]

However, into the 1990s, the first practical acknowledgement by Middle Eastern nations that the nascent Irish economic boom had potentially valuable lessons came in October 1998 when a group of London-based Arab ambassadors made a three-day visit to Dublin.[2] Since that time the Irish economic involvement in the Middle East – in Morocco, Saudi Arabia and the other Gulf States, as well as the three countries focused on here – has 'developed considerably',[3] as then Minister for Foreign Affairs Brian Cowen put it during a 2003 tour of the region.

EGYPT

By 2000 Egypt was the largest single market for Irish beef exports in terms of total volume, with Irish firms providing almost 80 per cent of Egypt's beef import requirements in 1999 (157,000 tonnes).[4] Despite this the dawn of the new century saw Irish–Egyptian relations develop in a number of other areas of economic activity. In part this was due to the damage done to the bilateral trade relationship in beef by the 1996 decision of Egypt, as well as a number of other Arab countries, to place an embargo on European beef products and live cattle imports following the BSE scare in the United Kingdom.[5]

However, the shift in the bilateral relationship away from beef was also due to the changing nature of the Irish economy which saw a new Irish effort to engage across all sectors of the Egyptian economy from textiles and agri-business to Information Technology (IT). This is evident in the sharp increase in Irish direct investment into Egypt from US$59,000 in 1996 to almost US$16 million in the following year. In 1997, Ireland was the sixth largest EU investor in Egypt, only behind the United Kingdom, Germany, France, Denmark and The Netherlands. In 1999, Ireland was the fourth largest EU investor in Egypt, with US$25.5 million, only behind the United Kingdom, France and Denmark and ahead of major global and European investors such as Germany, Italy, The Netherlands, Spain and Sweden.[6]

Irish companies have also won some flagship contracts. In September 2003, International Development Ireland Ltd signed a major agreement with the Gulf of Suez Authority in which the Irish body was appointed the external adviser on the establishment of a Special Economic Zone in the Gulf of Suez. Then Minister for Foreign Affairs Brian Cowen described this key Irish role in the 'prestigious and flagship' project as an 'acknowledgement of the success of Ireland's own industrial and economic transformation in recent years'.[7]

Similarly, the success of the Irish architectural firm Heneghan Peng, in beating off 1,557 competitors from eighty-three different countries in 2003 to win the contract to design Egypt's new Grand Museum in Cairo (a design which adorns the cover of this book) has also underlined the Irish capacity to compete on a global level in the area of cultural and creative industries. While in September 2006 the oil and gas group Aminex signed a production sharing agreement for the West Esh El Mellahah area in Egypt, following both Egyptian parliamentary and presidential approval of the deal.[8]

Despite the rapid growth in the bilateral relationship (embodied in the above flagship projects that Irish firms have been awarded), the success of the 'Celtic Tiger' is still not as widely appreciated, or known, in Egypt as the achievements of the 'Asian Tiger' economies who were at the forefront of the world economy during the 1980s and 1990s. Nevertheless, according to Dr Ashraf Mishrif, a consultant to the Egyptian embassy in London on culture and education and a leading expert on foreign direct investment into the country there is 'definitely an awareness of the Irish economic miracle in Egypt over the past decade, most notably there is a wide understanding among relevant government officials, the business community and economists that Ireland has made tremendous strides in economic growth in the past ten years'. Mishrif further adds that the

> Irish experience is [a] very good model for developing countries... This is basically because Ireland does not possess vital physical and natural resources. This makes the experience so valuable to developing countries and thus a number of lessons can be drawn from it.[9]

Moreover, attracting Foreign Direct Investment (FDI) is a key priority of Egyptian policy-makers. The recent establishment of the Ministry of Investment has been one of the most significant developments in this respect. In December 2006, the Cairo Investment Forum in conjunction with the Ministry of Investment hosted 1000 leaders from the Egyptian Private and Public sectors to discuss ways to improve the investment climate in Egypt.[10] As such, Ireland's phenomenal success in attracting FDI, not only offers Egypt encouragement and provides good examples of best practice that its investment promotion agencies can adopt, but also highlights the failings in Egypt's existing investment strategy.

The Irish success in attracting FDI is unprecedented. According to the UN World Investment Report for 2004, Ireland received US$25 billion in FDI in 2003 – more than the UK received (US$14bn) in the same year. By far the biggest reason for this has been investment by US firms, particularly those in the information and communication technology sectors, healthcare and pharmaceuticals. By 2000 40 per cent of all US 'green-field' investment into Europe went to Ireland. By 2003, US investment in Ireland was more than two and half times greater than investment in China. Indeed, over 40 per cent of all US overseas software investment has gone to Ireland, while over 300 US entities have been licensed to trade in the International Financial Services Centre (IFSC) in Dublin. Overall, an estimated 600 US companies, including Intel, Microsoft, Google and Dell, employing over 100,000 people, have set up in Ireland and the US multinational sector, even accounting for the fact that its contribution to GDP is hugely inflated by transfer pricing, is a key sector of the economy alongside agriculture and the tourism industry.[11]

This Irish success in attracting FDI by offering a deregulated marketplace and a low tax regime gives credibility to those in Egypt who have been calling for economic liberalisation at home. In particular, unlike in Egypt, where the majority of FDI is made in petroleum and natural gas projects, the majority of Irish FDI inflows have been invested in the financial sector and manufacturing – the two most dynamic sectors for economic growth. The concentration of between one-third and one-half of Ireland's FDI in Dublin's IFSC has boosted economic activities and increased the total value of Irish domiciled funds to US$500 billion (total funds serviced, including non-domiciled fund, reached US$768 billion) in 2005 up from US$21 billion ten years earlier. This in turn has provided Ireland with significant capital for the implementation of national development programmes.

As such, Egypt has looked closely at the Irish FDI experience in the financial services sector in developing the Egyptian Financial Market Authority. The same is true in the area of IT. In 2003, the same year that Egypt established its first business park dedicated to IT (the Smart Village Pyramids project[12]), it also set up an IT Marketing Support Office in Dublin, which created the brand of 'Software from Egypt' on behalf of nine of Egypt's leading offshore software developers.

At an institutional level, Irish–Egyptian economic relations have also developed greatly since 2000. In 2003, Egypt and Ireland established the Joint Ireland–Egypt Business Council to boost their trade and investment ties. Though this council is a non-governmental consultative body, its role has been quite significant as it forms the basis for establishing direct business relations between Irish and Egyptian business organisations, firms and entrepreneurs. This adds to the role of the Egyptian–British Chamber of Commerce, which attempts to boost Irish–Egyptian economic relations, and the role of Egypt's Investment Promotion Office (IPO Egypt) in London, which has responsibility for promoting Egypt's investment potential in the United Kingdom, Ireland and the wider EU.[13]

LEBANON

While the Irish institutional relationship with Lebanon over the last few years has not developed to the same extent as it has with Egypt, the Irish role in developing the infrastructure of Lebanon in the early part of the 'Celtic Tiger' era was far greater than that undertaken in any other Arab country. For example, the Irish Electricity Supply Board played an important role in the Lebanese government's economic reconstruction plan throughout the 1990s.[14] While in 1999, Aer Rianta began managing the duty free operation at Beirut's new airport terminal as part of a US$225 million venture that by 2002 saw it managing (but not owning) the duty free shops in airports in Bahrain, Oman, Kuwait and Qatar, as well as the Lebanese capital.[15]

Moreover, as the most Westernised of all the Arab states, Lebanon has been very receptive to Ireland's growing cultural influence on the world stage, which paralleled and overlapped with the Irish economic boom. In

2002, for example, Michael Flatley's 'Lord of the Dance' show headlined the twenty-fifth Baalbek International Festival.[16]

While even more than in Egypt, senior Lebanese officials and the domestic media have been very open publicly about the need to follow the Irish model in order to prepare the economy for the global, hi-tech era.

In a keynote address to the 'Towards e-Lebanon' conference in Beirut in June 2003, Dr Nasser Saidi, then first vice governor of the Bank of Lebanon, expressed his vision that 'Lebanon should become the Ireland of the Middle East',[17] a view reiterated on several occasions by the Beirut *Daily Star*, the Arab world's leading English-language daily newspaper, which has argued that Ireland provides 'a path for Lebanon's economic rebirth'.[18]

There are three areas in particular where the Irish success has been identified as offering important lessons for Lebanon. The first is in reducing the red-tape and bureaucracy that makes it difficult for foreign firms to set up business. This is a major problem for Lebanon. In 2003, after eighteen months of negotiations with the Lebanese government over opening an office senior Hewlett Packard officials were on the verge of giving up because of the red tape, with Constantine Salameh, the Lebanese vice-president and general manager of financial services for Hewlett Packard Europe despairing: 'I could write a book about it'.[19]

Another key area where Ireland offers a model is in the Lebanese attempt to modernise its tax system. In 2001, for example, Jim Somers, an Irish-born partner in Ernst & Young, and a member of a five-man committee established by the Lebanese Finance Ministry to advise on tax, told Lebanese officials that their government needed to rapidly modernise the tax system if the country wanted to meet the challenges of globalisation. In particular, he gave the example of Ireland as a country that had used Value Added Tax (VAT) as a way of earning revenues to fund development.[20]

More recently, in May 2006, on the eve of the Lebanon war between Hezbollah and Israel, the first conference on technology development in Lebanon was held at the prestigious Massachusetts Institute of Technology (MIT) in the United States. This meeting attempted to provide momentum and ideas for pushing forward Lebanon's tech industry by addressing key issues such as developing infrastructures, setting regulatory frameworks, improving market access and mobilising financial resources.

The conference looked at the successful hi-tech ventures that Lebanon could build on and, in particular, focused on what the conference chair Loai Naamani, a doctoral student at MIT, termed 'models of technology-driven economic development in countries like Ireland, India, and Eastern Europe'.[21]

Among the speakers at this event was Kevin Carroll, a senior official in Ireland's Industrial Development Agency (IDA). He argued that Ireland's success has been built largely on the strength of its hi-tech industry, which in the early years had been concentrated in attracting manufacturers and call centres, rather than focusing on R&D and indigenous growth.[22]

Another speaker, who gave a keynote address, was John Cullinane, head of The Cullinane Group, and the founder of the first successful US software products company (Cullinet Software Inc. in 1968). Cullinane has extensive experience of the Irish software industry and has promoted peace through jobs and economic development in Northern Ireland, where he was named Special Economic Adviser for Belfast in North America. He also established the Friends of Belfast in North America, an informal network of people from the United States and Canada whose 'social capital' could be of value in creating jobs and economic development, thus contributing to stability and economic prosperity in Northern Ireland.

Cullinane told the audience that Lebanon has to invest in 'smart' call centres as Ireland had done in the past adding that 'I believe call centres would create job opportunities exponentially' and that such an initiative would, in turn, attract multinationals servicing this area, as well as local companies which are realizing the importance of outsourcing their call centres.[23]

This is a hugely important issue because without a sophisticated and low cost communications infrastructure, including call centres and back office support – two areas where Ireland has thrived – Lebanon cannot compete in attracting multinationals looking to outsource production.[24] Cullinane's advice had an immediate impact and within weeks of the MIT meeting the Lebanese Telecommunications Minister Marwan Hamade promised to set up a call-centre unit under his supervision and to take the appropriate measures to reduce cost barriers to the establishment of call centres in Lebanon.[25]

ISRAEL

Cullinane has not only been involved in sharing his knowledge of the Irish economic model and his Northern Irish experience in promoting the economics of peace in Lebanon. Indeed, he has invested much effort in also promoting the economics of peace in Israel and the Palestinian Authority (PA). Cullinane helped organise the Conference on Technology Investment and Partnering Opportunities for Israel, Ireland and Northern Ireland sponsored in conjunction with the University of Massachusetts and the Sloan School of Management at the Massachusetts Institute of Technology. He also organised a conference hosted by the University of Ulster on the issue of using jobs and economics to promote peace that was attended by Israeli, Palestinian and other key participants in the Middle Eastern peace process.[26] This led to the 2003 launch of an ambitious project promoting Arab–Israeli peace through economic development that aimed to create 20,000 jobs across the region.[27] He also promoted the Israel–US Binational Industrial Research and Development (BIRD)[28] project as a model for a job-creating vehicle in Northern Ireland and the six border counties, the first cross-border economic initiative in the history of the island of Ireland.

The efforts of Cullinane, and others, including many senior Irish politicians (from the North and South) to use their experience of promoting an end to conflict in the North to aid the search for peace in the Middle East, have done much to increase awareness of Ireland's recent history – both political and economic.

But even without such efforts, nowhere in the Middle East have the potential benefits of emulating the Irish model been more widely, publicly and consistently embraced than in Israel. As a 1999 report by Bank Hapoalim, a leading Israeli financial institution, noted the Irish economy had 'excelled in performance...and provides a means of learning about methods that can be employed to improve the performance of the Israeli economy'.[29]

Despite the fact that Ireland's economic involvement in the Middle East in the 1970s and 1980s was dominated by trade with the oil producing, and meat importing, Arab and Muslim states, it is not surprising that Israel, which like Ireland, has a small domestic market, a lack of any mineral resources (especially oil) and past experience of major fiscal and budgetary challenges, identifies great potential in the Irish economic success. Moreover, by the early years of the 'Celtic Tiger' Irish–Israeli economic ties had increased dramatically, in part due to Israel's increased integration into the world following the commencement of the Oslo peace process in 1993,[30] and in part due to the rising Irish interest in entering the wider Middle East market in these years (as seen in the case of both Lebanon and Egypt also).

By 2000, Ireland and Israel were experiencing unprecedented economic ties and the media was describing Israel as Ireland's 'most dynamic trade partner'.[31] In particular, there was widespread excitement over the long-term potential for growth in the area of scientific instruments, data processing and photographic and optics equipment.

However, what excited Israeli politicians even more than existing, and potential, bilateral trade ties was the opportunity Ireland offered as a model for Israel's evolving economic policy. This was clearly seen during the period of Likud government between 2002 and 2005. Benjamin Netanyahu, currently head of the Likud opposition party, but Ariel Sharon's finance minister between 2003 and 2005, regularly cited Ireland as an economic success story made possible by the adoption of free market economy policies. 'What did they do?' Netanyahu once asked rhetorically before answering

They lowered taxes, cancelled monopolies, made incentives to work, cut bureaucracy, privatized companies, and increased competition. There is a word for it: they implemented free market economics. They persevered for at least a decade, and they passed us by.[32]

This admiration for the Irish success in replacing 'a welfare ethic with a business ethic',[33] as Netayahu termed it on another occasion, was echoed by other senior politicians at the time. Meir Sheetrit, then a junior minister under Netanyahu at the Israeli ministry of finance, vowed to copy the methods used by Ireland to attract hi-tech inward investment so that Israel would offer an 'improved version of Ireland' to foreign investors.[34]

Even now, with the free-marketers of Likud in opposition and a centrist-left coalition of Kadima–Labour in power, there are still regular expressions of a desire to emulate the Irish example. This was highlighted in a statement made by Israeli Prime Minister Ehud Olmert following a meeting with renowned US investor Warren Buffett in September 2006. Olmert thanked Buffett for the large investment of US$4 billion he had made in the Israeli firm ISCAR and encouraged him to invest in more projects in Israel adding that 'Israel is open for investment. In terms of taxation levels, Israel is in a very competitive place compared to other places in the world, including Ireland'.[35]

What is interesting is not only the fact that Netanyahu or Olmert have been drawn to the Irish model, but that members of the Israeli left, who espouse socialist economic principles, have also held out the Irish model as a way forward for dealing with the growing disparity between rich and poor in Israel.

Israel's current Labour party leader and minister of defence, Amir Peretz, visited Ireland in November 2004 when he was still the head of the Histadrut, Israel's largest and most powerful trade union. On his return he expressed admiration for what he saw in Ireland, stating in an interview in the *Jerusalem Post* in May 2005 that:

> we view Ireland as a model from which we can learn a great deal, in relation to upgrading workers' rights and welfare rights, as well as in the attempt to reach national agreement between all sectors of the economy: the government, the employers, the unions, and social groups. Our idea is to establish a national council for society and economy, according to the Irish model, that would help Israel mimic the Irish economy.[36]

Following Labor's accession to government as part of the coalition with Kadima in mid-2006, Peretz was urged by some to make good on such promises by copying the Irish Social Partnership agreement. However, some commentators have argued that it is wrong to look to the Irish experience precisely because the Irish success has been due to 'many components that no government in Israel would want to adopt: A long-term social convention with professional unions, the renunciation of an independent currency, and early participation in the euro bloc'.[37]

Certainly, the EU factor cannot be ignored and the Irish membership of the Euro-Zone does mean that it has lost control of setting its own interest rates. It is also true that membership of the EU, and especially the significant level of EU money that has been pumped into Ireland over the last three decades, has been partly responsible for developing the nation's infra-structure and facilitating economic growth. But it is also true that a number of other EU member states have received similar levels of EU funding over the last few decades yet have failed to match Ireland's economic success. This is underpinned by the fact that Irish GDP per capita as a per centage of the core EU-15 states rose from 103 per cent in 1998 to 126 per cent in 2004. Over the same period EU receipts as a per centage of Irish GDP declined sharply.

Others have used the Irish success to dismiss the Israeli security situation as a valid reason for Israeli economic problems over the same period. Unlike Israel, one such argument went, Ireland

> never sat back whimpering about its own security problems, quite the contrary: it took advantage of its economic boom to improve its security situation. Its economic growth played a key role in bringing the Irish and British governments to reach an agreement on Northern Ireland.[38]

This is a weak argument as the Republic of Ireland did its own share of 'whimpering' even though the security problems it faced were almost negligible compared to those faced by Israel and Northern Ireland. It is also simplistic to argue that Ireland's economic success played a 'key role' in bringing about the Northern Ireland peace process. In fact most informed observers believe the opposite is true – that the peace process that began in 1998 was key to the success of the Irish economy.

As in the case of Egypt and Lebanon, what attracts Israeli interest more than any other factor is the Irish success in gaining FDI, which has not only been very important in providing a base for broad economic growth, but has ended the traditional high unemployment that plagued Ireland (and Israel) for decades. But it is also true that Ireland's reliance on FDI leaves it very vulnerable to the whims of foreign multinationals which could abandon the country at any time for cheaper locations.

This reality is made worse by the fact that with the exception of a limited number of companies, including Ryan Air, Ireland lacks locally established world-beating innovative firms like Finland's Nokia. It also has low domestic expenditure on research and development (R&D) and it has one of the worst records among developed countries in terms of Internet use and registering patents. Moreover, the literacy of Irish students in maths and science is close to the EU average, the number of PhDs in these areas is below average, and the government spends little more than the EU average on education.[39]

While this far from impressive list of statistics still puts it way ahead of Egypt in terms of development, R&D investment and educational standards, it places Ireland far behind Israel in similar areas. In 1996, *Newsweek* magazine noted that Israel was the only serious rival to California's silicon valley in the hi-tech sphere. A decade later, despite the downturn in the global hi-tech sector and the collapse of the Oslo peace process post-2000 Israel has managed to maintain its position as a global technology leader.

By 2005 hi-tech industries accounted for almost 15 per cent of Israel's GDP. It had the highest rate of R&D investment per GDP in the world and spent a record 5 per cent of GDP on R&D. Seventy Israeli companies were quoted on Nasdaq, more than any other country outside North America. Israel could also boast more US-registered patents than China, India and Russia combined. In proportion to its population, Israel had the largest number of start-up companies in the world, and in absolute terms, had more start-up companies than any other country in the world apart from the US (3500, mostly in hi-tech). Israel was also ranked second in the world (again behind the US) for venture capital funds, and on a per capita basis, had the largest number of biotech start-ups.[40]

The Israeli success in investing in R&D and of funding technology incubators to nurture hi-tech talent not only makes it by far the most advanced economy in the Middle East, but it also places it far ahead of Ireland in terms of indigenous growth and development. Indeed, the success of the Irish hi-tech sector has been fuelled primarily by attracting major overseas (usually American) firms. In the World Economic Forum's Global Competitiveness Index (GCI) rankings for 2006–07, Israel was in fifteenth place, while Ireland was twenty-second, but what was significant was that Israel was ranked third worldwide in the area of technological readiness. While on the basis of the 2006 Digital Opportunity Index (DOI) that evaluates the opportunity, infrastructure and utilisation of Information and Communication Technologies (ICTs) for 180 economies worldwide, Israel came thirteenth while Ireland was ranked thirty-first.[41]

Some Israelis have woken up to this reality. When Sol Gradman, chairman of the High-Tech CEO Forum in Israel, was invited to give a lecture to an Irish software company on Israel's hi-tech success he began researching the 'Celtic Tiger' and soon realised that despite the way Ireland was lauded by Israeli politicians:

> The overwhelming majority [of the Irish exports] come from American companies... Ireland, which in effect is a logistics centre with no added value or technological innovation... At the end of the day, Ireland isn't necessarily the right model. They have attracted investment and the country is thriving, and I'll tip my hat to them for that. But it's not based on local entrepreneurship, and the advantages can melt away fairly easily.[42]

Interestingly, this reality has not dented the enthusiasm of the majority of Israel's political or business elite who still look to emulate the Irish success. At the January 2006 Herzliya Conference, Israel's annual get-together of movers and shakers from around the world (jokingly referred to as 'Davos on the beach'), Irish economist Dr Sean Barrett of Trinity College, Dublin, was flown in to explain to an 800-strong audience, including such eminent figures as Stanley Fischer, former managing director of the International Monetary

Fund, the secret of Ireland's success. In his speech Barrett said that over the last decade and a half Irish success had been due to 'two main pillars: free trade and order in the public finances'; Barrett also drew particular attention to the importance of FDI from the US and the positive developments in the Northern Ireland peace process as there would have been 'no growth without peace', concluding that the Irish model is 'a good one and might be worth exporting'.[43]

Even taking into account the weaknesses in the Irish model, Barrett is correct about the opportunities that it offers Israel. By 2001 it was estimated that over forty Israeli hi-tech companies were doing important business in Ireland. More recently *Globes*, the Israeli business newspaper, reported that Irish software companies were planning to introduce Israeli products into the European market in a strategic collaboration. Under the project, which would include fifteen Israeli software firms, joint companies would be set up in Ireland to introduce Israeli products into the Irish market via Irish companies, and through Ireland, boost sales throughout the EU. As Israel–Ireland Chamber of Commerce President Dr Ben Nachman explained, the idea was to combine Israel's advantages in software with Ireland's strong software industry.[44]

In March 2006 Rafi Hofsten, President of Hadasit, the technology transfer company of Hadassah University Hospitals in Jerusalem, and co-chair of Biomed Israel, the country's national life science and technology convention, was similarly optimistic. Following a visit to Ireland he expressed the view that Israel's strengths in innovation could complement Ireland's ability to translate inventions into products.[45]

For over a decade such co-operation with Israel has appealed to the Irish government precisely because it has hoped to emulate the Israeli success in developing world-class indigenous hi-tech start-ups. In 1999, Mary Harney, at the time Tanaiste and Minister for Enterprise, Trade and Employment welcomed the signing of a Framework of Co-operation Agreement in Indus-trial Scientific Research and Technological Development, specifically because of Israel's 'international reputation for a combination of strong aca-demic infrastructure along with prudent government support for Research and Development. Ireland has clearly earmarked further investment in this area as a key priority'.[46]

Other government ministers expressed similar sentiments subsequently, with Tom Kitt, telling a meeting of the Oireachtas Joint Committee on Enterprise and Small Business, that co-operation with Israel, a country with a 'successfully developed knowledge based economy [and] high rates of business related research and development' provided Ireland with an opportunity to develop its own priority objective of Research, Technology and Innovation (RTI).[47]

An awareness of the lessons to be learned from the Israeli case has not simply existed on a political level. As far back as 1997 John Cullinane's organisation, the Cullinane Group, produced a study entitled *Israel: A Model for Indigenous High Tech Development in Ireland?*, while a number of Irish journalists also noted how Ireland could learn from Israeli practices in R&D and the hi-tech sphere.[48] As of now, Ireland has not achieved these ambitious goals, something that Dr Maurice Treacy, director of biosciences and bioengineering at Science Foundation Ireland, acknowledged in mid-2006 when he noted that the vibrant venture capital community focused on investing in Israel in the life sciences sector is 'a distinguishing factor that we are developing in Ireland but are not at the level that they have in Israel'.[49]

As Treacy's comments remind us, while Middle Eastern nations do have much to learn from the 'Celtic Tiger', they also have something to teach us.

NOTES

1 'Arab-Irish Chamber of Commerce', *DFA Bulletin*, No. 1037, May/June 1987, p. 15.
2 'Arab Envoys start Visit to Dublin to Cement Ties', *Arabic News.Com*, 29 October 1998; Arab ambassadors visit Ireland', *Arabic News.Com*, 4 November 1998.
3 'Minister for Foreign Affairs to visit the Middle East', DFA press release, 24 June 2004.
4 Sean MacConnell, 'Egypt Reopens its Beef Market to Ireland', *Irish Times*, 14 November 2001.
5 John Murphy, 'Irish Meat is Safest', *Examiner*, 30 April 1996. This was followed by a renewed ban on Irish live cattle and beef exports to the region in 2000–01 in response to another BSE scare in Europe.
6 Statistics on Irish investment in Egypt in the decade between 1995 and 2004 can be found in Ashraf Mishrif, 'EU Foreign Direct Investment into Egypt: 1972–2004', Unpublished PhD Thesis, University of London, 2006.
7 'Minister Cowen Welcomes Agreement Between International Development Ireland Ltd (IDI) and Gulf of Suez Authority', DFA press release, 23 September 2003.
8 'Aminex signs deal to drill in Egypt', *Irish Times*, 19 September 2006.
9 Author interview with Dr Ashraf Mishrif, Cultural Adviser to the Egyptian embassy in London, 15 September 2006.
10 See 'Egyptian Investment Strategies', 2006, Ministry of Foreign Affairs, Cairo, September 2006, http://www.mfa.gov.eg/MFA_Portal/enGB/Foreign_Policy/International_Relations/intereco/egyperfom/79_Investment+in+Egypt.htm.
11 James Kenny, 'Looking Back on a Remarkable Journey as US envoy', *Irish Times*, 10 October 2006.
12 Issandr el Amrani, 'Egypt's Smart Village wants to be Regional IT Hub', *Daily Star* (Beirut), 3 December 2003.
13 Author interview with Dr Ashraf Mishrif.
14 'Fears Over Safety to Delay Return of Irish UN Soldiers for Week', *Irish Times*, 15 April 1996.
15 'Aer Rianta is Emphatic that the US$225 Million Beirut Deal is not Void', *Irish Times*, 11 June 1999. Mark Hennessy, 'Aer Rianta as Advertised Welcomed Defended as a Matter of Protocol', *Irish Times*, 3 October 2002.
16 Ramsay Short, 'Lord of the Dance to reign in Baalbek', *Daily Star* (Beirut), 26 April 2002.
17 See Dr Nasser Saidi's keynote speech at the, 'Towards E-Lebanon' conference, 13 June 2003, republished in *Government Technology Magazine*, June 2003, http://www.centerdigitalgov.com/international/story.php?docid=57564.
18 Louis G. Hobeika, 'Recent History in Israel, Ireland and the Gulf Suggests a Path for Lebanon's Economic Rebirth', *Daily Star* (Beirut), 1 August 2005.
19 Dani Saadi, 'Government Hurdles Confound HP's Vision', *Daily Star* (Beirut), 3 August 2003.
20 Osama Habib, 'Preparations Under Way to Introduce VAT', *Daily Star* (Beirut), 9 July 2001.
21 Raed el Rafei, 'MIT Gathering Believes in Hi-tech Lebanon. Measures include Call Centres, Arabization of Software', *Daily Star* (Beirut), 10 June 2006.

22 'Business Sector Selection for Developing Countries', *The Monash Report*, 23 May 2006, Thhttp://www.monashreport.com/2006/05/23/70/.
23 Raed el Rafei, 'MIT Gathering Believes in Hi-tech Lebanon'.
24 Tarek el Zein, 'Lebanon Cut Out of Foreign Outsourcing Boom', *Daily Star* (Beirut), 29 March 2004.
25 Raed El Rafei, 'MIT Gathering Believes in Hi-tech Lebanon'.
26 See biography of John Cullinante, http://www.cullinane-group.com/ . See also Cullinane's opinion piece in the *Daily Star* (Beirut) 'Belfast says: "Jobs make friends"', 7 November 2003.
27 'US Software Entrepreneur Aims to Bring Regional Peace Through Development', *Daily Star* (Beirut), 22 November 2003.
28 BIRD is a US$108 million endowment funded by the US and Israeli governments that provides capital for joint projects between Israeli and US companies that will lead to commercialisation in the United States.
29 *Ireland and Israel: A Tale of Two Economies, Bank Hapoalim, Economic Report*, Issue 121, 25 October 1999.
30 *Dáil Debates*, Vol. 450, col. 1792, 22 March 1995.
31 David McWilliams, 'Big Ideas for a Small Country', *The Sunday Business Post Online*, 17 June 2001.
32 M. Plaut and Yated Ne'eman, 'Netanyahu: Israel will be Among the Richest 10 Countries Within 15 Years' http://chareidi.shemayisrael.com/archives5765/metzora/anetnyhumtz65.htm, 13 April 2005.
33 Allister Heath, 'Netanyahu Pledges Government Cuts and Tax Reform', *The Business*, 30 January 2005.
34 *Ha'aretz*, 4 April 2003.
35 Buffett 'World Must know about Israeli Wonder', *Israel Today*, 19 September 2006http://www.israeltoday. co.il/default.aspx?tabid=178&nid=9549.
36 'Q&A with Amir Peretz', *Jerusalem Post*, 23 March 2005.
37 Sever Plocker, 'Not quite, Bibi', *Ynetnews.com*, 11 April 2005.
38 Guy Rolnik 'Loss to Ireland', *TheMarker.com*, 29 March 2005.
39 For an interesting and informed account of the negative, as well as positive, aspects of the 'Celtic Tiger' see Michael J. O'Sullivan, *Ireland and the Global Question*, Cork, 2006.
40 'General Economy: Israel', Organisation for the Promotion of Israel–Netherlands Trade, http://www.optin.nl/geneco.php.
41 See World Economic Forum, Global Competitiveness Index, 2006, http://www.weforum.org/en/initiatives/gcp/Global%20Competitiveness%20Report/index.htm and Digital Opportunity Index, 2005, http://www.itu.int/osg/spu/statistics/DOI/ranking2005.html.l
42 Efrat Neuman, 'Begorra it's the Hora', *Ha'aretz*, 6 September 2005.
43 Sean Barrett, 'Investment to Spur Economic Growth and Reduce Poverty', 6th Herzliya Conference 24 January 2006, , http://www.herzliyaconference.org/Eng/_Articles/Article.asp?ArticleID=1487&CategoryID=215.
44 'Israel and Ireland in Joint Software Project', *Newsletter of Israeli Embassy*, Dublin, 3 March 2006, http://dublin.mfa.gov.il/mfm/web/main/document.asp?DocumentID=92355&MissionID=116.
45 Claire O'Connell, 'Israeli-bio-technology expert keen to forge links with Ireland', *Irish Times*, 7 March 2006.
46 'Tanaiste signs Science and Technology Agreement with Israel', Department of Enterprise, Trade and Employment press release, 27 October 1999.
47 'Presenting the Ireland–Israel MoU for Co-operation in Industrial, Scientific and Technological Development', speech by Tom Kitt, Minister for State at the Department of Enterprise, Trade and Employment to the Joint Committee on Enterprise and Small Business, 7 March 2000.
48 See, for example, David McWilliams, 'Calvinists and Cavaliers', *Business & Finance*, 11 January 1996, p. 21; Barry O'Halloran, 'Land of Milk and Telephony', *Business and Finance Magazine*, 29 June 2000, p. 14.
49 'Israel Bio-Technology Expert Keen to Forge Links With Ireland', *Newsletter of Israeli Embassy*, Dublin, 24 March 2006, http://dublin.mfa.gov.il/mfm/web/main/document.asp?DocumentID=93203&MissionID=116.

Index